The Market System

Introduction to Economics Series

Kenyon A. Knopf, *Editor*

The Market System

ROBERT H. HAVEMAN
Grinnell College

KENYON A. KNOPF
Whitman College

SECOND EDITION

John Wiley & Sons, Inc.
New York · London · Sydney · Toronto

Introduction to Economics Series

Teachers of introductory economics seem to agree on the impracticality of presenting a comprehensive survey of economics to freshman or sophomores. Many of them believe there is a need for some alternative which provides a solid core of principles while permitting an instructor to introduce a select set of problems and applied ideas. This series attempts to fill that need and also to give the interested layman a set of self-contained books that he can absorb with interest and profit, without assistance.

By offering greater flexibility in the choice of topics for study, these books represent a more realistic and reasonable approach to teaching economics than most of the large, catchall textbooks. With separate volumes and different authors for each topic, the instructor is not as tied to a single track as in the omnibus introductory economics text.

Underlying the series is the pedagogical premise that students should be introduced to economics by learning how economists think about economic problems. Thus the concepts and relationships of elementary economics are presented to the student in conjunction with a few economic problems. An approach of this kind offers a good beginning to the student who intends to move on to advanced work and furnishes a clearer understanding for those whose study of economics is limited to an introductory exposure. Teachers and students alike should find the books helpful and stimulating.

Kenyon A. Knopf, Editor

Preface

All of the chapters of this second edition of *The Market System* have been revised to deal more directly and more clearly with the analysis of a price and profit economy. For example, the first and last chapters have been reorganized for a more logical development of the material with which they deal, while Chapter 5 has been split into two chapters, one to develop market mechanics and the other to analyze a perfect market system.

There are two important additions. One is the use of marginal utility analysis in developing the theory of household demand in the body of Chapter 3. The other is the introduction of a simple money market operation in the presentation of general equilibrium in Chapter 6.

The most substantial departure from the first edition involves the placement of some of the more technical and complex material into appendixes to Chapters 1 and 3. This permits an instructor who prefers the less-elaborate marginal utility approach to household decisions and the theory of demand to utilize the body of Chapter 3. The instructor who prefers indifference curve analysis can substitute the appendix to Chapter 3 for certain sections of that chapter without loss of continuity. In this sense, we have tried to broaden the usefulness of the book rather than to move it from one level to another. We point out, however, that even if the appendixes are avoided, the text develops and makes use of the graphic techniques and model-building framework of economic analysis.

ROBERT H. HAVEMAN
KENYON A. KNOPF

Preface to the First Edition

It is always amazing to contemplate a society such as ours, which efficiently produces and distributes about $700 billion[1] of final goods and services a year without the direction of a central authority. Indeed, it is not less remarkable to discover how prices and markets are used in such a society to organize and direct its economic activity. This system of price and market direction is the central theme of this volume.

In studying the nature of a market system, however, the gap between an ideal market-directed economic system and what really goes on in the world must not be overlooked. Hence, not only is it necessary for citizens living in a market system to understand how an ideal and perfectly functioning system operates but they must also understand when they can and cannot rely upon the protection of market forces in the imperfect real-world economy. They must understand the reasons for and the effect of private economic power attempting to supersede impersonal market forces. They must understand those circumstances in which market forces, although operative, produce results in conflict with the goals of society. They must understand that in some cases the market system fails to operate at all. In this volume, therefore, we not only view the functioning of the ideal system, but we also investigate the reasons why it sometimes fails to operate in the public interest.

This volume introduces the market system to the reader by focusing attention on a single model framework abstracted from the complex real-world economy. In constructing this model, we use the method of deductive logic, first positing well-defined premises, then erecting analytic models upon these premises, and

[1] Since the publication in 1966 of the first edition, this figure has changed to $1000 billion.

Preface to the First Edition

finally drawing conclusions. The models which we erect are specifically tailored to isolate the effects of a limited number of the multitude of variables which determine economic behavior. Although they admittedly fail to give a comprehensive and complete explanation of economic activity, such models do fasten onto certain important determinants of economic behavior.

What we are saying, then, is that this is a volume of economic theory and, consequently, much of its contents abstract from the real world. Just as physical scientists abstract from reality, so too must economists. The physical scientist does not tell us, for example, that bodies fall with an acceleration of 32 feet per second. Rather his claim is that *if* there is a perfect vacuum, bodies will fall with such acceleration. And just as no one calls the physical scientist a madman upon seeing a snowflake drift down with no acceleration at all, so too must one not label the abstractions of the economist nonsense because they fail to provide a literal account of daily life.

This having been said, however, it must be recognized that the laboratory of the social scientist is something quite different from the laboratory of the physical scientist. While the economist, dealing with groups of people, cannot hold "all other things constant"[2] like the physical scientist, this is not to say that he is unable to experiment. His experiments, however, must be largely carried on in the mind rather than in the laboratory and hence the powers of his experiments are less ideal than those possessed by the physical scientist. Although not ideal, this method is an acceptable, indeed a necessary, way of "searching out the world." Professor Phelps-Brown put it this way:

Cannot [some salient properties of those phenomena familiar to us in our daily dealings] be held in the mind's eye, so that we can set up an experiment with them, and watch it work out, in the laboratory of the imagination? We all of us make such experiments. If we suppose a burning match put to the edge of a dry piece of newspaper; or one who cannot swim falling overboard at night in mid Atlantic, with nobody to see him fall and bring him help: we know what then will happen. The instances seem childish, and yet the method of our thought in them deserves attention, because it is the method of our

[2] This property of "all other things constant" is, in economics, generally stated in Latin: *ceteris paribus*.

economic theory. What we have done is to set up in the mind's eye a situation, of whose materials some salient properties—that paper catches fire and water drowns—are well familiar and ascertained; before the same mind's eye the situation so constructed works its story out. In economic theory we do the same. In such [trains] of thought, hypothesis and experiment [are] one. It is in this sense that we claim that the economist can work in a laboratory of the imagination.[3]

Thus, the theory presented here has both substantial power and significant limitations. The basic principles which will be developed are applicable to all problems of allocating scarce resources to maximize certain objectives, and are essential to rational decision-making in any system at any time. This is true even though our specific models, with their narrow premises, exclude much economic activity. And while our theory is further limited by real-world distortions such as irrational behavior, immobility, lack of knowledge and so on, all efforts to produce a better theory draw upon our theory for both an understanding of problems and a basic language. As witness of its importance in the decision-making process, consider the testimony of a high-level Defense Department analyst:

The tools that we in the Department of Defense use are the simplest, most fundamental concepts of economic theory, combined with the simplest quantitative methods. The economic theory we are using is the theory most of us learned as sophomores. The reason Ph.D's are required is that many economists do not believe what they have learned until they have gone through graduate school and acquired a vested interest in marginal analysis.[4]

It is for these reasons, then, that we claim the study of prices and markets to be worthwhile. Not only does it provide an understanding of the basic tools for rational decision making, but it gives training in the "language of economists." We make this claim fully recognizing the argument of others concerning the unsatisfactory state of existing theory.

ROBERT H. HAVEMAN

KENYON A. KNOPF

[3] E. H. Phelps-Brown, *The Framework of the Pricing System*, Chapman and Hall, London, 1936, pp. 34–35.
[4] Alain C. Enthoven, "Economic Analysis in the Department of Defense," *American Economic Review*, May, 1963.

Contents

**Chapter 5 The Organization and Functioning
 of Competitive Markets**

1

Economies and Economizing

The United Nations Secretariat classifies countries into market economies and centrally planned economies.[1] This book is about market economies, such as that of the United States, or Canada, or the countries of Western Europe. It is not a description of any of these economies; rather, it is a statement of the logic of a pure market economy. Because it is difficult to recognize the components of this logic in any existing market economy, we must also consider in what ways real world economies deviate from our description, and why they do so.

In the American economy millions of decisions are made about spending income at the same time that millions of other decisions are made about what to produce in order to earn income. Amazingly, the two sets of decisions match up fairly well. Where they match poorly, there are forces at work which will lead them to match better. This would not be so remarkable if households produced a high proportion of what they consume, or if they purchased a high proportion on special order from friends and neighbors. But this is not the case. Most production is for a vast number of unknown and unseen potential customers; in short, production is for impersonal markets.

[1] The Secretariat also distinguishes between developed market economies and developing market economies. This book presents the logic of market relationships abstracted from dynamic change in an economy. Another volume in this series, *Economic Development and Growth*, by Robert E. Baldwin, is concerned with analysis of developing market economies.

People living in Chicago sleep peacefully at night oblivious to the fact that a fantastic array of decisions must be made and acted on, some of them having occurred years earlier, in order that all of the store shelves in the city be stocked in the morning. As a community, they do not fear famine, nor do they often experience gluts of some goods. The same is true for other communities in the United States. Yet there is no superior authority, no board of directors, seeing to it that all of the decisions mesh, that the system is orderly. The reconciling of these millions of individual decisions would be beyond human mental capacities and beyond the capability of the most sophisticated computer imaginable.

The central concern of this volume is this observed economic order. What does produce order out of decentralized decision making in economic affairs? The answer we shall give is that the economic system possesses a very special mechanism to reconcile the many conflicting interests, to solve the problems of economic choice. We shall call this mechanism the market mechanism and the system that embodies it the market system.[2]

I. THE LOGIC OF THE MARKET SYSTEM

All societies face the same basic economic questions of *what* goods and services to produce, *how* to produce them, and *for whom*.[3] All societies make choices among alternative answers to these questions by means of a socioeconomic system. Many developed economies answer these questions through a market system, one in which the basic decisions are made, not by some central authority, but by individual producers and consumers acting in markets in response to prices. The essence of the system is that goods are produced for exchange and exchanges are money transactions. All inputs and outputs have prices that are set in markets by the actions of a host of competitors, each seeking his own advantage.

Households spend incomes to purchase the goods and services

---

[2] We shall use the terms "price system" and "market system" interchangeably throughout our discussion.

[3] See pp. 11-13 below as well as the appendix to this chapter for a detailed treatment of these questions.

that they most desire from the businesses that produce them. On the other hand, households sell their labor and the services of the capital and natural resources that they own for income. Businesses buy resources from households and sell products and services to each other and to households in the expectation that the revenue from sales will cover the costs of production and that some profit will remain.

This system would appear to be quite chaotic. How can a society hold together if individuals, or small groups in association, each pursue their own self-interest? How can reliance on selfish motives produce an optimum in economic welfare for society? Adam Smith supplied the answer by pointing to the "unseen hand" of competition among buyers and sellers as an effective regulator.

If business firms have a number of competitors for both their customers and their suppliers, pursuit of self-interest by each will be channeled to provide for the social welfare. Shoe manufacturers, for example, are given incentive to charge the lowest price consistent with continued operation, and production will tend to conform to the most efficient methods. If one shoe manufacturer charges a higher price for his shoes than that which covers all of his costs, his competitors will find it profitable to undercut his price and win away his customers. Since competition keeps the sales price down, a high-cost firm would suffer losses and would have to get its costs down or go out of business. Just how the price system produces these beneficial results under the guidance of competition is the substance of this volume. We shall also study how our real-world economic system deviates from this idealized model of a price system.

II. THE EMERGENCE OF A MARKET SOCIETY

Some of the logic of market societies and some of their institutional structure may be better understood from the perspective provided by a short historical excursion. Market-directed societies are relatively new. Elements of such societies appeared at various points in time in the life of tradition-directed societies, the kind of economic system which historically preceded the market economy. Despite the great differences in detail and institutional arrangements, the primitive societies studied by anthropologists, ancient China, ancient Greece, and Medieval Europe, all made their economic choices largely by tradition. A tradition-directed society is one whose economic choices are made by following patterns established by prior generations. Its technology is based on "rule of thumb," with skills passed on from father to son. Economic relationships are closely intertwined with social relationships and are subsidiary to them. Change in the social fabric, hence the economic fabric, occurs very slowly. The same is true of technology.

Much of the groundwork for market societies was laid in Western Europe in the late Middle Ages with the development of certain practices which facilitated the rapidly growing commercial activity. Long-distance trade had fallen off sharply with the end of the Roman Empire, in the fifth century A.D., and local exchange of goods and services came to be barter transactions.[4] From this time, the feudal arrangements of rights and obligations dominated local economic activity in Europe for centuries. The gradual development of peace in the countryside and a period of rapid population growth encouraged growth of local trade and the establishment of annual fairs for the sale of exotic goods from the Near East. The Crusades provided more contact with the Near East and more interest in its products.

These events created new pressures for the *monetization of transactions*. Italian merchants were among the leaders in the long-distance trade which then experienced rather rapid expansion, and it was in the Italian city states that several important practices developed. One was the emergence of banks of deposit which transferred funds within the bank from one person to another on written request—a primitive form of our check-writing practice. These banks also discovered that in normal times all depositors would not appear at once to withdraw their deposits, so it seemed safe to lend some of the deposits to people who wanted to borrow. Banks extended credit based on the holding

---

[4] See Henri Pirenne, *Economic and Social History of Medieval Europe*, Harcourt-Brace, New York, 1937, also *The Cambridge Economic History of Europe*, The University Press, Cambridge, 1944, Volume II.

of less gold and silver in reserve than would be necessary to cover 100% of the deposits. These practices made easier the transfer of wealth from those who held it to those enterprisers who would put it to productive use. Development of this fractional reserve banking also laid the foundation for bank credit as money that can expand and contract in quantity according to the needs of the economy.

Double-entry bookkeeping is another important practice that developed in the Italian city states. This method of accounting for business transactions provides an accurate check on entries in business books. More important, it gives the enterpriser a clear picture of where the business stands whenever he wants it, regardless of the complexity of the business. As a result of this invention, business accounts became separated from the family housekeeping account of the great merchant families. As a further result, business decisions became more clearly a weighing of changes in revenues relative to changes in costs, since businesses could get more current information on the state of the business. It put the spotlight on profits.

Two more developments were necessary for the emergence of a market economy that was to be sharply distinguishable from the traditional economies of earlier times. In ancient Greece, as well as in Italian cities of the fifteenth century, money was used as a medium of exchange and products were priced in terms of a money common denominator. One could reasonably identify markets for many products, but these nevertheless were not market-directed societies. The missing ingredients were markets for resources—labor and land were not allocated according to prices established by labor and land markets. Instead, they were largely subject to the forces of tradition and status.

The free exchange of land for money, based on the concept of private property, is a fairly recent phenomenon. Although the idea of private property was known in Roman law, the feudal forms, tenure and proprietorship, grew in importance in Western Europe in the fourth century A.D. and were the dominant forms of control into the eighteenth century. Tenure control of land involved the generalized right of use for immediate needs only, a form of control that dominated Western Europe from the ninth to the eleventh centuries. A serf could gather only as much wood from the manor forest as he needed for his own use. The right of use applied to the gentry as well as to the peasants.

Proprietorship control of land involved specified and limited rights for the gentry as well as the peasants. Rights of peasants on arable land were limited to the time from planting to harvesting. After harvesting, all members of the community had the right to turn their livestock out to graze indiscriminantly on all of the arable land. Sometimes these specified rights had begun as obligations in the feudal system but had become abusive. For example, in the early days of the manor, the lord had accepted the obligation of protecting the peasants and their crops from the depredations of wild animals. This later turned into the specified right to hunt through the fields, to the injury of the peasants' crops.

In the late Middle Ages, serfs in some areas of Western Europe had had their dues-in-kind converted to money payments. This might create the impression that serfs were paying rent for land "owned" by the lords. Whereas conversion to money payments was a necessary prerequisite to the formation of a land market, the dues-in-kind had been largely a *quid pro quo* for protection and administration of justice by the lord of the manor. Dues-in-kind were more a tax for government than rent for land. The money payments continued to be of this same character.

In neither the tenure nor the proprietorship form of control was there exclusive control. There was no freedom for private persons to transfer property as they chose. Private property as a form of control is distinguishable by this full freedom of transfer, added to the right of use and the right of abuse. Private property, encompassing this exclusive control, has been a dominant form of property control for no more than two centuries, and for a limited area of the world at that. This concept with some modification has been a basic one in the United States economy.[5]

---

[5] It should be noted that some restriction of private property rights has occurred in the United States in the twentieth century. A few states require that owners of strip coal mines replace the overburden of dirt that they scrape aside rather than leave it, helter-skelter, in piles that subject it to leaching, to the destruction of its fertility and of its future use. Local governments have passed zoning laws which restrict certain tracts of land to

A market-directed economy requires a labor market as well as a land market. In a mythical society made up entirely of single proprietors, each producing a product or service for exchange with others, laborer and entrepreneur are one. Although there is no labor market, there could be a market economy. In a society where some men work for others, labor is allocated by prices in markets only where certain conditions exist. Labor must have a price that changes with changes in market conditions rather than a price that reflects some customary "fair" standard in the medieval or ancient tradition. Labor must be free to move about in response to price differentials.

For example, Karl Polanyi argues that England did not have a labor market until the Poor Law Reform of 1834 eliminated parish relief.[6] Although serfs had long been emancipated, the administration of poor relief tended seriously to restrict worker mobility until that date. An unemployed worker could be assured of sustenance only in his home parish. Cities and towns were often inhospitable to new arrivals for fear that they might become public charges. While movement did occur, workers nevertheless were inhibited from freely moving from areas of unemployment to areas of expanding employment, or from areas of low wages to areas of high wages, by the working of the poor relief system. To the extent that free movement was inhibited, prices failed

---

particular uses, or which regulate smoke and odor emission by factories. The Anti-Trust Division of the Justice Department of the United States has the power to bring suit to prevent the transfer of the property of a company through merger where the result would be to lessen competition substantially. Thus, restrictions have been put upon the rights of private property in the United States where the use or abuse of property adversely affects people other than the property owner.

While a property owner does not have full and exclusive rights of use, abuse, and transfer, this society can hardly be said to have returned to the proprietorship form of control. The modern prohibitions are far less limiting than the earlier specifications of rights. It should also be noted that restriction on the use of private property in the United States is not limited to those cases in which the use (abuse) of the property inflicts costs on others. Sometimes a segment of the whole society will restrict the property rights of its members so that the segment may benefit at the expense of the rest of society. Many have claimed that this is what the state of Texas does when it controls the rate at which owners may pump oil out of their wells.

[6] See Karl Polanyi, *The Great Transformation*, Beacon Press, Boston, 1957.

to direct labor resources. A price system working in a pure market economy requires that the prices of all resources as well as all products be determined by the interaction of many buyers and many sellers in many markets.

Today, in addition to market-directed and tradition-directed societies, we recognize the centrally planned economy as a third way of organizing economic activity to make the basic economic choices that all societies must make. Centrally planned economies, often referred to as command-directed societies, include countries such as Russia, mainland China, and many of the countries of Eastern Europe. A command-directed society is one in which an individual, or a limited group, makes the economic choices for the whole of society and then directs that they be carried out. The decisions of the central body may be overlarded with tradition so that change occurs slowly, or the central group may operate so as to induce rapid change. The central planning group may be highly responsive to the members of the society, or weakly responsive. Modern centrally planned societies try to plan for rapid economic growth, but ancient military oligarchies combined command with strong overtones of tradition.

Details will differ among societies that fall under the same classification. Furthermore, most societies exhibit some aspect of all three forms of direction, although one form will predominate. Tradition has played a relatively small role in the making of economic choices in the United States. Command has played a role if by "command" we refer to some choices being made by authority, rather than by tradition or markets. Government taxation and expenditure, or regulation of international trade, involve command direction even though they may constitute a small portion of the total number of economic decisions as they did in nineteenth-century America. Just as no economy is a pure representation of one of these three categories, so also do economies shift the proportion in which economic decisions are tradition-directed, market-directed, or command-directed. These changes are readily apparent in various national economies today, regardless of whether one accepts the convergence hypothesis that Soviet Russia is accepting more and more market price direction while the United States adopts a larger and larger role for government direction of economic decisions.

III. THE LOGIC OF ECONOMIZING: SCARCITY AND CHOICE

The words economy or economizing conjure up many images, all of them restrictive or repressive in some sense. At the personal or family level, for example, an "economy kick" often means less total spending as well as reallocating some expenditures from the more frivolous to the more basic, from entertainment to meat and potatoes. In the larger social organization of community, state, or nation, economy in government again means reduction of expenditure and a shift from low priority expenditures to those that are considered more important. Family argument and political debate quickens, since we each have different views of what is frivolous or necessary, high priority or low. In each case, however, choice must be made because our limited means are insufficient to acquire all that we desire.

A. *Scarcity: The Basis for Economy*

Scarcity is an ever-present fact of existence for most persons and all societies. Few men and no society can achieve all of their economic objectives simultaneously. Indeed, nature is seldom so bountiful as to provide even the necessities of life in the quantity and form needed without human labor. Primitive societies constantly face destruction by starvation, by the rigors of the elements, or by the predatory activity of man and beast. Respite from these forces is the scarcest commodity in such societies. Whatever respite has been achieved has been the result of organizing society in such a way as to increase the production of goods and to alleviate hunger, exposure, and attack.

Over the centuries some societies have learned to increase production to such an extent that today we speak of an affluent society, such as the United States, rich in goods and leisure. Yet even an affluent community constantly strives against scarcity, admittedly at a different level, but scarcity nonetheless. Using all of its accumulated knowledge, its abundant natural resources, its vast stock of productive equipment, its highly trained labor force, and its highly advanced technology, the United States cannot produce enough to achieve all of its goals at once. *Scarcity of the means of production relative to the social goals to be met with them is the first central and universal fact of economics.*

B. *Choice and the Principle of Opportunity Cost*

When means of production are scarce relative to what people want produced, choices must be made. Only a few individuals and no societies possess the means to obtain all of the goods and services that they desire. Most of us have to pick and choose: if we choose to have some more of this, we must forego some of that. If a family spends more on transportation services in the form of monthly payments on a new car, it must reduce its allotment of income to some other purposes. It may spend less on shoes, or on recreation, or postpone painting the house, or put less in savings for the children's education. It may cut back a bit in several kinds of spending, or take it all out of one. It is obliged to choose, whether by prior planning or by struggling to adjust after buying something new on impulse. The decision is much easier if family income increases, but choice is still necessary. The cost of the new item is clearly the loss of the opportunity to spend that income for other purposes. And, in our example, the choice can only be made after comparing the value of the additional transportation with the value of the things which are being sacrificed. This is the opportunity cost principle applied to individual consumer behavior.

The same principle applies to societies because of the scarcity of means relative to ends. If members of a society choose to produce more complex and costly weapons systems, they must forego building some day care centers, educating some children, rebuilding inner cities, laying some highways, or producing some consumer goods. The choice of one thing eliminates the opportunity to choose another because productive resources are limited relative to all of the things that the members of society would like to produce with them.[7]

---

[7] At times a society may have idle resources, in which case it can increase production in many directions simultaneously until those resources are fully employed. To have idle resources at the same time that there are unfulfilled needs is, of course, wasteful, although a society may be willing to experience some amount of unemployed resources if it is a prerequisite for other goals such as freedom to quit one job to look for another, or to introduce new, more efficient equipment even though the old machinery is not worn out.

C. Choice: What to Produce, How, for Whom?

Because of scarcity, every society, primitive or highly developed, is confronted with the choice of *what* goods and services to produce and how much of each kind; *how* to produce these goods and services and *for whom* the production is undertaken, that is, who receives what quantities of the product. In each case there is an enormous range of alternatives: shoes or cars, urban renewal, armaments, schools, or food; using primitive technology and large amounts of labor or new technology and heavy capital equipment; distributing to the already wealthy and well educated or to the poor, minority groups and those with fewer opportunities. Moreover, societies may organize in different ways in order to answer these questions. Regardless of what economic system is adopted, all of these questions continue to exist. *The necessity to choose what to produce, how, and for whom is the second central fact of economics.*

Today the United States has a fixed amount of resources available to produce the things that its citizens may want. The population is of a particular size. The labor force is a relatively fixed proportion of that population, being determined by the age distribution and by those social mores that control how long young people remain in school, at what age old people retire, and whether women are housewives or work in the fields, factories, and offices. The skills and abilities of the labor force cannot be changed in the short run. Further, there is only a certain amount of land in productive use and it will take time and effort to bring more into production. Similarly, the productive capability of the nation's mines is not changed quickly. To enlarge the rate of exploitation or to find and open new mines is a time-consuming enterprise. Only a certain number of factories contain a specific quantity and kind of machinery. Thus, in a society at a point in time the quantity and quality of resources is relatively fixed.

We can, however, choose what to produce because resources may be shifted from what is presently produced to the production of other things. The extent of this flexibility was demonstrated dramatically in the conversion from peacetime goods to war goods at the start of the second World War and the swift reconversion at the end of the war. Tens of thousands of manufacturing plants stopped producing cars, cocktail dresses, and bed sheets and started making tanks, khaki pants, and bandages. Large numbers of people stopped producing personal services and started to work in war plants. Under conditions of full employment, this kind of reallocation so as to produce more of certain kinds of goods requires that less of other goods be produced. To get more of one thing entails the loss of another. Hence, scarcity requires that society determine what goods to produce, and how much of each. It forces society to make choices.[8]

How to produce is also a matter of choice. As we know, resources can be shifted from the production of one thing, such as highways, to the production of another, such as missile silos. Here we are concerned with the choice of what resources to use to produce a particular product. A highway can be built of gravel, concrete, or asphalt. We may use a very large number of men and few machines, or many and more complex machines with fewer men. To carry rocks to an airport site, many laborers may carry the rocks in baskets on their heads. Fewer laborers might carry the same amount of rocks by using wheelbarrows, a substitution of capital for labor. Animals drawing wagons might be substituted for the wheelbarrows and some of the remaining labor. Dump trucks powered by internal combustion engines, representing more machinery (and a change in its form), might be substituted for still additional labor in transporting rocks from quarries to roadbed.

Sometimes it appears that factors of production must be used in fixed proportions, but appearances can be deceiving. Imagine a production process which stamps out metal parts for automobiles. A quantity of one of the parts is produced on a line of 20 punch presses, each with one operator. The particular quantity is produced by 20 men working an 8-hour day. These men are responsible for getting their materials to the presses, removing the stamped pieces to a polishing line, and keeping the area around each machine clean. Obviously, the same output could be produced with fewer machines if more labor were applied in the form of overtime or additional shifts. Less obviously, other workers could be hired to haul the metal blanks to the presses and

---

[8] See the appendix to this chapter for a more detailed treatment of the choice of what to produce.

truck away the barrels of stamped parts. This would permit the press operators to devote more time to machine operation so that the same daily output would be produced with fewer machines but more labor. Even fewer machines would be needed if janitors were hired and more intensive use made of the remaining machines. Production processes differ in the extent to which proportions among factors of production can be varied, but the possibility of variation almost always exists. Each society must develop a process of choosing *how* to produce.

A society must also have some institutional arrangement to answer the question: For whom are the goods produced? There may be different answers in different societies, with the product being distributed equally among the members in one society and distributed with varying degrees of inequality in others. Criteria for some people getting more and others less also may differ from society to society. In one society people may receive income according to their inherited status. In another, income may reflect contribution to production. In yet another, political contributions may be specially regarded. In any event, the members of every society must somehow choose how to distribute the social product.

IV. MARKET ECONOMY: SELF-REGULATING OR SOCIALLY REGULATED?

If we put together money, prices, markets, and self-interest and then install competition as the regulator of relationships, will the economy proceed to operate satisfactorily without further social intervention? This is the first and most basic question which must be posed in evaluating a market system. As we shall see, the levels of social intervention necessary to sustain a market system are substantially more than many realize.

Adam Smith in *The Wealth of Nations*[9] argued for a reduction of government activity in the economy because at the time that he wrote, government had often created monopoly where it need not have existed, and regulated economic activity where competition could have existed and regulated with more widespread social benefit. He recognized that government had to provide the

[9] Modern Library edition, Random House, New York, 1937.

society with defense from foreign invasion because citizens could not, individually, produce that "product." In today's world, defense has become an enormous enterprise, with tens of billions of dollars being spent by each of the great powers for development of new armaments, and the maintenance and distribution of old. Both major and minor powers direct a large proportion of their resources to the military budget.

Government also must maintain internal order—it must provide police and a system of justice for the same reason that it must provide defense. Also, if a society adopts exploration of the unknown as a major goal, government is likely to become heavily involved. Exploration has been a government-sponsored activity since before the fifteenth century. Space exploration is no exception today. In research and development, as well as actual exploration, the resource requirements are so large and the economic benefits so remote that a national government is the only feasible organization for its pursuit.[10]

Closer to the direct functioning of the economy is the necessity for government to establish and regulate a money supply. Since a market-directed economy attaches prices to all quantities, the society, through government, must establish a stable monetary unit. Similarly, there is a necessity to establish collectively standards of weights and measures. Further, government is required to adopt and enforce a body of commercial law to provide confidence in the contracts into which private buyers and sellers enter.

Private enterprise and decision in the production of some additional kinds of services will not serve the public interest. For any society, there is a category of services from which some members of the society might be excluded, but their exclusion would substantially reduce the national welfare.[11] For example, sewage disposal facilities could be provided only to a selected few. However, to enhance the public health of the entire city, these facilities must be provided to all through the power of government. Likewise, education produces both economic and noneconomic benefits to society which are not directly reflected in the incomes of

[10] International governmental cooperation appears to be the only alternative.
[11] See Chapter 8 for further discussion of this topic.

the buyers of education. Consequently, if its provision were made by private enterprise, too little education would be produced from society's point of view. Therefore, the government must play a role in the provision of education. Here, as in many other areas, we as a nation do not accept the ethic of one dollar, one vote.

There are some kinds of production which by their nature must be provided by only one seller, so that the regulation provided by competition cannot come into play. Adam Smith named these natural monopolies and argued that they had to be regulated by government if they were not operated by government. The number of natural monopolies has probably increased over time owing to technological developments that give great advantages in efficiency to large-scale operation. A good modern example is the provision of telephone service. We cannot conceive of the effects of a very large number of telephone firms competing with one another in a modern city. The enormous duplication of poles and lines obviously would be wasteful and a nuisance. The inability to call a subscriber to a different company (if the firms were competing rather than cooperating) would be frustrating. Although there are many telephone companies in the United States today, each company has a monopoly in each locality that it serves, granted in a franchise from the local government. Regulation provides for the interchange of calls. The reader undoubtedly can think of other cases of natural monopoly.

The accumulation of a large capital sum frequently is necessary today if a business is to reach optimum size with low costs and efficient technology. Sometimes this optimum size produces natural monopoly. Sometimes it produces few enough firms that competition is not an effective regulator in the public interest. To enable accumulation of the large capital sums which are necessary to achieve these economies, government has recognized certain kinds of business organization, and has granted privileges to them.

The modern corporation, for example, is a creature of the state, receiving a charter which grants its owners (or shareholders) a limitation on their liability for the debts of the business. The corporate charter typically will limit shareholders' liability to the amount paid for the shares. Also, the corporate charter usually is issued for a long period, such as 99 years, or in perpetuity, so that a corporation's life is not limited to the lives of the initial owners.

A single proprietor, on the other hand, is liable for his business debts to the full extent of his personal wealth. Further, the business organization of a single proprietor dies with him. The net assets, of course, can be transferred to someone else, but creditors can claim full settlement before transfer, which can seriously interrupt the flow of business. In a similar way, partners are generally liable beyond their initial payment into the business, and partnerships are reorganized each time a partner is added or withdraws.

Government-granted privileges such as limited liability and perpetual life make possible the accumulation of a very large capital sum from a great many individuals, few of whom have the time, knowledge, or inclination to keep close enough track of the company's operations to be willing to accept unlimited liability.[12] Furthermore, capital accumulation is encouraged because shareholders can sell their shares to other parties without interrupting the business. A legal entity created by government, the corporation is an expression of ingenuity in social organization to keep abreast of technical possibilities.

Although the achievement of large size is often necessary if a firm is to take full advantage of technical possibilities in production, in other instances, firms will grow to large size simply to reap the benefits of market power. Where market power exists, prices are not established by the interaction of many buyers and sellers in markets;[13] rather, prices are set or administered by those private individuals or groups with the power to do so. To that extent, the economy and the allocation of resources are not directed by the tastes and preferences of consumers. Society through government often has decided to interfere and regulate those institutions possessing market power. Government has often attempted to regulate so as to maintain competition where the realities of tech-

---

[12] Adam Smith considered the corporate form of organization to be inappropriate both because of the power of large size and because he believed that hired managers would not be as diligent in running the business efficiently as owner-managers.

[13] The technical requirements of pure competition are that there must be a sufficient number of buyers and sellers so that no one of them, by his actions, can affect price. See Chapters 5 and 6.

nology make that possible, thereby avoiding the more detailed regulation that is found necessary in the case of natural monopolies.

There are other ways in which government may act to support and maintain the market system. A market system frequently is described with the assumption that buyers and sellers know relevant facts so that they can act rationally. Others describe markets as institutions that find the facts. Such propositions may be applicable to small, local markets. But remarkable advances in transportation and communication have established huge national and international markets.

Facts are not known unless they are explicitly gathered. The markets do not gather them, yet markets will not function smoothly unless facts are provided impartially. In the United States, for example, the government provides an extensive crop-reporting service that is invaluable for agricultural markets. Similarly, government surveys of labor markets and the operation of government employment exchanges can provide information to firms and households that the private economy will not provide. It should be pointed out that labor markets would function more smoothly if households and firms were not so reluctant to use these government services.

Today private firms or their trade associations try to forecast their sales with some precision not only to plan their production schedules but also to plan major, long-term investment in capital equipment. They base their forecast of particular markets on a government or private forecast of what total production, called gross national product (GNP), will be. This forecast of GNP, in turn, is based on government-collected statistics of GNP for past years. In most instances, government is the most effective organization for the impartial provision of the facts necessary for private forecasts and informed private decisions.

Most participants in a modern market-directed society are employees who produce very little for their own direct consumption. When they are unemployed, their incomes are reduced or cease, creating serious hardships or debilitating poverty. Market systems, as they have operated, contain within themselves neither guarantee of full employment nor self-correction of general unemployment. Countries of the western world have faced recurrent crises of unemployment during the nineteenth and twentieth centuries. Government has been called on to cope with widespread and persistent unemployment. Virtually all governments have taken action to prevent general unemployment as well as to deal with it after the fact.

Considerable government activity, then, is necessary to establish the conditions for a healthy market-directed economy. Other government activity is necessary where the economy cannot function through markets or will not function if left to itself. Still other government activity is necessary for essentially noneconomic reasons, although that activity may have a substantial impact on the economy. In all of these cases, public command replaces private command. Whether private or public, the existence of command modifies the market-directed character of the economy.[14]

V. UNDERSTANDING THE PRICE SYSTEM

In this volume we shall present the theoretical structure of a simple, market-directed economy. It is so severe an abstraction from reality in the United States today that many readers will think it irrelevant. Our assumptions about business motivations may not correspond to the complexities that lie behind decisions in a modern economy where most business leaders are not owners, and are somewhat insulated from the pressures typical for profit-seeking owners. Also, we may assume too much rational judgment by consumers in choosing their purchases or the sale of their services in an affluent society. How relevant is a description of a market-directed economy to a society in which many prices are set, not in markets, but by producers who are to some degree isolated from the pressure of competition?

However, we would argue that there are many reasons for the student to begin with the study of a price system such as that presented here. One is the pedagogical reason of moving from the

---

[14] This is true whether the command stems from democratic expression or dictatorial fiat. Although the source of command makes no difference in the categorization presented here, it makes a tremendous difference to the people of the society.

simple to the complex, learning about concepts, relationships, and patterns that will be useful as one moves closer to reality. For example, some current efforts to construct a new theory of the business firm make use of the theory of political process. Yet, the profit concept that our simple model is based on is present as one measure of success and, therefore, as one element in decisions. And the decisions themselves involve the kinds of marginal changes—a bit more of this or a bit less of that—which we shall discuss. Similarly, the cost and revenue concepts that we shall develop are basic notions in real-world decision making. And although costs, revenues, and profits may not be the only crucial matters considered in the actual economy, they are important and they do act as constraints on management freedom to make decisions based on other criteria. We can read the ground-breaking literature with more understanding having started from this base.

A society may have many goals associated with its economic activity. It may wish to have equity in economic opportunity, justice in economic relationships, economic growth so that its citizens may look toward a better life, full employment so that resources seeking employment are not idle while there are unfulfilled needs, and economic efficiency so that resources will be used to produce the things that consumers most desire. To understand our economy and how it relates to the economies of other societies, we must consider all of these economic goals. In this volume we are especially concerned with the goal of economic efficiency, since a price system provides a way of allocating resources to alternative uses. The market system presented here in elementary form is applicable to any society whose primary aim is maximum satisfaction of consumer wants. It is as applicable to a socialist economy which subscribes to this end as to a capitalist economy,[15] although the distribution of income will differ.

We have already indicated that a market-directed economy involves prices for resources as well as for products. Resource incomes may be distributed differently in a socialist economy than in a capitalist one but, in both cases, prices should reflect relative scarcity. In a capitalist society all resource prices become incomes

---

[15] See, for example, Oskar Lange and Fred M. Taylor, *On the Economic Theory of Socialism,* The University of Minnesota Press, Minneapolis, 1938.

paid to the private owners of the resources,[16] but in a socialist economy property incomes are recieved by the state since private property ownership is limited to personal property. Although socialists consider that interest, rent, and profit incomes should not go to private individuals, these resource prices must be calculated if resources in society are to be allocated efficiently.

The rent of land, for example, is a value derived from the value of the product of the land, whether that be wheat or a downtown building site. If land is used for one purpose, its use for other purposes is foregone. The cost of its use is the cost represented by the value of its next, slightly less preferred use. This, it will be recalled, is the opportunity-cost principle. Calculating of opportunity cost and its assignment as the price to the piece of property in question will assure that the property will be used for its most preferred use, and no other. Clearly, the building of alternative users will establish the most preferred use. If consumer tastes change, some other use of the land may become the preferred use. The old use will have less value and the land will be shifted to its new use. The point is that arbitrary assignment of use of the property which is not based on opportunity cost is less likely to produce the best allocation of the land. Moreover, the land use is even less likely to shift with changing circumstances if new demands and new costs are not reflected in prices. The price system will allocate land most efficiently[17] in either capitalism or socialism, the only difference between the two systems being who gets the rent. Similarly, interest must also be calculated and entered into costs if scarce capital funds (and, therefore, capital goods) are to be allocated most efficiently in the provision of goods and services.

Profits provide a measure of efficiency for a production unit. Unusually high profits indicate that production of this sort should be expanded, while unusually low profits or losses indicate that such production should be contracted. High profits in one production unit relative to another producing the same thing may indicate that the prices and uses of resource inputs need to be adjusted. It may be that management skill is superior in the one

[16] Except where taxes are a part of the price quoted.
[17] With the exceptions noted in Chapter 8.

unit and this is not reflected in the price of management. Or it may be that one location is superior to another and this is not reflected in the rent of the land. Competition for superior management or land would raise the price and, at the same time, extend the use of the superior resource relative to the inferior one.

A few years ago, Russia made public some of its problems of production efficiency. An Associated Press dispatch appeared in the *Des Moines* (Iowa) *Register* as follows.

. . . A front-page editorial in *Pravda*, organ of the Soviet Communist Party, called for less central planning in light industries. It urged consumer industries to plan their own production on a profit basis. . . .

The *Pravda* editorial said, "It is time to give more independence to the [consumer] enterprises so that they will be economically interested in producing high-quality goods popular among the customers. . . .

"The plans of production of consumer goods are very often approved without taking into consideration the demands of trade organizations and the requirements of the population. . . .

"This is a wrong practice. The planning of almost all indexes from the top is interfering with the initiative of the factories and plants.

"We still have quite a number of enterprises which do not take into consideration the requirements of the customers and produce goods of low quality—badly finished and old fashioned."

Pravda said 20 per cent of the clothing produced in Russia this year (1964) was either returned to factories or sold only by cutting prices.

This year, the paper [*Pravda*] said stores have been burdened by unsold consumer goods worth $2.3 billion.

To avoid this, *Pravda* said, individual plants should be allowed to plan production on the basis of customer demands. In this way, production, quality and efficiency would increase and also improve the competitive position of Soviet goods in foreign markets, it added.

Proposals for abolishing tight government planning from above and making profit the basic measure of a factory's efficiency were first advanced two years ago by Prof. Yevsey Liberman of Kharkov University. . . .[18]

A dispatch the following month stated that:

Obviously convinced of the tonic effects of capitalist-style profit-making, the Soviet government Friday disclosed it would extend the idea on a trial basis to heavy industry and mining. . . .

[18] November 16, 1964, page 1.

The experiment will be carried out at a plant producing loading machines, a factory making television sets, the Zarya textile enterprise, and the Velkomostovskaya No. 9 coal mine. . . .

The new experiment obviously was designed to see whether the system would work in heavy industry and raw material industries.

The television and textile plants, being consumer goods factories, will make their own plans on the basis of orders direct from retail stores.

In both cases, profits may be distributed to plant personnel as bonuses and used for cultural and workers' welfare purposes.

"The higher the profits, the bigger the bonus fund," *Izvestia* explained. "Under these circumstances, it will be advantageous for the enterprise collective to take on more strenuous plans, exploit reserves to the limit and to turn out production that the consumer really needs."[19]

Use of profit as a measure of factory efficiency does not imply that Russia is moving swiftly to capitalism. Capitalism involves private ownership of natural resources and capital goods, which means that the returns of rent, interest, and profit are paid to private individuals as owners. In Russia, these returns belong to the state and are used as government officials see fit. However, adoption of profit as a measure of efficiency does mean that Russia has incorporated a large part of the price system which evolved with the development of capitalism. It signifies more decentralized decision making in the parts of the economy that are adopting the profit measure. It denotes more substantial use of a pricing system to allocate resources according to consumer wants, rather than directing economic activity so much by command. Distribution of part of the profit to management and workers in the form of bonuses assures that production incentives will be related to efficiency considerations. An understanding of the simple model of a price-directed economy presented in this volume will help us to understand why Russia has adopted such a sharp change in economic policy.[20]

Another reason for studying the price system is to understand

---

[19] *Des Moines* (Iowa) *Register,* December 26, 1964, page 5.

[20] A volume in this series, *Welfare and Planning: An Analysis of Capitalism vs. Socialism,* by Heinz Kohler, discusses in depth the difference between planned and price-directed economies.

the stringent conditions required for a truly self-directing economy which would automatically operate in the public interest. The conditions are numerous and demanding and require, for example, competition on both sides of every market, perfect information, and perfect mobility. Many argue that government should not interfere in the economy on the assumption that we *have* the kind of self-directed economy that will automatically result in the general welfare. An understanding of the logical requirements of such a system will demonstrate that the United States economy does not meet the conditions, and that, in so far as it does not, there will be market failure or the exercise of private power by a few sellers or buyers. Such results have led to increased government interference in market economies. For example, in both Britain and the United States there has been growth in the number of economic decisions made by command of government.

It is one thing for the system to require that its participants behave in the public interest; it is quite another for the participants to have the power to decide whether or not to behave that way. It may be the decision of society to rely on the good will and "social responsibility" of those who have either a small or a great amount of private power. Or the society may wish to inject the pressure of government where competition is not an effective force. Before making up our minds on such policy questions, we must determine if there are "built in" social forces other than the simple, purely competitive model presented in this volume.[21] An appraisal of the effectiveness of *all* of the significant forces must be made if the nature and extent of government intervention is to be decided on pragmatic rather than ideological grounds. The simple model presented in this volume is not intended to catalogue all of these forces. Nor is it designed to be "the ideal" against which reality should be measured, to which reality should be made to conform. On the contrary, understanding this model is but a first step in understanding how our price system operates, and the public policy questions that arise from the failure or success of its operation.

[21] See Chapter 8 in this volume; also see *Case Studies in American Industry*, by Leonard W. Weiss, in this series.

VI. CONCLUSION AND SUMMARY

While economies may be classified into tradition directed, market directed, or command directed, they all face certain common economic problems. One is scarcity. Another, stemming from scarcity, is the necessity to choose what to produce, how, and for whom. This volume describes how a market-directed economy goes about dealing with these basic questions. Market direction involves response to impersonal market prices by economic participants—households and businesses. There must be markets for land and labor resources as well as for consumable products and services. While these markets organize a fantastic array of facts and produce an amazing number of decisions, they do not work perfectly. In addition to describing an idealized market system, this volume is concerned with ways in which any real market economy deviates from this ideal and the consequences for economic policy.

QUESTIONS

1. What is the strongest evidence of scarcity in the American economy today? Explain how this example may be used to illustrate the opportunity cost principle.
2. Can you think of a production process in which the proportions of all of the factors of production are fixed so that the question of how to produce is irrelevant?
3. "The market system, as it has developed in Western civilization, has embraced the principle for income distribution of 'to each according to his contribution to production.'" Appraise this statement. Can you think of any social institutions which modify this principle of income distribution?
4. Some argue that income should be distributed equally among all in a society. Others say that even if this were done, it would not be long before those with ability would hold the wealth and income would be distributed about as unequally as it is at present in the United States. Discuss.
5. What manner of competition must there be for the market system to function efficiently? What are the criteria of efficient functioning?

APPENDIX: WHAT, HOW, AND FOR WHOM —SOME BASIC RELATIONSHIPS

A. *What to Produce: The Production Possibilities Curve*

The social choice of what to produce involves the consideration of a vast number of alternatives. However, to simplify the problem, suppose that we can only choose between two classes of goods: capital goods and consumer goods. Capital goods are products that are used to produce other things. These include such things as factory buildings, shoe machines, and barber chairs. Consumer goods are those final products which satisfy consumer wants, such as shoes and haircuts.

At one extreme we might choose to use all of our resources to produce only capital goods, a conceptual possibility, although clearly not a realistic one. In this event we could produce OA_1 of capital goods, an amount which is plotted on the vertical axis of Figure A1-1. At the other extreme we could produce only consumer goods, in the amount of OB_1, plotted on the horizontal axis of the figure. Realistically, a society must choose some capital

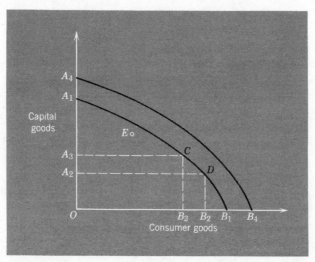

Figure A1-1 Choice of what to produce: the production possibilities curve.

goods and some consumer goods, since it must provide for both current and future consumption needs. All such possibilities lie along the curve joining point A_1 to point B_1. A society must decide where along the curve it is to produce, whether at point C yielding A_3 units of capital goods and B_3 units of consumer goods, or at point D yielding more consumer goods and fewer capital goods, or at some other point on the curve.

The points on this curve represent possible choices of what to produce given the quantity of the various available resources and given the state of technology. Should the quantity of one or more resources increase, more of both goods could be produced. The curve would shift outward, for example, from $A_1 B_1$ to $A_4 B_4$, indicating that it is now possible to expand the production of both capital goods and consumer goods. The same type of shift would occur if new, more efficient techniques of production were discovered. Again, production of both kinds of goods could increase. Because of either of these changes, the economy would experience economic growth. Nevertheless, growth in quantity of resources and technological change only occur over time and then not at an infinite rate. At any moment in a society's life, choice must be made of what to produce and that choice is constrained by the position of the *production possibilities curve.*

A society that gives a high priority to economic growth will choose a point relatively close to the OA axis, for instance, point C on the production possibility curve. This represents the production of a relatively large volume of capital goods and a relatively small volume of consumer goods. On the other hand, a community that gives a high priority to present consumption and low priority to growth might produce at D. Because capital goods are a productive resource, expansion of their quantity will permit greater production in the next time period, causing the whole curve to shift outward over time.

Shape of the production possibilities curve. This production possibilities curve is concave to the origin at zero because of the law of increasing costs (opportunity costs). Costs of producing one product will increase as resources are successively shifted from it to another product because some resources are rather specialized. Some are specialized in the production of capital goods and would be less efficient when used to produce consumer goods, while other resources are specialized in the production of consumer goods and would be less efficient when used to produce capital goods. If some quantity of both classes of goods is produced, those resources most suitable to each can be put to their most effective use.

Suppose that we start from point B_1 in Figure A1-1 with all resources devoted to production of consumer goods. Now let us take away some resources from consumer goods production and use them to produce capital goods. Naturally, we would select resources which are most advantageously used to produce capital goods. In doing so, we must give up B_2B_1 of consumer goods to get OA_2 of capital goods. The shift of resources will increase capital goods more than if no resources were especially efficient in capital goods production. As resources continue to be shifted, we shall have to select those that are rather specialized in the production of consumer goods and of low productivity in the production of capital goods. Hence, by giving up an amount of consumer goods B_3B_2, which is equal to the quantity B_2B_1, we gain an amount of capital goods A_2A_3, which is smaller than the previous increase of OA_2. Stated alternatively, we have to give up more consumer goods production to get an increase in capital goods equal to the first increase. The opportunity cost of the second increment of capital goods is greater than that of the first increment.

The existence of increasing costs and a bowed-out production possibilities curve can also be understood by recognizing that different products are produced most efficiently with different proportions of resources. For example, the production of food requires relatively more land, as compared to the production of electronic components which requires relatively more capital. Starting from a position in which all resources are devoted to the production of electronic components, the shift of some land to food production would involve very little sacrifice of output of electronic components. Successive shifts would eventually involve greater sacrifice of electronic component output as capital is moved from the production of components into the production of food. If resources were completely neutral in their use, the production possibilities curve would be a straight line, for example, between A_1 and B_1 in Figure A1-1.

Production possibilities curves can illumine many economic relationships. For example, point E in Figure A1-1 represents a situation in which some resources are unemployed. It is not on the society's production possibilities curve because the curve is drawn on the presumption of full employment of resources. By employing the unemployed resources, the society can obtain more of both classes of goods, moving out to the production possibilities curve.

It is also interesting to note that if the labor force is inefficient because of poor diet, education, or other causes related to consumer goods, we might find a greater outward shift in the curve from one time period to the next if resources were shifted to consumer goods from capital goods. This would, in effect, increase the labor input. From this it is clear that what to produce is a critical choice facing underdeveloped countries.[1]

B. *How to Produce: The Isoquant Curve*

Substitutability among factors of production may be illustrated simply by a curve known as an isoquant curve. Each curve in Figure A1-2 is made up of points representing all of the combinations of labor and machinery that will produce a specified output. In this hypothetical example, engineering information provides us with the fact that 100 units of output can be produced with 30 units of machinery and 75 units of labor (point A), with 20 units of machinery and 125 units of labor (point B), with 10 units of machinery and 225 units of labor (point C), or with any other combination of machinery and labor described by points on the same curve.

In the figure it can be seen that as labor is substituted for machinery, moving from A to B to C and holding output constant at the 100 unit level, more and more labor is required to replace each machine. The isoquant curve is convex to the origin. This shape occurs because factors of production are substitutes for one another, *but not perfect substitutes*. As labor is added and machinery subtracted, the additional labor has less and less machinery to work with. The effect of this change in proportions is

---

[1] For a discussion of the subject, see *Economic Development and Growth*, by Robert E. Baldwin, in this series.

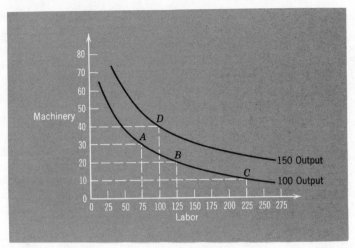

Figure A1-2 Choice of how to produce: the isoquant curve.

to require more and more labor to replace each machine that is withdrawn. At the extreme there is so much labor relative to machines that an additional unit of labor would contribute very little to output, while one less unit of machinery would subtract a relatively large amount from output. Hence a very large quantity of labor must be added if output is to be held constant while a machine is subtracted.[2]

Combinations of machinery and labor that could produce a larger output would be represented by points on a curve that would lie farther out from the origin. The curve in Figure A1-2 labeled "150 output" is such a curve. Point *D* illustrates that it takes 10 more units of machinery and 25 more units of labor to produce 50 more units of output than the input-output combination represented by point *A*. It takes more resources to produce more output, but along the new curve representing 150 units of output, labor and machinery may again be substituted for one another to produce this output.

We might digress here from the general proposition of social

[2] A more thorough explanation of the principle of substitutability is discussed in the appendix to Chapter 3 with the example of consumers substituting one consumer good for another in making choices. See also question 6 at the end of Chapter 4 (page 137).

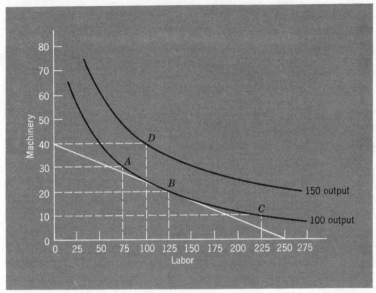

Figure A1-3

choice in combining factors of production to discuss a "best combination" in a price-directed economy. Suppose that the relative
prices of machinery and labor are 6 1/4 to 1. Converting this
ratio to dollar prices, one unit of labor will cost $1, while one
unit of machinery costs $6.25. If total outlay on resources were
$250 it would be possible to spend it all on machinery and buy
40 units. If all were spent on labor one could buy 250 units. A
straight line between those two points would describe all of the
combinations of machinery and labor that could be bought for
$250.

In Figure A1-3, this constant outlay line is tangent to the isoquant curve representing 100 units of output, the point of tangency being at *B*. The best combination of resources is 20 units
of machinery and 125 units of labor so long as the firm faces these
conditions of total outlay, techniques of production, and relative
prices of resources. Any other combination of labor and machinery involving a total outlay of $250 will be a point on a lower
isoquant curve representing a lower volume of total output.

A larger total outlay by the firm would be represented by a total

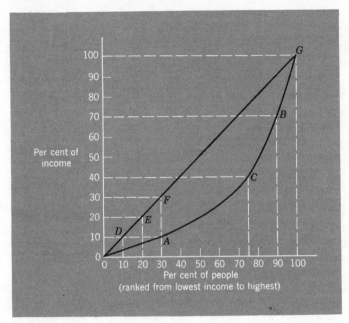

Figure A1-4 Choice of for whom to produce: the Lorenz curve.

outlay line farther out from the origin, and it would be parallel to the first outlay line so long as the relative prices of machinery and labor remain the same. There will be a tangency point with an isoquant curve representing a larger output. That tangency will indicate the "best" combination of factors of production under the new conditions.

C. *For Whom to Produce: The Lorenz Curve*

The character of the distribution of total product (or income) may be visualized by reference to a Lorenz curve (Figure A1-4). If the curve is bowed toward the "people" axis, the distribution is shown to be unequal. For example, at point *A* on the curve *OACBG*, the poorest 30% of the people are seen to receive only 10% of the income.[3] At point *B* the richest 10% of the people are shown to receive 30% of the income. At the intermediate point,

---

[3] See *The Economics of Poverty,* by Alan B. Batchelder, in this series, which discusses causes and effects of low income.

C, the richest 25% of the people receive 60% of the income. Clearly, the more bowed the curve, the more unequal is the distribution of income. The reader can satisfy himself that this is true by drawing in a more bowed curve and reading the percent of income associated with percent of people at various points along it.

A straight line through the origin of Figure A1-4, bisecting the 90° angle, represents perfect equality in the distribution of the total product or total income. It is evident from the line *ODEFG* that in a society with such an income distribution, each 1% of the people get 1% of the income, and so on. Again, the reader can test the proposition by reading off more points along the line.

If we were to draw Lorenz curves for many societies, we could see at a glance how societies have made different choices regarding for whom the product is produced, and which societies possess the more unequal distribution.

QUESTIONS

1. How might the production possibilities curve be used to aid in deciding whether to build the Aswan hydroelectric dam in Egypt? Use the notion of opportunity costs explicitly in your answer. Are there elements of the what-to-produce problem that cannot be handled by the production possibilities curve or a mathematical extension of it to more than two variables?

2. Consider the example of Figure A1-3. Discuss what would happen if the price of labor were to double to $2 while the price of machinery stayed the same. Trace out the impact on total outlay, total output, and the "best" combination of resources.

3. Many people through the years have treated the distribution of income as a purely ethical question. Others have argued that the economic effects are so great that the decision on how to distribute income must be dominated by considerations of economic growth and productivity. Discuss. Will the shape of the Lorenz curve illustrate which basis for decision a society has adopted?

2

A Price Economy—The Model
of a Simple Economic System

In this chapter we shall begin to analyze the nature of a price system. We shall attempt to cut through the complexity and confusion of everyday economic events in order to see more clearly the basic underlying relationships which determine how the economy functions. To do this we shall construct some simple and abstract models. These models will explain how a market system answers the economic questions, "What?" "How?" and "For whom?" Consequently, they can properly be called decision models. These models not only illustrate how individual households and businesses formulate decisions, but they also illuminate the process by which the entire system reconciles the conflicting desires of a multitude of individuals.

In this chapter we shall develop a simplified model of an entire free market economy. In succeeding chapters we shall investigate the individual sectors of this economy.

In our simple economy we shall recognize only two kinds of decision makers: *households* and *business firms*.[1] Moreover, this

---

[1] The concept of the business *firm* should be distinguished from both the concept of a *plant* and the concept of an *industry*. The firm contains all of the parts of an enterprise which are under one management. A plant, on the other hand, refers to a location where production takes place. One firm may have many plants. The industry is a group of firms all of which produce the same product. The Ford Motor Company is a firm; its assembly facility

economy will be assumed to exist in isolation, engaging in no trade with other nations. As for institutional arrangements, we shall assume private ownership of property and pure competition among buyers and sellers.[2] We shall look into our economy at a moment when consumers have certain tastes for products and certain quantities of factors of production to sell. We shall assume that firms have a given amount of production know-how and facilities at their disposal. Under these circumstances, the pattern of exchange in a market economy forms a configuration well-described as a *circular flow*. Let us see how it works.

The household sector is the consuming sector and the business sector is the producing sector. Each sector operates from quite different sets of goals or motivations just as each serves a different function in the economy. We shall assume that the force that motivates behavior in the household sector is the desire to maximize the satisfaction of wants through consumption. We assume that each household knows best the pattern of consumption that will maximize its satisfaction. Because we are basically concerned with human welfare in this study, the center of our concern will be the way in which the working of the economy affects the household sector. In fact, we can state that our chief job is to evaluate how any economic change affects this sector and its welfare.

The business sector, we shall assume, is motivated by the desire to maximize profits. Although real-world businesses respond to many other objectives, we shall assume that the central reason for business activity is to make a profit. Thus, for both households and businesses, self-interest is the driving power. As Adam Smith has said:

It is not from the benevolence of the butcher, the brewer, or the baker

---

at Dearborn, Michigan, is a plant. All of the producers of automobiles taken together form the automobile industry.

[2] Pure competition is one of four distinct market structures recognized by economists. The others are monopolistic competition, oligopoly, and pure monopoly, which are discussed in Chapter 7. In pure competition there are so *many firms* producing each *standardized product* that no single firm, by itself, can influence the price of that commodity. There are *no barriers* of any sort to either the entry of firms into an industry or the exit of firms from the industry.

that we expect our dinner but from their regard to their self-interest. We address ourselves, not to their humanity, but to their self-love, and never talk to them of our necessities, but of their advantages.[3]

In what kinds of activities does each of these sectors engage in order to attain its goals? Most basically, both sectors exchange their commodities and services, they buy and sell, and through the exchanges attain their goals. But this answer, by itself, is incomplete, since buying and selling could not take place unless there were something to buy and sell, some goods or services to be exchanged. Besides exchange there must be production. Through production and exchange, then, the goals of both the business and the household sectors are attained. Profits are earned by businesses and wants are satisfied by households.

I. THE HOUSEHOLD

The household sector is composed of all of the families in our model economy. Each household is an individual decision-making unit. The primary decisions made by each household revolve about the questions: "What and how much should we buy?" "What and how much should we sell?" The household must be aware of its alternatives. It must know what can be bought and what can be sold. Because the household is a want-satisfying entity, the things it desires to buy are consumer goods; goods such as shoes, shirts, food, and theater tickets whose use gives the consumer satisfaction or utility. The quantities of these goods which the household can buy is limited by the income which it earns. The higher its income, the more consumer goods the household can purchase.

But where does this income come from? The answer is clear. The income of the household is obtained by selling what it possesses. These possessions are called *factors of production* because they enter into the process of production and are transformed into output. Economists divide factors of production into three mutually exclusive categories: labor, capital, and natural resources. *Labor* does not simply mean work done with the hands

[3] Adam Smith, *Wealth of Nations,* Random House, New York, Modern Library edition, 1937, page 14.

or in a factory but any effort expended in producing goods or services. Carpenters, lawyers—even college professors—provide labor. For the economist, *capital* also has a special meaning. It usually refers only to real goods such as buildings, machines, tools, or inventories which are used in the process of production. *Natural resources* mean much the same in economic theory as they do in everyday usage. Virgin land, raw mineral deposits, even climate, all qualify as natural resources.[4] Sometimes economists speak of a fourth factor of production: innovation or entrepreneurial activity. This factor is the special creative ability which leads some people to organize production in new ways or to produce new things—in general, to perform creative activities that cause change and growth in the economy, often at some risk. The contributions of this factor swell the circular flow.[5] The payments for these factors of production are labeled wages, interest, rent, and profits.[6] These payments accrue to households as income.

Thus, from selling the services of its factors of production, the household receives income and, with the income received, purchases consumption goods which satisfy its wants. In both buying consumer goods and selling factor services the decisions of the household are guided by its goal of maximum satisfaction of wants.

II. THE BUSINESS FIRM

The other sector in the circular flow economy is the profit-maximizing sector. The business firms in this sector buy factors of production (labor, natural resources, and capital) as inputs, combine these factors in the production process to produce consumer goods, and sell the consumer goods as outputs. We have seen that the payments to the factors of production are income to the household, but to firms these same payments are costs of production.[7]

---

[4] Often, what is thought to be a natural resource, say, a river, is a combination of natural resource and capital. Any man-made improvement, such as dredging a navigation channel for barge traffic, is as much a capital improvement as adding a new machine to a factory.

[5] Within the circular flow there is need for more routine managerial abilities involving organization and direction. We classify these as labor.

[6] These factor payments are discussed at greater length in Chapters 1 and 8.

[7] Economists consider costs of production to be those payments necessary to

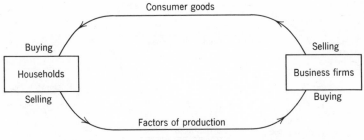

Figure 2-1

To earn revenue to cover these costs, firms sell to households the consumer goods they have produced. Profits are earned if the costs of production are less than the revenue earned by selling the output. In both buying factor services and selling consumer goods, business decisions are guided by the goal of maximum profits. Adding the buying and selling of households, the circular flow is completed (Figure 2-1).

III. PRICES AND MONEY

In our model we have not yet spoken of prices or money. Surely if our model is to depict a price system, these concepts must find their place in it. In a simple economic system such as that which we have constructed, money serves primarily as a lubricant. Without it all trade would be barter; all payment would be payment-in-kind. With it, money is traded for goods and goods for money. Money, then, is a common denominator, it is the medium of all exchange. As such, money is a standard of value. The values of all goods and services are expressed as so many units of money: one dress equals $10, one tie equals $1 dollar (removing the common denominator, one dress equals ten ties).[8]

---

bring forth the services of the factors of production. Some of these may be implicit costs rather than out-of-pocket costs. The return to the independent farmer for his own labor is an example of an implicit cost. Since the entrepreneurs are members of households, profits also flow as income to households. See Chapter 4.

[8] Money is also a store of value. It may be held over time and used in future

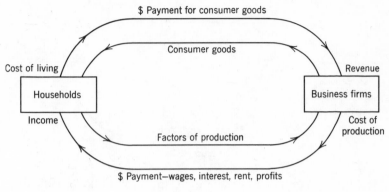

Figure 2-2

The number of units of money attached to each unit of a good or service is the *price* of that good or service. One theater ticket, for example, has $2 attached to it; one car has $2000 attached to it. $2 and $2000 are prices. In a price system, when trade or exchange occurs, money invariably serves as one-half of the transaction: one hour of labor is given up for $2; one pair of sox is traded for $1. For this reason, we find the flow of real goods and services matched by an equal and opposite flow of money. This property is incorporated into a revised circular flow model shown in Figure 2-2. What we have called wages, rent, interest, profits, costs, income, and revenue are all seen as flows of money in this revised scheme.

IV. MARKETS

Now that we have added money and prices to our model of exchange between households and businesses, we can introduce that social device through which both prices and quantities exchanged are determined. This device, or institutional arrangement, is called a *market*. A market is simply the sum of contacts between buyers

---

periods to purchase goods and services. It is a way of holding wealth that is more flexible than holding it in physical objects such as wheat or land or buildings.

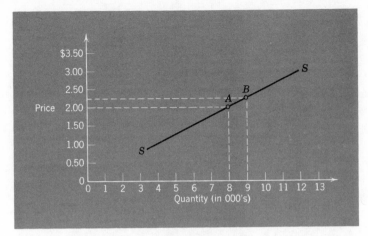

Figure 2-3

and sellers of a product or service. Markets may be formally organized and geographically centered, as are the New York Stock
Exchange or the Chicago Board of Trade, or they may be neither.
The market for shoes or for structural steel shapes is not formally
organized as is the stock market, nor can either of them be located
at some particular place on a map. To repeat: markets are institutions through which buyers and sellers interact and in which
prices and quantities exchanged are determined. It is not surprising that "market system" has long been synonymous with
"price system."

When businesses carry their goods or services to market, they
are acting as suppliers. In seeking maximum profits, they strive to
secure high prices for their wares. The higher the price per unit
of goods, the better off they are. Moreover, the higher the price,
the larger the quantity of goods that businesses will want to sell.
The quantity of a product supplied increases as its price increases.[9] This relationship is illustrated by the supply curve SS
in Figure 2-3. If price rises from $2 to $2.25, the quantity of the
product supplied by the firms in our example will rise from 8000

[9] At this point the reader is asked to accept this relationship as describing
observed behavior in the real world. A theoretical explanation of the relationship is presented in Chapters 3 and 4.

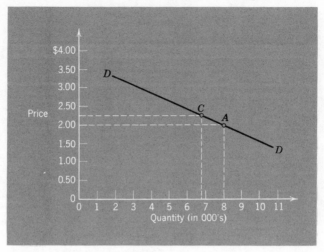

Figure 2-4

to 9000 units. An increase in price of $.25 elicits 1000 additional units of output—suppliers move from point A to point B on the market supply curve.

Households are demanders in the markets which are supplied by businesses. As demanders, they desire to exchange a part of their income for consumption goods and services. They cast their "dollar votes" for the items they most strongly desire. Being demanders (rather than suppliers) in these markets, households desire to give up as little money as possible for each unit purchased. The lower the price, the better off they are. Moreover, at lower prices buyers will be induced to buy more of the product than otherwise and some households not yet in the market will buy the product for the first time. Quantity demanded increases as prices falls. This relationship is illustrated by the demand curve DD in Figure 2-4. If price falls from $2.25 to $2, households want to increase their purchases from 6800 to 8000 units. Household demand moves from point C to point A on the market demand curve.[10]

---

[10] As we shall see in Chapter 5, the demand and supply curves for a particular commodity do not stay fixed in place over time. They can shift up or down in response to various forces. For example, if the costs of producing

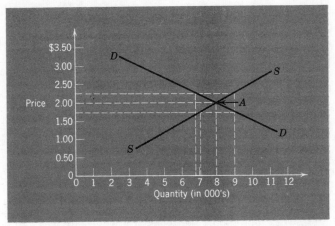

Figure 2-5

With demanders competing freely among themselves to buy goods cheaply and suppliers competing freely among themselves to sell goods dearly, the market conflict is on. Resolution of this conflict will occur when one particular price is established in the market. This is the price which will equate the quantity that demanders are willing to buy with the amount suppliers are willing to sell. In Figure 2-5 this price is $2. It is the price that will clear the market. At any price higher than $2, businesses want to sell more of the product than households stand ready to buy. For example, at the price of $2.25 in Figure 2-5, suppliers desire to sell 9000 units, while demanders are willing to buy only 6800 units. There is a surplus on the market which will tend to depress price. At a lower price than $2, for instance, $1.75, households want to buy more than businesses are prepared to sell. In this case, there is a shortage of goods and the price will be bid up. There is only one price in a market which will produce neither a *shortage* nor a *surplus*. This price will just clear the market. It is known as an *equilibrium price*.[11] In Figure 2-5, the equilibrium price is $2, the

---

a good were to rise, the supply curve of that good would shift upward. In much the same way, the demand curve will shift outward if peoples' incomes increase or if peoples' tastes shift toward the good in question.

11 In economics, as in physics, the concept of equilibrium refers to a balance of forces; hence it signifies a state of rest. An equilibrium price balances the

equilibrium quantity is 8000 units, and the equilibrium itself is denoted by A.

In the market for the services of the factors of production, the roles of households and businesses are reversed. Businesses are demanders and households are suppliers. To maximize their profits, businesses attempt to buy the factor services (labor, natural resources, and capital) for as low a price as possible. The lower the price, the larger the quantity of factor services that businesses will demand. Again, quantity demanded varies inversely with price.

Households, to maximize their satisfaction, desire to sell their factor services for high prices. The higher the price, the more factor services they will be willing to sell. A worker would be willing to work more hours per week at a wage rate of $5 an hour than he would at a wage rate of $2 an hour. As in the goods and services market, quantity supplied varies directly with price.[12]

Again a conflict is posed; again through free competition the market secures a resolution of the forces of factor supply and factor demand; again an equilibrium price is established which equates quantity supplied with quantity demanded. Again the market is cleared with no surplus and no shortage.

With this analysis of the factor market, we can complete our diagram of a purely competitive price system. By interposing markets in the exchanges between households and businesses (Figure 2-6), the circular-flow economy is completed. In the top half of the diagram the markets for consumer goods and services are shown. Here several things occur. (1) Households as demanders interact with businesses as suppliers. (2) Both the prices of goods and the quantities exchanged are determined. (3) The flow of goods and services from businesses to households is equated in value terms with an equal flow of money from households to businesses.

---

quantity demanded with the quantity supplied, and *ceteris paribus,* shows no tendency to change.

[12] There are situations in which a labor market will experience a different relationship between price and quantity supplied. Likewise, if the quantity of a natural resource is fixed, its supply curve will be a vertical straight line at the fixed quantity. We shall discuss some of the peculiarities of factor supply in Chapter 3.

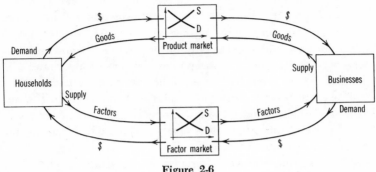

Figure 2-6

In the bottom half of the diagram the roles played by the participants are reversed, as are the flows of money and of services. Factor services flow from households to businesses. This flow is matched in value terms by an equal and opposite flow of money from businesses to households. Again the market forces of supply and demand determine prices and quantities exchanged.

In our simple model we have simplified the real world drastically. First, we have only considered trading relationships between households and firms, not between firms and firms or households and households. Moreover, we have assumed that there would be no change in the total quantity and quality of resources available. Because of this assumption, changes in the particular goods exchanged, changes in incomes, and changes in prices result only from changes in consumer tastes. We have excluded growth in the quantity of or change in the quality of the labor force, capital goods, or natural resources. Because of these assumptions, the size of the flow in the top half of the diagram will equal the size of the flow in the bottom half. The value of consumer goods exchanged is equal to the value of factor services exchanged. The revenue from sales of the business firms is completely absorbed in payments to households.

This is clearly an artificial set of conditions. In the real world, the quantity and quality of factors of production change because of such things as population growth, technological change, or discovery of new mineral deposits. Suppose, for example, that the population grows so that more people enter the labor force. Households now will supply more labor at each and every possible price than they would have before. This increased supply will tend to depress the price of labor and businesses will hire more workers. With more labor, businesses will produce more goods which, in turn, will affect supply in the consumer-goods markets. Moreover, the changes in the population will create changes in the demand for products. New equilibrium prices and quantities will be established in both factor and product market.[13] The circular flow of economic activity will now continue its newly established pattern until some other change occurs which will jar the system into still another circular-flow pattern.

Of course, the real-world circular-flow economy is constantly interrupted by extraneous changes in tastes and technology. Consequently, it is not possible to identify a general equilibrium situation at any time. Nevertheless, it is useful to stop the world mentally to try to determine what is going on. This mental experiment compares to the physical experiment in which one understands the real world with its air friction by carrying on experiments in an artificially created vacuum.

V. CONCLUSION AND SUMMARY

We have arrived at a simple model of the economy, stripped of many of the complexities of everyday activity in order to make clear the essence of a price system. Succeeding chapters will add many of the missing details. Our hope is to develop a sufficiently detailed framework to enable the reader to analyze most policy problems with some degree of accuracy and sophistication. Our simple model has highlighted the circular-flow mechanism through which incomes are earned and spent, and goods and services are purchased and consumed. The pervasive interdependence among

[13] Yet additional complexities will enter the picture in the real world and would have to be accounted for by relaxation of more of our implicit and explicit assumptions. For example, particular prices and quantities would be affected by participants exercising control over supply or demand, by lack of knowledge, and by uncertainty. Price and quantity levels would be affected by involuntary unemployment, the effects of international trade, or changes in the money supply. See *National Income and Employment Analysis* and *Toward Economic Stability,* in this series, for a more detailed discussion of these effects.

the economic units in the system is clearly evident. As Joseph Schumpeter has stated with respect to such a system:

How much meat the butcher disposes of depends upon how much his customer the tailor will buy and at what price. That depends, however, upon the proceeds from the latter's business, these proceeds again depend upon the needs and the purchasing power of his customer the shoemaker, whose purchasing power again depends upon the needs and purchasing power of the people for whom he produces; and so forth until we finally strike someone whose income derives from the sale of his goods to the butcher. This concatenation and mutual dependence of the quantities of which the economic cosmos consists are always visible, in whichever of the possible directions one may choose to move.[14]

Moreover, our simple model of a free enterprise economy has pointed up the key role played by the prices of commodities and services. By equating quantities supplied with quantities demanded and clearing markets, these prices organize the economic activity in the system. They determine incomes, organize output, and ration consumption. In general, they provide the mechanism in a market society for answering the basic economic questions asked of any society: What is to be produced? How is it to be produced? For whom is it to be produced?

QUESTIONS

1. What is meant by the word "system" when we speak of the "market system" or the "price system?"
2. Nearly all people serve as both "demanders" and "suppliers" during the course of a day. In which ways does the behavior of a person change when he, say, changes from a demander to a supplier? Do his basic motivations become altered?
3. It is often said that prices and profits guide the allocation of resources in a market economy. What is the basis for this statement? Describe how the allocation of resources would be altered in a market economy if, say, the government decreed that the price of shoes would be fixed at $5 *above* the equilibrium price.
4. From your observation of the United States economy, describe the differences in the retail market for groceries and the market for

---

[14] Joseph Schumpeter, *The Theory of Economic Development,* Harvard University Press, Cambridge, 1934, p. 7.

school teacher services. In each case, which sector serves as buyer? Seller? What are the characteristics of the buyers? Sellers? How many of each are there? Where is the market for each located? Name some extraneous forces which might make the equilibrium price in each market change.

5. In the text it states that ". . . the size of the flow in the top half of [Figure 2-6] will equal the size of the flow in the bottom half." Show what the existence of profits has to do with this equality.

3

The Household—A Decision-Making Unit

The household does not exist in a vacuum but is a part of an entire economic system, whose decisions both affect and are affected by other parts of that system. The signals it receives from other parts of the system affect the decisions which it makes. Conversely, in making decisions, the household sends signals to other parts of the system. For example, if a household should decide to buy a car, the decision of what make, style, and price to choose is affected by many signals received from other parts of the economic system—the prices of smaller cars relative to larger cars, the relative effectiveness of the advertising campaigns of the various auto companies, the incomes paid by the businesses which employ members of the household, the prices of all other goods, and other things. Household decisions, in turn, affect many other sectors—for example, the business firms that produce cars, the employees of these businesses, and the businesses that supply the car producers. It is this taking in and giving out of signals that will interest us in this discussion of the household sector.

In discussing the behavior of the household we shall rely on deductive logic. We shall make some basic assumptions about the household and then, on the basis of a model developed from these assumptions, deduce the behavior of the household in making economic choices. We shall present here a basic model of household choice; a more rigorous model will be offered in an appendix to this chapter.

I. MOTIVATION AND RATIONAL CHOICE

The household as a family unit is forced to make a multitude of decisions—what food to buy, what kind of a house to rent (or buy), how much to spend on entertainment, where to work, and the like. Because of the household's position in the circular flow of an economic system, all of these economic decisions can be placed into two groups. On the one hand, there is the choice of which and how much of each of its factors of production are to be sold, and on the other, the choice of which and how much of each of the available consumption goods and services are to be purchased.

In considering these two kinds of choices, the question of motivation immediately arises. For an individual to choose rationally, he must have some goal which he is trying to achieve. With a basic objective, the decision maker can approach each decision with the question: "Which of the alternatives available to me will lead to the most progress toward my goal?" In constructing a model of consumer behavior, we shall assume, not unrealistically, that the drive which motivates the household is the desire for something called *utility* or *satisfaction* or *pleasure*. As a decision-making unit, the household chooses among available alternatives in order to maximize its satisfaction or pleasure. Consequently, when a housewife in the supermarket picks up a package of doughnuts, hesitates, and sets them down again, we conclude that she considers the 49¢ that she would have spent on the doughnuts capable of giving more satisfaction if spent on other things.

II. THE DETERMINANTS OF CONSUMER CHOICE

For a household to choose rationally it must consider and weigh a number of factors. If we are to understand the behavior of the household—why it chooses as it does—we must isolate the most important factors and determine how they influence household decisions. In analyzing a household buying goods and services, the basic question is: What factors determine which commodities the household will buy, and of those it chooses, how much of each will be purchased?

The list of factors affecting a household's choice is long. At the top is something we shall call the household's set of *preferences* or its *tastes*. In calling this a determinant of choice, we assume that the decision maker knows himself sufficiently well to be able to say, for example, "I prefer three loaves of bread to one pair of socks but I prefer one pair of socks to one theater ticket." According to his set of preferences, the household is able to "order" or rank its alternatives. This ranking is a most important consideration in determining what alternatives the household will eventually decide upon. Clearly, a decision maker's tastes and preferences are determined by all of those forces, physiological, psychological, sociological, or religious, which influence a person's attitude toward alternative goods and services.

However, a consumer's tastes and preferences are not the only determinant of his consumption pattern. A second important determinant of consumer decisions is the *income* of the household. By observing the world around us, we can readily discern how the level of income influences consumer behavior. It is more than a difference in tastes which causes some people to live in Beverly Hills while others live in Watts. In general, an increased income will cause a household to increase the quantity purchased of those goods already chosen and, in addition, to choose a larger assortment of commodities. For example, poor people generally have fewer clothes than rich people and clothes of a much narrower range of styles and types. Few sharecroppers own the latest style tuxedo!

The third primary determinant of a consumer's decisions is the set of *prices* placed on the various commodities which he confronts. Again, observation of the real world demonstrates that the prices of commodities importantly influence the bundle of goods that a consumer actually chooses as well as how much of each he stands ready to buy. Were the price of a dozen doughnuts $2 instead of 49¢, the housewife would not give them a second thought. Were the price 10¢, she would probably buy a dozen— or maybe even two.

III. THE DEMAND FUNCTION FOR A
SINGLE HOUSEHOLD

Having described the major determinants of consumer choice, we can now specify more accurately the relationship between the household's demand for a good and those things that determine this demand. With respect to any of the alternative goods facing a consumer, say, good x, the quantity of x demanded (D_x) depends on the following four determinants: the price of the good (P_x), the prices of other goods (P_n), the consumer's income per unit of time (I), and the consumer's set of preferences or tastes (T). This can be written as follows:

$$D_x = f(P_x, P_n, I, T)$$

in which f signifies "a function of."

All of the variables in this demand function are free to change. A change in any of those on the right-hand side of the equation —the determinants—elicits a change in the variable on the left-hand side of the equation—the determined. Within this equation, we are especially interested in one particular relationship. This is the relationship of the price of x (P_x) to the household's decision of how much x to buy—the demand for $x(D_x)$. Assuming all things other than P_x to be constant (that is, P_n, I, T), how will the quantity of the good demanded vary as its price changes? How will the number of packages of doughnuts bought by the housewife change when the price of doughnuts changes but the income of her household, their tastes, and the prices of other goods all remain unchanged? This relationship can be written as:

$$D_x = f(P_x) \ ceteris \ paribus^1$$

To derive this relationship, we shall, in the next section, investigate each of the determinants of demand in more detail, evaluating the influence of each on the household's decision-making process. Beginning with an analysis of the consumer's tastes and preferences (T), we shall, in turn, analyze the impact

---

[1] In economics, the property of "all other things held constant" is often stated in Latin, *ceteris paribus*.

of income (I) and prices (P_n, P_x) on the decisions of the consumer.

QUESTIONS

1. What does the economist mean when he speaks of "rational behavior"? Is it possible to determine whether a particular individual is making rational choices? Is there a basis for asserting that any particular choice is or is not rational? If it is granted that cigarette smoking is cancer inducing, can one use this fact to assert that Mr. X's decision to smoke cigarettes is an irrational decision?
2. It is often noted that a person's cultural background has a good deal to do with the choices and decisions which he makes. Is this influence included in the three determinants of consumer decisions or is it in addition to them? If it is included in the three determinants, where does one find it?
3. In the demand function, the variables on the right-hand side of the equation determine the value of the variable on the left-hand side. Can the variables on the right-hand side influence each other? Can changes in the variable on the left-hand side of the equation cause changes in one or more of the variables on the right-hand side? For the first equation shown on p. 50, how many separate *ceteris paribus* equations are there?

IV. CONSUMER TASTES AND PREFERENCES: MAXIMIZING UTILITY[2]

To construct a model of consumer behavior, let us assume the existence of a perfectly rational individual who maximizes his satisfaction or utility. Clearly, this is an abstraction. The behavior pattern of such an individual cannot be found in the real world. Who among us is perfectly rational in framing choices among alternatives? Who always chooses the good or service that brings him the most satisfaction per dollar? However, although

[2] Sections IV, V, and VI contain a basic analysis of how the determinants in the demand relationship affect the quantity of x demanded by a household. It is based on marginal utility analysis. A somewhat more rigorous analysis of the demand relationship and derivation of the demand curve is presented in the appendix to this chapter. It is based on indifference curve analysis. The appendix can either be used in place of sections IV, V, and VI (with no loss of continuity) or be treated as a supplement to Chapter 3.

man is not perfectly rational, neither is he completely irrational. By dealing with such an abstraction, we shall be able to discover, in idealized form, some very real characteristics of actual human behavior. The economist's model of human behavior is much like the model airplane of the small boy. Although the model airplane makes no pretense at describing the complete reality of aerodynamics, it does clarify some of the principles of flight. The economist's abstraction, too, is not a complete explanation. However, it does clarify some principles by which humans make choices.

Let us, then, assume that this rational, utility-maximizing individual has a set of tastes and preferences—likes and dislikes— which define his attitude toward the myriad of goods with which he is confronted. That each person has such an unique set of tastes is indisputable. For Mr. Jones, red Thunderbirds convey enormous pleasure. For Mr. Smith, a stereo recording of a Bartok quartet conveys the same satisfaction. If we presume that satisfaction is measurable, an individual's tastes can be summarized in a set of "utility curves" of the type shown in Figure 3-1. For

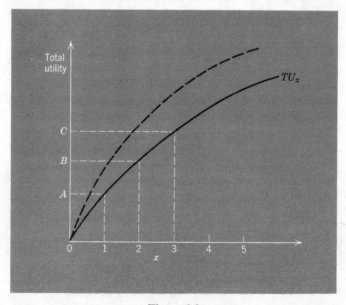

Figure 3-1

each good or service, the consumer will have a separate utility curve. The curve in Figure 3-1 is for the good x. On the horizontal axis, we have plotted the number of units of the good x; the total amount of utility provided by the consumption of x is shown on the vertical axis. The curve is labeled TU_x to stand for total utility derived by consuming good x. On the diagram we can see that the consumption of one unit of x (say, one glass of tomato juice) gives an utility of OA. If two units are consumed, total utility increases to OB, implying that the second unit of x adds AB units of utility to the OA units of satisfaction already experienced. Similarly, if three units are consumed, total utility is OC with the third unit adding BC to the OB units of satisfaction previously obtained.

Clearly, the level of the TU_x curve describes the extent of the consumer's enjoyment of good x. The higher the TU_x curve, the more satisfaction good x gives to the consumer. For example, the dashed curve in Figure 3-1 implies a greater preference for good x than does the TU_x curve. For any number of units consumed, the level of satisfaction on the dashed curve exceeds that for TU_x.

Similarly, the shape of the total utility curve must be noted with care. With but few exceptions, total utility curves must possess the general shape of TU_x in Figure 3-1. This is so because of a most basic characteristic of human beings. It can be described as follows. *As a person consumes equal additional units of a good or service, his total satisfaction may well increase continuously. However, after some point, the addition to total utility conveyed by each additional unit of the good or service will decrease.* Because this characteristic holds in all circumstances, it is referred to as a law in economics—*the Law of Diminishing Marginal Utility.* The marginal (or additional) utility obtained by consuming one more unit of a good or service is, after some point, smaller than the marginal utility obtained by consuming the previous unit. Thus, in Figure 3-1, the additional utility obtained by consuming the second unit of x (AB) is less than the additional utility obtained by consuming the first unit (OA); the additional utility obtained by consuming the third unit of x (BC) is less than the additional utility obtained by consuming the second unit (AB); and so on.

It is because of the Law of Diminishing Marginal Utility that

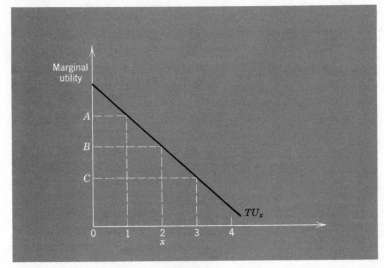

Figure 3-2

the TU_x curve of Figure 3-1 is bowed downward—each additional unit consumed adds less to total utility than did the previous unit. This same property can be shown in a diagram in which the amounts of additional utility—the *marginal* utilities—are related to the number of units of the good which are consumed. Figure 3-2 plots the marginal utility curve which corresponds to TU_x in Figure 3-1. This curve, labeled MU_x, shows that the first unit of x consumed yields satisfaction of OA. This exceeds the addition to satisfaction gained by consuming the second unit—OB—which exceeds the addition to satisfaction obtained by consuming the third unit (OC), and so on.[3] Because of the Law of Diminishing Marginal Utility, the marginal utility curve for virtually all commodities for each and every consumer must be downward sloping like MU_x of Figure 3-2.[4]

[3] It should be noted that the distance OA in Figure 3-2 corresponds to OA in Figure 3-1. Similarly, OB and OC in Figure 3-2 represent the same increments to satisfaction as AB and BC in Figure 3-1.

[4] It would be a good exercise to draw the marginal utility curve which corresponds to the dashed total utility curve in Figure 3-1. How does this marginal curve relate to MU_x in Figure 3-2?

Given the notions of total and marginal utility and the Law of Diminishing Marginal Utility, we can easily describe what is meant by "consumer tastes and preferences." Basically, a consumer's preferences are defined by the complete set of total utility curves—one for each good or service—which he possesses. Because each total utility curve has a marginal utility curve which can be derived from it, the consumer's tastes and preferences are also defined by the whole family of marginal utility curves—one for each good or service which gives him satisfaction.

QUESTIONS

1. Draw a typical person's total utility curve for alcoholic beverages or drugs. Does the stupor-inducing or habit-forming character of these commodities affect the general shape of the total utility curve? Draw a typical person's total utility curve for minutes of attendance at an unconscionably dull lecture. (*Hint.* If there is utility, there must be disutility.) Draw the marginal utility curve of each of these total utility curves.
2. Describe the implication of a total utility curve which turned down after reaching a peak. What would the corresponding marginal utility curve look like?
3. What is likely to happen to the typical person's total utility curve for cigarettes as the link between smoking and lung cancer becomes more firmly established?
4. What would happen to a typical person's total utility curve for drinking water over time if he found himself lost in a hot and arid desert? Also show what would happen to the marginal utility curve.
5. Complete the following table.

Number of Pairs of Shoes	Total Utility	Marginal Utility
0	0	—
1	20	—
2	—	—
3	50	—
4	60	—
5	66	—
6	—	—
7	72	—

V. THE OTHER DETERMINANTS OF DEMAND
—INCOME (I) AND PRICES (P_x, P_n)

In addition to consumer tastes, there are other determinants of how much a consumer will demand of a particular good or service. As we noted earlier, his income (I) will surely be a factor. In general, we can assert that the greater a consumer's income, the more he will demand of any good. This relationship, however, may not hold for a few, rather unique, goods. For example, it is possible that a consumer will reduce the amount of hamburger purchased as his income rises. He may substitute more exotic varieties and cuts of meat for the less exquisite hamburger. Goods whose demands respond in this way to changes in income are referred to as *inferior* goods. In sum, for most goods, the relationship between the level of demand and a consumer's income is a positive one; for inferior goods the relationship is negative.

Prices are the remaining determinants of consumer demand for a good. Two types of prices are pertinent to the level of demand —the price of the good itself (P_x) and the prices of the n goods which are related to x (P_n). For example, the number of packages of doughnuts which a housewife puts in her shopping basket depends on the price of doughnuts but also on the price of related goods, say, cookies.

If the price of doughnuts rises, the housewife will be discouraged from buying as many packages of doughnuts as before and, in all likelihood, will reduce her purchases of the good. In general, the relationship between the amount of a good demanded and its price is a negative one.

The influence of the prices of *goods related to* doughnuts on the quantity of doughnuts demanded is slightly more complicated to discover. The difficulty here stems from the fact that some goods go well with doughnuts while others are substitutes for them. An example of a good which is *complementary* to doughnuts is milk. On the other hand, cookies are *substitutes* for doughnuts. The more milk a typical consumer has, the more doughnuts he desires; on the other hand, the more cookies he has, the *fewer* doughnuts he desires.

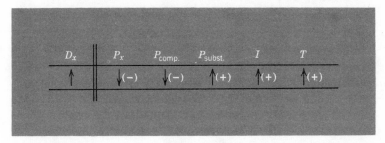

Figure 3-3

What now is the influence of changes in the prices of these related goods on the demand for doughnuts? Let us assume that the price of both milk and cookies goes up. As we have seen, this means that the consumer will try to buy less of both of these goods. Now, let us take them one at a time and see how the change in price (of milk or cookies) affects the quantity of doughnuts which a consumer demands. First, consider milk. Because the consumer has decreased his purchases of milk because of its higher price, he will tend to want fewer packages of doughnuts than before. For *complementary* goods, then, the relationship of the *price* of one good and the *quantity demanded* of its complement is *negative*.

Next, let us look at the substitute good—cookies. We have seen that the higher price of cookies has led the consumer to purchase fewer packages of them than he would otherwise have. With fewer cookies in hand, the consumer would tend to buy *more* packages of doughnuts. When the price of cookies rises, the consumer will tend to substitute doughnuts for cookies. For *substitute* goods, then, the relationship of the *price* of one good and the *quantity demanded* of its substitute is *positive*.

In the above paragraphs, we have explored the complex of relationships between the demand for a good x (D_x) and the determinants of that demand (P_x, P_n, I, T). In Figure 3-3, this complex of relationships is summarized. This chart can be read as follows. If the price of x falls ($\downarrow$), the quantity of x demanded will rise ($\uparrow$)—the relationship is a *negative* one. On the other hand, if the consumer's tastes for good x increase ($\uparrow$), the quantity of good x which is purchased will also rise ($\uparrow$)—the relationship is a *positive* one.[5]

QUESTIONS

1. Describe the likely effect on the quantity of good x demanded if:
   (a) The price of a good complementary to x rises.
   (b) The price of a good which is a substitute for x falls.
   (c) The tastes of the consumer for a good complementary to x increase.
   (d) The income of the consumer falls.
2. How would you describe the relationship between two goods, x and y, if, when the price of x increases by 10 percent, the quantity demanded of y shows no change? Suggest a pair of goods which are likely to have such a relationship to each other.
3. Consider two goods, x and y. Would it be possible for the quantity demanded of x to fall by 10 percent and the quantity of y demanded to fall by 5 percent, if a 2 percent increase in the price of y was the only economic change to which the changes in quantity demanded were reacting? Discuss.
4. Which of the following items would be likely to generate an increase in the quantity of ties demanded by a man and through which of the determinants of the demand function would each of these changes work?
   (a) The decision of his wife to seek a part-time job.
   (b) An increase in his taste for soup at lunch.
   (c) The death of a rich uncle.
   (d) A decrease in the price of steel.
   (e) A change in fashions to wider ties with bright colors.
   (f) An increase in the price of suits.
   (g) The hiring of a young and attractive secretary.
   (h) Having a new red car.

VI. $D_x = f(P_x)$ *CETERIS PARIBUS*— THE DEMAND CURVE FOR GOOD X

In this section, we shall pick one particular demand relationship and explore it in some depth. This is the relationship of the quan-

---

[5] While the relationships shown in Figure 3-3 hold generally, one should be careful to allow for aberrations. For example, we have seen that it is not always true that the quantity of a good demanded will increase as a consumer's income rises.

tity demanded of a good (D_x) and the price of that good (P_x). From this relationship we shall derive the *consumer's demand curve* for a given product. Stated most basically, the demand curve relates *THE QUANTITY OF A GOOD, X, DEMANDED* (D_x) *TO THE PRICE OF THAT GOOD* (P_x), *WHEN ALL OF THE OTHER DETERMINANTS OF* D_x (namely, P_n, I, T) *ARE CONSTANT.*

To help us in logically deriving the demand curve, we shall build a simple model. With this model, we shall be able to see clearly the basis for what we shall call the Law of Demand. First, then, let us assume a rational consumer with an *income* (I) of, say, $6. This consumer can buy only two goods, x and y, and by chance, his *tastes* for these two goods are identical. These tastes are shown by the identical marginal utility curves (MU_x and MU_y) of Figure 3-4. Finally let us assume that the price of both x and y (namely, P_x and P_y) is $1.

Given these assumptions, the first task is to determine how the consumer will allocate his $6 of income between x and y. Let us take it dollar by dollar. On which good, then, will he spend his first dollar? Because the consumer is rational, he will spend that dollar on the good for which the marginal utility is the greatest. In our model, however, the marginal utilities are equal. Being indifferent between spending the $1 on x or y, the consumer, let us say, flips a coin and on the basis of the outcome chooses x.[6] The utility which the consumer receives is shown by the shaded area labeled ① on the diagram for good x.

The question now is, on which good will he spend his second dollar. Obviously, if he spends it on x, he receives less additional utility than he received by spending the first dollar on x. This is so because of the Law of Diminishing Marginal Utility. However, because the utility from y is as yet untapped, the consumer will gain greater utility by spending the second dollar on y than by spending it on x. This additional utility is shown by the shaded area labeled ② on the diagram for y. By similar reasoning the con-

---

[6] It should be emphasized that the flip of the coin is only used as a crutch in this example. In trying to keep the model simple, we have assumed that the marginal utility curves for the two goods are identical. This gives us no basis for choosing one over the other in allocating the first dollar of income so as to achieve maximum utility.

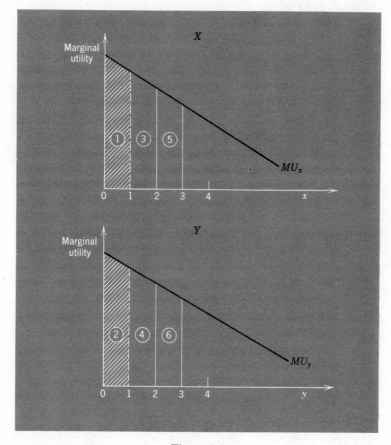

Figure 3-4

sumer will spend his third dollar on x (if the flip of the coin yields the same results as the first time), his fourth dollar on y, his fifth dollar on x (again, if the flip of the coin so decrees), and his sixth dollar on y. The result of this sequence is shown in Figure 3-4. With identical tastes for the two goods and with each good bearing the same price, it is not surprising that the consumer will allocate his income equally between the two goods —purchasing three units of each.

In order to derive a demand curve, we must observe how the

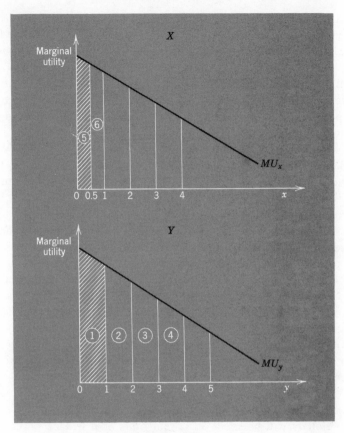

Figure 3-5

quantity of a good demanded changes when *its* price changes. In working through this exercise, let us concentrate on good *x*. We shall alter its price and observe how the quantity demanded of *x* changes in response to the new price. Let us assume that the price of *x* rises from $1 to $2, while the price of *y* (P_y) the consumer's income (I), and his tastes (T) all remain unchanged. We shall refer to the marginal utility curves in Figure 3-5 in working through this exercise. They are identical to the curves in Figure 3-4.

How will the consumer allocate his income between *x* and *y*, given the increased price of x? Again, let us take it dollar by dollar[7] and see how a rational consumer would behave. For the first dollar the consumer can buy either one-half unit of x or 1 unit of y. By comparing the pertinent shaded areas, it is clear that the utility from purchasing one unit of y is greater than the utility from purchasing one-half unit of x. The first dollar will go to y. The utility gained is shown by the shaded area labeled ① in the graph for y.

Now, how will the consumer allocate the second dollar? With that dollar, he can purchase either the second unit of y or the first one-half unit of x. By the same reasoning as above, the consumer will spend the second dollar on y as well. The marginal utility from obtaining a second unit of y exceeds the marginal utility from obtaining the first one-half unit of x. Again, by comparing areas (marginal utilities), it is seen that the third dollar and the fourth dollar will also be spent on y.

In the allocation of the fifth dollar, however, comparison of the marginal utility areas shows that the greater gain in satisfaction is obtained by purchasing the first one-half unit of x rather than the fifth unit of y. The decrease in the marginal utility of y (as more of it has been obtained) has been sufficient to compensate for the higher price of x. By the same comparison, the sixth dollar of income will be allocated to x.

The results of this allocation exercise can now be easily summarized. Four of the $6 of income will be allocated to y, two of the dollars will be spent on x; four units of y will be purchased and only one unit of x. Because of the increase in P_x from $1 to $2 (with nothing else changed), the consumer has reallocated his income from x to y, has decreased his purchase of x from three units to one unit, and has increased his purchase of y from three units to four units.[8]

---

[7] Implicit in working through the example the first time was the assumption that the consumer could not break the dollar down into smaller units (say, pennies) and allocate them one at a time. We retain that assumption here.

[8] From the logical exercise of Figures 3-4 and 3-5, one question rather naturally arises. If the consumer could shift his income between x and y in very small amounts, where would he find the optimal allocation; what characteristics would this allocation have? The answer to this question is that the consumer would allocate his income between x and y so that the ratio

By allowing only the price of one of the commodities to change —nothing else—we have performed precisely the kind of logical exercise necessary to derive the demand curve for x. It will be recalled that the demand curve of any commodity (x) relates the quantity demanded (D_x) of that good to its price (P_x), when nothing else changes. In the diagram of Figure 3-6, we have plotted the quantity of x on the horizontal axis and the price of x (P_x) on the vertical axis. In our first exercise, we found that three units of x would be demanded when the price of x (P_x) is $1. This is shown by point A in Figure 3-6. Point B was derived from the second exercise; at the $2 price of x, only one unit would be demanded. By connecting points A and B, the demand curve for x $[D_x = f (P_x)$ *cet. par.*$]$ is derived.

The shape of this curve is precisely that which our initial thoughts led us to incorporate into the table of Figure 3-3—the relationship between the quantity of a commodity demanded and its price is a negative one. This shape has become for economics

---

of the marginal utility of x to the price of x would just equal the ratio of the marginal utility of y to the price of y $(MU_x/P_x = MU_y/P_y)$. Let us again use some numbers to see why this is so. Assume that the consumer found himself in a situation in which the ratios were unequal—say, $MU_x/P_x = 20/\$2$ and $MU_y/P_y = 20/\$1$. We could write this $MU_x/P_x < MU_y/P_y$ or $20/\$2 < 20/\$1$. The consumer in this situation would find that he could increase his total utility by reallocating his income from one of the commodities to the other. How would he do this?

It makes sense to experiment by taking the first dollar away from the good with the lowest marginal utility-to-price ratio—in this case, x. If $1 is taken away from x and spent on y, the consumer sacrifices 10 units of utility (by decreasing his consumption of x by one-half unit) but increases his utility by 20 units (by increasing his consumption of y by one unit). On balance, he gains 10 units of satisfaction by making the shift. Clearly, it would be in his interest to continue this process as long as $MU_x/P_x < MU_y/P_y$. However, as he reallocates his income, these two ratios begin to converge. Because of the Law of Diminishing Marginal Utility, the MU_y will tend to *fall* as more of y is consumed. For the same reason, the MU_x will tend to *rise* as less of x is consumed. At some point the two marginal utility ratios will become equal $(MU_x/P_x = MU_y/P_y)$. In our example this would happen when the marginal utility of x rises to 30 and the marginal utility of y falls to 15. When this adjustment occurs, the equal ratio condition will hold $(30/\$2 = 15/\$1)$. This equal ratio condition is called the *equilibrium* condition for the consumer. In equilibrium, the amount of utility experienced by the consumer is as great as it can possibly be—utility is maximized.

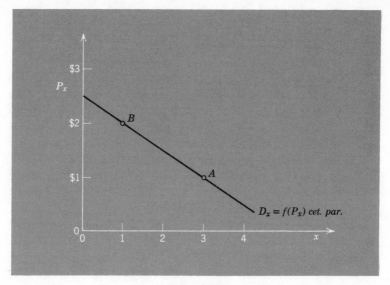

Figure 3-6

what the gravity hypothesis is for physics: a stable law on which a large superstructure of further analysis has been built. This law in economics is called the *Law of Downward Sloping Demand.* It says that *because of the nature of rational consumer decision making, more of a good will be demanded when its price falls and less of a good will be demanded when its price rises.* But we must do more than simply state the law; we must also defend it.

Without question, the Law of Diminishing Marginal Utility is the basic reason for the shape of the demand curve. Because of this law, the satisfaction gained from consuming the *next* unit of a good is less than the utility gained from consuming the previous unit. Consequently, there is a point in the consumption of each good at which the money spent to get one more unit of it could be used to acquire more utility by purchasing another good. It follows that if the price of a good rises, the level of consumption at which that point is reached will be less than at the lower price.

This effect is called the *substitution effect.* It states that as the price of a good, x, falls relative to the price of another good, y, the consumer will tend to buy more of x, which is now relatively cheaper, and less of y, which is now relatively more expensive. He will substitute the consumption of x for the consumption of y. Hence a decrease in the price of x results in an increase in the quantity demanded.

There is another effect which, in most cases, also causes the demand curve to be negatively sloped. It is called the *income effect*. It states that, when the price of one good, x, *decreases* while the prices of all other goods remain constant, the consumer has, in effect, experienced an increase in his purchasing power. His real income has been augmented. This increase in purchasing power will cause the consumer to buy more of all his choices, including good x.[9] Again, the quantity of x demanded rises as its price falls. The combined income and substitution effects therefore cause an inverse relationship between the price of a good and the quantity of it which is demanded—in other words, the Law of Downward Sloping Demand.

Before continuing, however, we would do well to explore briefly how changes in the other determinants of the demand for x (D_x) could be examined in terms of our simple model. In Figure 3-4, it was noted that the pair of marginal utility curves picture the consumer's tastes for the two goods. What would happen to the level of the two curves if the consumer's tastes, say, shifted from x toward y? How would this shift in tastes be reflected in the allocation of the consumer's income between x and y? What would happen to the demand curves of x and y? Or consider how a change in the level of consumer income would affect the consumption of x and y. If the price x were \$2 and the price of y were \$1 (Figure 3-5), how much of each good would the consumer buy if his income rose to, say, \$10? What would happen to the demand curve for good x shown in Figure 3-6? All of these questions can be answered by again working through the simple model using the same logic of allocation which we used in deriving the demand curve.[10]

[9] This, of course, assumes that none of the goods which the consumer is buying are inferior goods.

[10] In order to understand more clearly the complexities of the demand function $D_x = f$ (P_x, P_n, I, T) and the demand curve $D_x = f$ (P_x) cet. par., the reader would be well advised to work through the model.

QUESTIONS

1. The marginal utility curves of a consumer for goods A, B, and C can be drawn from the following table. Assume that the consumer has an income of $20 and that the prices of A, B, and C are $1, $2, and $1, respectively.

Quantity of A, B, or C Consumed	Units of Marginal Utility—A	Units of Marginal Utility—B	Units of Marginal Utility—C
1	50	105	25
2	45	100	20
3	40	95	15
4	35	90	10
5	30	85	5
6	25	80	0
7	20	75	0
8	15	70	0

(a) On a sheet of graph paper, draw the marginal utility curves for goods A, B, and C. (Each of these curves will be a straight line. Extend the line up to the y axis.)

(b) As we did in the chapter, allocate the consumer's income, dollar by dollar, among goods A, B, and C so as to maximize his utility. In making this allocation, assume that each successive dollar allocated can be spent on only one good; that is, a dollar cannot be divided among two or three goods. In addition, use the rule that if equal satisfaction is obtained by allocating a dollar to either of two goods, the decision will be made in favor of A rather than B or C and B rather than C. Record on the graph where each dollar is allocated.

(c) Assume now that the price of A rises to $1.50 while the prices of B and C, the consumer's income, and his tastes remain unchanged. With these new conditions, again allocate the consumer's income, using the rules stated in b.

(d) On a sheet of graph paper, draw the consumer's demand curve for A, using the conclusions of exercises (b) and (c).

(e) Describe (in a paragraph) what would happen to the demand curve for A if the price of B were to fall to $1 while everything else stayed the same. What would happen to the demand curve of A if the consumer's income doubled and everything else stayed the same? Why would these results occur?

2. In the chapter, we stated that both the income and the substitu-

tion effect would cause the demand curve to be negatively sloped. Would this be true for an inferior good? Does the demand curve for an inferior good have to be negatively sloped? What is the relationship between the income and substitution effects for a good which has a positively sloped demand curve?

3. In question 1, the amount of A purchased fell as its price rose from $1 to $1.50. Can we state that that change in quantity represents a "decrease in demand?" How would you portray a "decrease in demand" in your graph of the demand curve for A?

4. Consider the following demands. Which ones do you think obey the Law of Downward Sloping Demand—and why?

    (a) The family's demand for vacations.
    (b) A family's demand for children.
    (c) A man's demand for wives (assuming he could buy more than one).
    (d) A family's demand for doctor's services.
    (e) The household's demand for funeral services.
    (f) The household's demand for passports.
    (g) The family's demand for automatic dishwashers.

5. Mr. X consumes 200 loaves of bread per year. Mr. Y consumes one loaf of bread per week. The price of bread is the same for each consumer. Which consumer has the greater demand for bread? Which consumer would have the greater demand for bread if the price of bread to Mr. A were 15¢ per loaf and the price to Mr. B were 20¢ per loaf?

6. How would you respond to the person who asserted that the marginal utilities of all commodities would be equal in equilibrium?

VII. THE MARKET DEMAND CURVE FOR THE HOUSEHOLD SECTOR

Having derived the demand curve of a single household for a single good, we have taken the first step in describing the effect of price changes on the choice of goods and services by the entire household sector. To extend this analysis of a single household to the entire household sector—all households demanding goods and services—we must obtain the demand curve for each and every good from each and every household. This extension from one good to several and from one household to many is easily accomplished, however. By repeating the analysis of good x for goods $a, b, \ldots, z$, the entire set of demand curves possessed by a

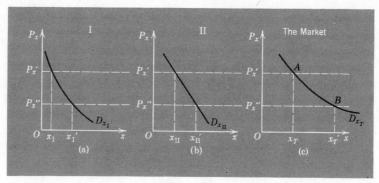

Figure 3-7

single household, say household I, can be derived. Similarly, by repeating this analysis for households II, III, . . . , N, the set of demand curves for each of the commodities—one curve for each good from each household—can be derived. By combining these individual household demand curves for each commodity, a market demand curve for each of goods a, b, . . . , z can be obtained.

Figure 3-7 shows the derivation of the market demand curve for a single commodity by combining the individual household demand curves. In Figures 3-7a and 3-7b the demand curves of two independent consumers, I and II, for good x are displayed. At a price of P_x' consumer I stands ready to purchase x_I units of the good and consumer II stands ready to take x_{II} units. Taken together, a total of x_T units ($x_I + x_{II}$) is demanded by the two households at a price of P_x'. This is shown as point A in Figure 3-7c. For example, if Mrs. Jones would buy 5 dozen doughnuts a month at a price of 29¢ a dozen and if Mrs. Smith would buy 2 dozen doughnuts a month at that price, the combined demand would be 7 dozen doughnuts a month at a price of 29¢. By the same summation process, a total of x_T' units ($x_I' + x_{II}'$) will be demanded at a price of P_x''. This is represented by point B in Figure 3-7c. The market demand curve, then, is produced by connecting points A and B in Figure 3-7c, and other points derived in the same way. It shows the quantity of good x which will be demanded by all consumers in the market at all possible prices.

By *horizontally* adding each of the individual consumer demand curves, a market demand curve has been derived. This market demand curve exists for each of the commodities which the household sector stands ready to buy. As we shall see, it plays a very important role in the process by which prices are set in a market system.

VIII. $S_f = f\ (P_f,\ L,\ T)$—THE SUPPLY OF FACTORS OF PRODUCTION

In a price system the household sector plays a dual role. Not only does it serve as a demander of consumer goods but it also acts as a supplier of the factors of production: labor, capital, and natural resources. Consequently, households not only have demand curves for consumer goods and services but they also have supply curves for factors. The household of the lady in the supermarket not only buys doughnuts and other consumer goods but also earns the income to buy these goods by selling its services or the services of its possessions—that is, by earning wages, rent, interest, and profits. To complete the analysis of the household sector, we must discuss the household's willingness to supply factors of production. By way of illustration, let us take the labor factor.

To derive the consumer's demand curve for a good or service, we worked with a pair of marginal utility curves showing the household's set of preferences between two desirable goods. We called them good x and good y. To analyze the behavior of the household in supplying the factors of production, we must again deal with the household's tastes and preferences. Again, choice must be made between alternatives. In the case of the labor factor, the household must choose between leisure, which a supplier of labor possesses by virtue of being alive, and money income, which he can obtain by trading leisure for money, namely, by working for wages.[11] He is able to substitute one for the other in the same way that the consumer was free to substitute cookies for doughnuts. He must decide how to allocate his time between

---

[11] It should be noted that in this analysis we are assuming that work is distasteful while leisure gives pleasure. While this is true for many people, it is clearly not true for all. However, this same mode of analysis could be applied in explaining the behavior of people who love to work and hate to loaf.

earning income (work) and leisure. The question we must answer is: How much labor does a possessor of leisure, a household, supply at different wage rates? From the answer to this question, we shall obtain the supply curve of labor, a curve showing the quantity of labor supplied by the household at all possible wage rates.

To derive the supply curve of labor, we shall proceed in the same way as in obtaining the consumer demand curve. We shall isolate the determinants that affect a household's willingness to supply labor and then single out one of them, the price of labor or the wage rate, for special consideration.

What are the determinants of how much labor a man will supply? They appear to fall into three categories. First, the absolute amount of leisure which a man possesses (L) will obviously have something to do with the amount he is willing to offer in the form of labor. To the labor-supplier, leisure plays the same role as income to the consumer—it is the scarce thing which must be allocated. It appears reasonable to say that the greater the amount of leisure possessed, the more of it he would be willing to offer in the form of labor. Second, the wage rate or the price offered for hours of labor (W) will also affect how much the possessor of leisure would be willing to give up. A man will be willing to devote different amounts of time to work depending on how much he can earn per hour. Finally, because the choice here is between income and hours of leisure, the household's tastes and preferences between these "goods" (T) will also be a determining factor. A born hater of work will probably supply less labor at any given wage rate than a person who likes to work. The supply of labor by the household, then, depends on the amount of leisure possessed by the household, the wage rate, and the household's set of preferences. This can be written as

$$S_l = f(L,W,T).$$

As we did for the demand function in the preceding section, let us set up a table summarizing the expected relationship between the determinants (W, L, T) and the determined (S_l) for supply of labor function. This is done in Figure 3-8. We have asserted a positive relationship between each of the determinants

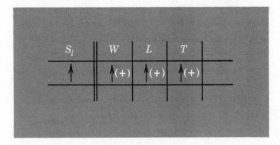

Figure 3-8

(*W, L, T*) and the determined. Let us take them one at a time and see why this should be so.

Consider first the most straightforward of these relationships—that between the quantity of labor supplied (S_l) and the worker's tastes for work relative to leisure (*T*). This relationship can be stated as $S_l = f(T)$ *cet. par.* How do changes in a person's tastes for work influence the number of hours of labor he is willing to supply, given that the wage rate (*W*) and the quantity of leisure available (*L*) remain unchanged? An example of such a change in tastes would be the individual who, after learning the details —the ins and outs—of his job discovers that he experiences a good deal less discomfort from spending time at work than he did while he was still learning the job. The disutility of working the last hour decreases; his tastes and preferences shift toward work and away from leisure. One would anticipate that such a person would be willing to increase his supply of work-hours (in response to the changed tastes) even though his hourly wage (*W*) or the amount of leisure available to him (*L*) showed no change. On this basis we assert that the relationship between a person's tastes and preferences for work and the quantity of hours he is willing to devote to work is a positive one.

Next, let us consider the relationship between the number of hours of available leisure (*L*) and the number of hours of labor a person is willing to supply (S_l)—all other things held constant. It must be kept in mind that in allocating leisure time (*L*) between nonwork and work, one is "buying" two kinds of things which convey utility—relaxation which conveys satisfaction and income which is valuable because it enables the purchase of goods and services which, in turn, convey satisfaction. Because both income and relaxation are "desirable," it is likely that any increment to available free time (L) will be allocated in some way to both of them. Similarly, a reduction in L is likely to result in a reduction in both the quantity of work hours supplied (S_l) and the quantity of relaxation hours experienced. On this basis we can confidently assert that the relationship between L and S_l, all other things held constant, is a positive one.[12]

Finally, let us deal with the relationship between the quantity of labor supplied (S_l) and the price paid for labor—the wage rate (W). It is this relationship which describes the demand curve for labor $[S_l = f\ (W)\ cet.\ par.]$. To analyze it, let us assume that the wage rate for a worker rises from \$3 per hour to \$4 per hour. Will this lead to a change in the number of hours of work which the laborer will supply and, if so, will S_l increase or decrease? In answering this question, we have to be concerned with the two effects which we encountered before—the income effect and the substitution effect. Let us take them one at a time.

First, the *income effect*. If the worker was working 50 hours per week when the wage rate was \$3 per hour, his weekly pay would be \$150 dollars. When the wage rate rises to \$4 per hour, his pay increases to \$200, if he does not alter the number of hours which he is working. What would one expect the influence of this increased income to be on the worker's allocation of L? As we learned in analyzing the consumer's demand curve, an increase in income tends to be allocated among all of the items which convey utility to the decision maker—food, travel, theater tickets, and so on. Perhaps the worker can enjoy *both* more income *and* more relaxation time because of the increase in W if he cuts back on the number of hours which he is willing to work. For example, if the worker decides to work only 45 hours a week as W rises from \$3 to \$4 per hour, he experiences both an increase in his money income (from \$150 per week to $45 \times \$4 = \$180$ per week) and an increase in his relaxation time of five hours per week. Indeed, because of this reasoning, it is generally accepted that the

---

[12] As we mentioned earlier, the allocation of L between work (for income) and relaxation is analogous to the allocation of income between desirable consumer goods in analyzing the household's demand function.

income effect usually leads to a *negative* relationship between W and S_l—as W rises, S_l tends to fall.[13]

The *substitution effect* leads to an opposite relationship. When the worker was supplying 50 hours of labor per week, he was giving up enjoyable hours of relaxation for unenjoyable hours of work. He was willing to do this because he was being "paid off" for making this substitution at the rate of $3 an hour. If now the rate at which he is paid off rises to $4 an hour, he has added incentive to shift even more of his hours from relaxation to work. If this incentive works like other incentives in the real world, the worker will respond to the higher wage rate by supplying more hours of work—a *positive* relationship between W and S_l.

On balance, what can we expect concerning the relative sizes of the income and substitution effects? Will the income effect (generating a negative relationship between W and S_l) override the substitution effect (generating a positive relationship) or will it not? In truth this question cannot be answered definitively. However, most observers tend to feel that in most instances the substitution effect is the more powerful of the two. On this basis the supply curve of labor is often drawn with a positive slope as we have shown it in Figure 3-9.

It must be emphasized, however, that there is no *Law of Upward Sloping Supply* which we can call on, as we could in the case of the downward sloping demand for consumer goods. Indeed, it makes some intuitive sense to draw a labor supply curve with both positive and negative slopes—a supply curve which bends back on itself. We have pictured this curve in Figure 3-10. The reasoning for such a curve goes like this. When the wage rate (W) is low, the worker's income tends to be low. Consequently, an increase in the wage rate (W) is likely to induce additional hours of work from the laborer. The substitution effect will be dominant, and the supply curve will have a positive slope. However, when the wage rate is rather high, the worker's income will also tend to be high. In this case, an increase in the wage rate is likely to raise his income high enough that he would be willing

[13] The ability to alter the number of hours worked may be difficult for many workers, especially those employed in large plants or bureaucracies. In these cases, the hours of work are either set by management or by collective bargaining between unions and management.

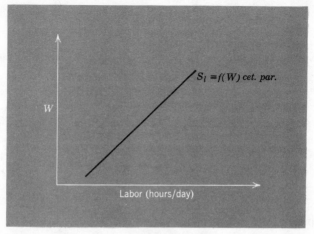

$S_l = f(W)$ *cet. par.*

W

Labor (hours/day)

Figure 3-9

to sacrifice some potential income in order to obtain additional nonwork time. The income effect will be dominant. If at the higher income he supplies less labor when W rises, a negatively sloped supply curve for labor will result. Because such a backward-bending supply curve would substantially affect our further analysis only under the most extreme circumstances, we shall use a supply curve of factors of production which bears a positive slope—which slopes upward and to the right as in Figure 3-9. The higher the factor price, the greater will be the quantity supplied.

As in the discussion of demand, our analysis would be incomplete if we stopped here. At this point we have derived a supply curve for only a single factor for a single household. Again, we must extend the analysis from a single factor to all of them and from a single household to all. But, as before, the task is not conceptually difficult. We must repeat the analysis of the labor-supply curve for natural resources and capital, for each and every supplier of these factors. Then we must horizontally add the resulting curves for each of the factors.[14] In so doing, we shall

---

[14] When the supply of labor curve is derived for a household of several persons rather than one, the backward-bending curve is even more probable. At lower wages, other members of the family are likely to supplement the

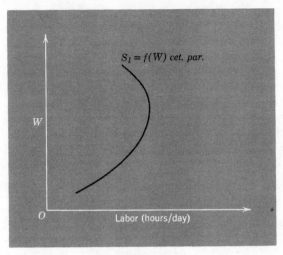

Figure 3-10

obtain the market supply curves for labor, capital, and natural resources.[15] These curves represent the factor-supply reaction of the entire household sector to changes in the price of the respec-

---

income of the primary income earner by working at least part-time. When the wage is high, other members of the household are likely to turn to pursuits other than work.

[15] The supply curve for capital and that for natural resources have peculiar characteristics just as we discovered in the supply curve for labor. The supply of arable land, for example, is fixed at any moment of time when technology, political boundaries, and the like, are given. In this case the supply curve is a vertical straight line. The same can be said for urban building sites in any of our cities.

Capital goods are produced and, therefore, are more closely related to consumer goods than to labor and natural resources. Because of the long, though finite, life of capital such as factory buildings, blast furnaces, and turret lathes, risk and uncertainty play important roles in the supply as well as the demand for capital. The time preference of a society is a factor—how people weigh present consumption versus larger future consumption. Because capital is productive, its use enlarges output. But it requires resources to produce capital which otherwise could be used to produce consumer goods. Given full employment, the production of capital goods has a foregone opportunity cost in consumer goods.

The wealthier (more productive, more capital using) a society, the less this opportunity cost "pinches" and the more the quantity of capital supplied will increase for any given price range.

tive factors. This is the concept we were after when we began the analysis—the quantity of the factors supplied by the household sector at all possible prices.

QUESTIONS

1. Consider the following things, each of which is likely to influence how much labor a worker would be willing to supply. Through which of the determinants of the supply of labor (W, L, T) would each of these effects influence the supply?
   (a) A heat wave drives the thermometer to 105° for a week.
   (b) The bus fare for commuting to work rises from 25¢ to 35¢.
   (c) The worker's wife sprains her ankle requiring him to take over some of the housework.
   (d) A rapid transit system is constructed enabling him to cut his commuting time in half.
   (e) The payment for overtime work rises from "time and one-half" to "double time."
   (f) A grouchy, unpleasant fellow is hired to work at the next desk.
2. In the chapter, we asserted that the income effect tends to cause the relationship between S_l and W to be a negative one. Does this imply that leisure (for which the worker has a demand curve) is a normal or an inferior good?
3. It is often asserted that: "The higher the hourly wage rate, the higher the worker's income." Is this necessarily true? Why or why not?

IX.   CONCLUSION AND SUMMARY

The road has been long and perhaps hard to follow. Having finished our analysis, we would do well briefly to retrace our steps. This will enable us not only to determine just where we are in the analysis of the entire price system but also how we got there.

In this chapter, we postulated some rather well-known and largely accepted elementary motivations possessed by human beings and, then, logically deduced the behavior or choice patterns which a rational animal with such motivations would display. We considered the household sector both as buyer of consumer goods and also as seller of the factors of production. We first isolated those factors that determine "the choice of which and how much of each of the available consumption goods are to be bought" and "the choice of which and how much of each of its factors of production are to be sold." We saw how subjective phenomena—preferences—and objective phenomena—prices and income—interact to determine the nature of demands and supplies. On the basis of these factors, we derived the demand and the supply curves presented by the household sector to the marketplace. We secured firm relationships between the prices of consumer goods and the quantities of them which households demand. We also explored the relationship between the prices of factors and quantities which households are willing to supply. With this result, we conclude the analysis of the household as a decision-making unit, one of two key decision-making sectors in a price system.

APPENDIX: THE INDIFFERENCE CURVE MODEL AND THE DEMAND CURVE

In Sections IV, V, and VI of Chapter 3, we presented a simple model from which the household demand curve for a particular good— good x—was derived. Basic to that model was the notion of marginal utility and the Law of Diminishing Marginal Utility. Implicit in both the concept and the law is the assumption that this thing called "utility" is measurable. However, no one has yet found a meter by which one's level of satisfaction could be estimated. As economists have become more concerned with the need to apply empirical tests to theory, the marginal utility approach has come under growing criticism. Economists have searched for a means of deriving the consumer demand curve and demonstrating the Law of Downward Sloping Demand without having to rely on the measurable utility notion. The model which was developed is called the indifference curve model. It is presented here.

The analysis in this appendix accomplishes much the same task as the marginal utility model in the text. It derives the consumer demand curve for a rational consumer using the $D_x = f\ (P_x,\ P_n,\ I,\ T)$ demand relationship presented in the chapter. As such it can be used to substitute for sections IV, V, and VI in the text or to supplement them.

A. *Consumer Tastes and Preferences*

To obtain a concept of consumer tastes and preferences appropriate for the indifference curve model, let us conduct an experiment. We shall take a typical rational consumer and ask him to choose between a series of *combinations* of two goods which we shall call "staples" and "luxuries." On the basis of his choices, we shall develop a picture of his tastes and preferences.

Being rational, the consumer is able to rank the desirability of any series of combinations of staples and luxuries with which we might confront him. For example, he is able to state that the combination of 50 units of staples and 20 units of luxuries is preferable to less of both goods, for instance, 25 units of staples and 10 units of luxuries. Such statements enable us to derive a basic Principle of Rational Behavior, namely, *more of both goods is preferred to less*. With this principle in hand, let us proceed to our experiment.

In beginning the experiment, let us give our subject a certain quantity of both staples and luxuries, say, 50 units of staples and 20 units of luxuries. We record this combination in Figure A3-1 as point *A*. Next, we shall give him a large number of other com-

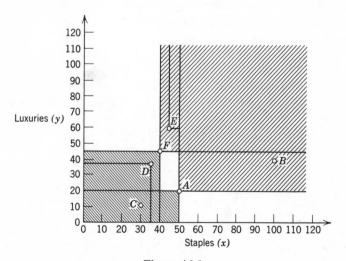

Figure A3-1

binations of these two goods, each time asking him to state how the new combination compares with A.[1] We allow him to give only one of three answers to each combination presented. He may state that (1) the combination is preferred to A, (2) it is not preferred to A, or (3) he is indifferent between them.

In the first combination which we present to him, combination B, we double both the amount of staples and the amount of luxuries; we give him 100 units of staples and 40 units of luxuries. We ask him, "Which combination do you prefer, A or B?" He states: "I prefer B to A. As a rational decision maker, I clearly prefer more of both goods to less." Because of this principle, any combination containing more of both staples and luxuries than combination A will be preferred to A. Therefore, imagining Figure A3-1 to be a map, any combination in the light-shaded area to the north and the east of point A will be preferred to combination A. By the same principle, combination A is preferred to any combination composed of less of both commodities than it. Thus, combination C, containing 30 units of staples and 10 units of luxuries is less desirable than A, as are all of the combinations in the dark shaded area to the south and the west of A.

We tell the subject to consider combination D. "Is it preferable to A?" He examines the two combinations and replies: "No, given my set of preferences, I would choose A." Because of the Principle of Rational Behavior, we immediately shade in heavily the rectangle south and west of D, since all points in it are less desirable than A. If A is preferred to D, it is surely preferable to combinations less desired than D.

Now combination E. "Combination E," the subject replies, "is preferred to combination A." Again, because more of both goods is preferred to less, we shade in lightly the quadrant north and east of E. Because E is preferred to A, all combinations preferred to E will be preferred to A.

Next, combination F is presented. It contains less of both commodities than combination E but more of both than combination

---

[1] In Figure A3-1, the quantity of staples is plotted on the x or horizontal axis and the quantity of luxuries is plotted on the y or vertical axis. For convenience, we shall use the letters x and y instead of staples and luxuries later in the analysis.

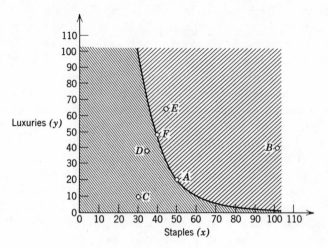

Figure A3-2

D. His answer comes, "I am indifferent between *A* and *F*." For the same reasons as above, we now shade in heavily the quadrant below and to the left of *F* because all these combinations are less desirable than *A*. We shade in lightly the quadrant above and to the right of *F* because all these combinations are preferred to *A*. In combination *F*, and this is the significant point, we have a point which lies on the borderline, the boundary, between those combinations that are more desired than *A* and those that are less desired. Combination *F* is the second point in Figure A3-1 at which the dark shaded area meets the light shaded area. By continuing this kind of experiment, clearly all of the points on the borderline can be found.

In Figure A3-2, we have pictured just such a borderline along with some familiar points. The outstanding characteristic of this curve is that at every point on it the consumer is receiving the same amount of satisfaction. He is *indifferent* between any two points on the curve. Because of the Principle of Rational Behavior, every combination above the curve—in the light shaded area—is preferred to any combination on the curve. Every combination below the curve—in the dark shaded area—is less desirable than any point on the curve. This curve is called an *indifference curve*.

Now, beginning with any point not on the original indifference curve, we can, by repeating the experiment, derive any number of indifference curves. In fact, an *infinite* number of indifference curves can be found. In Figure A3-3, a few of these are pictured along with some familiar points. This family of curves—this indifference map—is a picture of the consumer's tastes and preferences (T). Clearly, higher indifference curves represent greater satisfaction than do lower curves. That is, reading $<$ as "is less preferred than," we can say $U_1 < U_2 < U_3 < U_4, \ldots, < U_n$. Being a rational maximizer, the consumer will strive to reach the highest indifference curve possible.

Before we observe the consumer scrambling up the indifference map, let us look at three outstanding characteristics of the map itself. First, all of the indifference curves slope downward and to the right throughout their entire length. They have a negative slope. Second, no indifference curve intersects any other. Finally, all of the curves are drawn convex to the origin. They bow in toward point zero. Let us consider each of these characteristics in turn.

Consider first the need for indifference curves to slope downward and to the right. From studying Figure A3-1, it is seen that if an indifference curve should slope upward and to the right, the Principle of Rational Behavior would be violated. A consumer who possessed such a positively sloped curve would be indifferent between two combinations of staples and luxuries, one of which contains more of both commodities than the other. He would not prefer more of both goods to less. Such behavior would not be rational. Therefore, indifference curves must be negatively sloped.

By much the same sort of "negative proof," we can demonstrate that indifference curves cannot intersect. Imagine that the dotted line in Figure A3-3 is an indifference curve passing through both D and A. The following inconsistency results. A is indifferent to both D and F because it lies on indifference curves passing through both of these points. F is preferred to D because it contains more of both goods than does D. Because F and A are of equal utility and because F is preferred to D, A must also be preferred to D. Consequently, the impossible situation of A being both indifferent to D and preferred to D results. Hence, the indifference curves of a rational consumer cannot intersect.

To justify the convex shape of indifference curves, we need to

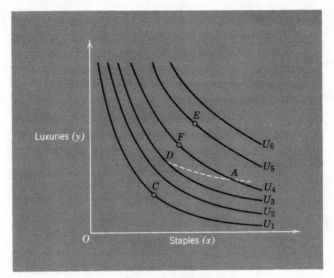

Figure A3-3

be introspective about our own tastes. Consider the single indifference curve displayed in Figure A3-4. We have drawn it convex to the origin or bowed in. As the consumer moves from A toward B along this curve, it becomes less and less steep, like a ski slope. Because the *slope* of a curve is defined as $\Delta y / \Delta x$ (read as the change in the value on the y axis over the change in value on the x axis, ignoring the sign), we can say that the slope of the curve decreases as the consumer moves from A toward B. This phenomenon of decreasing slope is known as the *Diminishing Marginal Rate of Substitution of x for y* (MRS_{xy}); as such, it describes the convex nature of the curve. The question now is: Why is there a Diminishing Marginal Rate of Substitution?

At point A on the indifference curve in Figure A3-4, the consumer possesses a relatively large amount of luxuries and a small amount of staples. The opposite situation prevails at point B where the consumer possesses a large amount of staples and a small amount of luxuries. Now, let us assume that the consumer performs two mental experiments. First, assume that he begins at point A and moves to point A', giving up some luxuries (Δy) and gaining some staples (Δx). Second, assume that he makes the

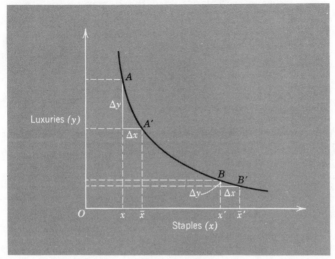

Figure A3-4

same sort of trade but that he begins at *B* and moves to *B'*. Beginning at points *A* and *B*, then, the consumer gains, say, a single unit of staples (Δx) and gives up just enough luxuries (Δy) to keep him on the same indifference curve. In both cases, he keeps his satisfaction unchanged.

The significance of the convex shape now becomes clear: when the consumer has an abundance of luxuries but only a few staples, he is willing to give up a rather large amount of luxuries to get an additional unit of staples, the movement from *A* to *A'*. When he is well stocked with staples he is willing to give up only very few luxuries to get one more unit, the movement from *B* to *B'*. Thus, while in each of these movements, *A* to *A'* and *B* to *B'*, the value of Δx is the same, the value of Δy is substantially larger when a small amount of *x* is possessed than when *x* is held in abundance. As one moves down the indifference curve, the slope of the curve ($\Delta y / \Delta x$) falls. For this reason, indifference curves are drawn convex to the origin and we speak of the Diminishing Marginal Rate of Substitution of *x* for *y* ($MRS_{xy} = \Delta y / \Delta x$).

With this discussion of the indifference map we have taken the first step in constructing our model of consumer choice. For a consumer choosing between two commodities, this map is an accurate picture of the variable in the demand function which we called consumer tastes and preferences (T). Let us complete our model by analyzing the remaining determinants in the demand function—the consumer's income (I) and the structure of prices $(P_n$ and $P_x)$.

B. *Consumer Income and the Structure of Prices: The Budget Constraint*

Considering only his tastes and preferences, a rational consumer will attempt to reach the highest indifference curve that he can. However, in making the climb up his indifference map in the real world, the consumer is constrained or limited by forces other than his set of preferences. He summarizes several of these in something he calls his budget. Thus, the housewife in the supermarket fails to buy the dozen doughnuts because of her inadequate budget. Or the accountant with a 1962 Ford fails to make a trade this year because he is constrained by his budget. The budget constraint must also be incorporated into the model.

The budget of a consumer is based on his income and the prices of the goods he purchases. At the same prices, a man with a higher income is less constrained than a man with a lower income, although both are constrained to some extent. Or, of two people with the same income, the one buying in a market with higher prices is more constrained than the one buying in a market with lower prices. Indeed, it is conceivable that a man with a high income in a situation with very high prices could be more constrained than a man with a lower income in a situation with very low prices.

Consider a consumer with an income of \$6000. Assume that he spends his income on only two goods, good x and good y, whose prices are \$100 and \$60, respectively. By confronting the consumer with both a fixed income and a set of prices, we are limiting his range of choice in a realistic fashion. Before we established his income or the prices of the goods he purchases, the consumer could conceive of himself choosing any point above and to the right of the two axes in Figure A3-5. However, with the imposition of the price and income constraints, this wide range of choice is cut back. Let us define more precisely the range of choice

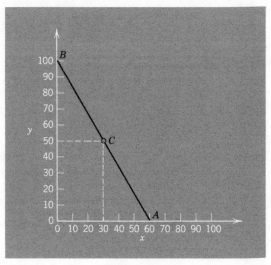

Figure A3-5

which remains open to the consumer after the constraints of his budget have been imposed.

Assume, first, that the consumer spends his entire income on good x. Given the price of x, the most that he could purchase with his income would be 60 units ($6000/$100). This is shown as point A in Figure A3-5. If he can purchase 60 units of x, he can surely purchase any amount less than 60 units. Next, assume that he spends his entire income on good y. In this case, the maximum that he could buy with $6000 would be 100 units which is represented by point B on the diagram ($6000/$60). If point B is attainable, any amount of y less than B can also be obtained. Finally, let us assume that the consumer divides his income equally between the two goods, spending $3000 on both x and y. Given the prices of these goods, he is able to purchase 30 units of x ($3000/$100) and 50 units of y ($3000/$60). This combination is represented by point C on the diagram. Not surprisingly, point C lies on a straight line connecting points A and B. In fact, if the consumer divides his income between the two goods in all possible ways—$6000 on good x, nothing on good y; $5999 on good x, $1 on good y, and so on—all of the combinations will lie on that straight line. By experimenting with a number of alternative ways of dividing up the income, the reader can easily demonstrate this.

To see this still more clearly, consider the equation

$$I = P_x(x) + P_y(y),$$

which is known as the budget constraint. Of the five symbols in this equation, three represent determinants in the demand function—I, P_x, P_y. By working with this equation, it can be seen that, given values for I, P_x, and P_y, any combination of two numbers for x and y which maintains the equality will fall on the line. We shall call this line *the line of attainable combinations* or, alternatively, *the budget line*.[2]

Quite legitimately, this line can be considered a boundary line between two distinct sets of combinations of x and y. It separates all combinations which the consumer can obtain with his income —all points on the line or below it—from all combinations out of his reach—all points above the line.

We have now incorporated all of the determinants of D_x into the indifference map (T) and the line of attainable combinations (I, P_x, P_y). What remains for us to complete the model of consumer choice is to put all of the determinants together and to analyze the impact of each determinant on the decision-making behavior of the consumer.

C. $D_x = f(P_x, P_y, I, T)$ —A Model of Consumer Behavior[3]

To analyze a consumer's behavior in deciding the quantity of good x to purchase, let us introduce his indifference map. It is pictured in Figure A3-6. By itself, it depicts the tastes and preferences (T) of an individual consumer faced with a choice between good x and good y. As a second step, let us provide the consumer with an income (I), the price of good x (P_x) and the

---

[2] Because the slope of a line (ignoring the sign) is given by the ratio $\Delta y/\Delta x$, it can be seen that the slope of the line of attainable combinations in the example just discussed equals 5/3 or 1 2/3. Using the symbols of our model, we can define the slope of the line of attainable combinations to be $(I/P_y)/(I/P_x)$, which reduces to $P_x/P_y = \$100/\$60$ or 1 2/3.

[3] In this model we assume that y is the only other good besides x. Hence, P_n becomes P_y.

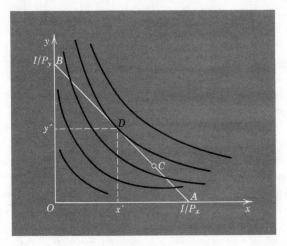

Figure A3-6

price of good y (P_y). In other words, let us provide him with a line of attainable combinations. By determining the value I/P_x, the maximum amount of x attainable is found. This is shown as point A in Figure A3-6. In the same way, I/P_y locates point B, the maximum amount of good y attainable. By connecting these two points, we obtain the line of attainable combinations, AB.

We are now prepared to investigate the process of rational decision making, the process of rational consumer choice. Let us again pose the basic question: "Facing a set of alternatives, any one of which is available, how will the household choose?" In answering this question, we must first isolate the "set of alternatives" open to the consumer. This set includes all of the combinations of good x and good y on or below the line of attainable combinations (AB), namely, all of the points in the triangle OAB. How will the consumer choose among these possibilities? The answer is easily obtained. Because he maximizes utility, the consumer will choose that combination of x and y which gives him the greatest amount of satisfaction; that combination which places him on the highest possible indifference curve.

For example, in considering *only* the combinations A, B, and C in Figure A3-6, a rational consumer would discover C to be the most preferred of the three and choose it. It lies on a higher indifference curve than the other two. Combination C gives him greater satisfaction than either A or B.

Now let us open up the consumer's range of choice to the entire triangle OAB. With this broader set of options, even C is replaced as the most preferred point. By moving along the budget line from C toward B—by exchanging x for y—the consumer attains higher and higher levels of satisfaction.

Until point D, each exchange leaves the consumer better off than he was before. He reaches continuously higher indifference curves. However, beyond point D, the reverse occurs; now additional substitutions of x for y give him successively lower levels of satisfaction. Each exchange places him on a lower indifference curve. At D, the consumer finds himself unable to move to any other combination which yields him a greater utility. Combination D places him on the highest indifference curve attainable given his budget constraint. As a rational maximizer, he will choose this combination from among all the others.

Two important characteristics of this choice immediately appear. First, point D is located on the line of attainable combinations, not below it. Indeed, if the consumer chose any point below the budget line, he would not be maximizing his satisfaction. Second, combination D is located at the only point where an indifference curve is tangent to the line of attainable combinations. Because it is the only point on the diagram from which he feels no desire to move, this point defines the consumer's equilibrium. At this point, the slope of the indifference curve (MRS_{xy} or $\Delta y / \Delta x$) is equal to the slope of the line of attainable combinations, or P_x/P_y. Thus, if the consumer is on the line of attainable combinations, we can locate the equilibrium (or utility maximizing) point where

$$MRS_{xy} = \Delta y / \Delta x = P_x / P_y.$$

This conclusion can be summarized as follows. When each determinant of the quantity of x demanded (D_x) is given (P_x, P_y, I, T), the consumer finds the most desirable yet attainable choice to be that combination which both exhausts his budget and maximizes his utility. With reference to Figure A3-6, the consumer will obtain the most utility from his income if he purchases x' units of good x and y' units of good y. For the assumed income, prices, and tastes, the value of the dependent variable, the demand for good x, is x' units.

The two equilibrium conditions of the consumer can be found from this discussion. First, in equilibrium, the consumer is on the line of attainable combinations—the amount which he pays for the goods exhausts his income,

$$I = P_x(x) + P_y(y).$$

Second, in equilibrium, the rate at which he is willing to substitute the goods is equal to the inverse of the ratio of their prices,

$$MRS_{xy} = \Delta y / \Delta x = P_x / P_y.$$

These two properties are the equilibrium conditions in the model of consumer choice.

D. $D_x = f(P_x)$ *Ceteris Paribus*—The Derivation of the Demand Curve

Our analysis of the demand function is not yet complete. Determining D_x for a particular set of P_x, P_y, I, and T is but a first step. We must also analyze how the quantity demanded of a good (D_x) changes in response to changes in its price (P_x) when all of the other variables remain constant. That is, we must derive the consumer's demand curve for a given product.

To derive this relationship, let us return to the consumer as we left him in equilibrium in Figure A3-6. This same equilibrium is redrawn in Figure A3-7. From the equilibrium represented by combination D, one point on the demand curve for x is observed; at a price of P_x, the consumer chooses x' units. We can plot this choice on a set of axes on which are measured the price of x (P_x) and the number of units of x demanded. Thus, in Figure A3-8, point D depicts one point on the demand curve for good x, the choice corresponding to point D in Figure A3-7. At a price of P_x, x' units are demanded.

Given our definition of the demand curve, we must now determine how the consumer will change the amount of x demanded when the price of x changes. We must find a second point on the demand curve which can be plotted in Figure A3-8. By definition, this new quantity demanded can be found only when the price of x—and nothing but P_x—has changed.

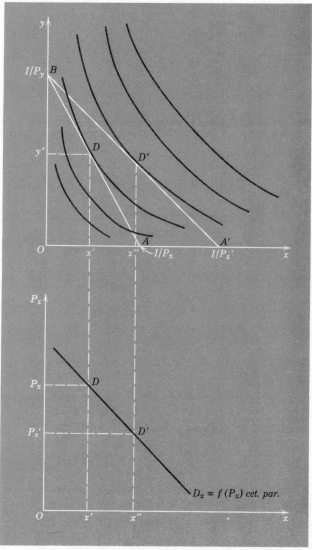

Figure A3-7 (*top*)
Figure A3-8 (*bottom*)

To observe how a price change will affect the quantity of x demanded, let us refer to Figure A3-7. By lowering the price of x from, say, P_x to $P_x{}'$, something in the diagram is going to change. Surely the indifference curves will not change. They represent the tastes of the consumer and these are independent of the price of the goods.[4] Thus, it is the line of attainable combinations, the consumer's budget, which must adjust to allow for the decrease in the price of x. But, just how will the line of attainable combinations be modified to take account of the price change?

The budget line AB in Figure A3-7 is drawn for a particular income (I) and for a particular set of prices (P_x and P_y). In fact, the slope of the line is equal to the ratio of the prices P_x/P_y. Thus, if the price of x decreases, the line will surely change its position. Point B, however, will not change when P_x changes. Its location is determined by the ratio of I and P_y (I/P_y), both of which remain constant. Because both the slope of the budget line, P_x/P_y, and the location of point A depend on the price at which x sells, both will be modified. If P_x decreases to $P_x{}'$, the slope of the budget line will decrease as the constant P_y is now divided into a smaller number. Likewise, the location of point A will move further out the x axis as the constant I is placed over $P_x{}'$, which is lower than P_x. Thus, with the lower price of x, we derive a new line of attainable combinations for our consumer, a line which again begins at point B but which now bears a smaller slope than line AB. This line is pictured as line $A'B$ in Figure A3-7.[5]

With the decrease in the price of x and the new line of attainable combinations, the consumer is back in the business of making decisions. Being thrown from his old equilibrium (point D) by

[4] In some cases this may not be true. Some people may value a good at a higher price more than at a lower price. This will occur when the purchase and display of an expensive item creates social prestige for its owner. In such cases tastes are not independent of price. See T. Veblen, *The Theory of the Leisure Class*, The Modern Library, New York, 1934.

[5] One very important thing to notice with respect to the line $A'B$ in Figure A3-7 is that, because of the decrease in the price of x, the number of attainable combinations—the range of choice—has increased for the consumer. Thus, such a decrease in price is looked upon most favorably by a consumer, since such a change can only work to his benefit. It will allow him to reach a higher indifference curve and thus cannot harm him. Although his money income has not changed, his real income has increased.

the price change, he must now reallocate his expenditures so as to again maximize his utility. By choosing that combination of x and y depicted by the tangency of an indifference curve with the new budget line, point D', the consumer again chooses rationally. He maximizes his satisfaction. Again an equilibrium position is achieved and the two equilibrium conditions hold; $I = P_x(x) + P_y(y)$ and $MRS_{xy} = P_x/P_y$.

The information supplied by this new equilibrium is precisely what is necessary to derive the demand curve for x. By changing only the price of x while holding all of the other determinants (I, T, P_y) constant, we observe how the quantity of x demanded (D_x) responds to a change in the price of x. Because of the change in P_x, the consumer has had to reallocate his income and adjust the pattern of his purchases. He has moved from D to D' in Figure A3-7, representing an increase in the quantity of x purchased from x' to x''. This new equilibrium is shown in Figure A3-8 as point D'. By definition, it forms a second point on the demand curve for x. Connecting this point with D and all of the other points derived from assuming different prices of x, we find the consumer's demand curve for good x. It is labeled $D_x = f(P_x)$ cet. par., in Figure A3-8.

The demand curve which we have derived is, in concept, identical to that derived in the chapter. Only the method of derivation is changed. We have substituted the indifference map for the marginal utility curves and the Diminishing Marginal Rate of Substitution for the Law of Decreasing Marginal Utility. In the appendix, it should be noted, we did not have to presume that utility was measurable; all the consumer had to do was to rank the various alternatives with which he was confronted.

QUESTIONS

1. What would an indifference curve between, say, cigarettes and automobiles look like if smoking made you sick?
2. "An indifference curve embodies the assertion that a consumer can substitute one good for another with no loss of utility." "By its very shape, an indifference curve implies that a consumer will not spend all of his income on one good." "If combination A (of two goods) is preferred to combination B, it can lie to the northeast, the northwest, or the southeast of B on an indifference map."

Draw an indifference map and discuss each of the assertions in terms of it.

3. What would the budget line look like if the more you purchased of a good the higher its price became?
4. How would you show a shift in tastes from good x toward good y on an indifference map for goods x and y?
5. Draw a set of indifference curves for right shoes and left shoes.
6. Show on an indifference map how the equilibrium would change when a consumer's income increases. Will both the old and the new equilibrium fall on a straight line which starts at the origin?
7. Can you relate the notion of the substitution effect which was discussed in the chapter to the change in the quantity of x demanded due to a change in the price of x which was discussed in the appendix? (*Hint:* The substitution effect showed how the amount of x demanded changed when its price changed, holding money and real income constant.)

4

The Competitive Business Firm—A Decision-Making Unit

The second basic sector in a market system is the business sector. While the household sector is known primarily for its role as a consumer of goods and services, the business sector plays the primary role in producing and distributing these outputs. In analyzing the household sector, we concentrated on the behavior of individual household units. Now we shall focus on the individual business units in the business sector. These units are the business firms.[1]

Because of their position in the circular flow, business firms perform certain specific functions—they purchase factors of production from the household sector as inputs, they transform these inputs into a useful and desired output, and then they sell the output back to the household sector. In performing these functions, firms make two basic types of choices. They must first decide how much to produce and offer for sale and then they must determine how much to buy of the available factors of production. The manufacturer of men's shoes, for example, must decide not only how many pairs of shoes to produce but also how much labor and how many machines to employ in producing the output.

[1] As noted previously, firms are clearly distinguishable from other kinds of business units such as plants and industries. General Motors, for example, is a firm. It produces automobiles in many plants. Together with Ford Motor Company, the Chrysler Corporation, and others, it forms the automobile industry. See footnote 1 of Chapter 2.

I. MOTIVATION, RATIONAL CHOICE, AND THE PROFIT CONCEPT

As in the case of the household, we immediately confront the question: What motivates the behavior of the firm? Why do they buy, produce, and sell? What do they get out of it? What is their goal? In order to answer the question of motivation, we must determine what the firm is and who (or what) makes its decisions.

Basically, the firm is a production process, absorbing inputs (land, labor, natural resources) and producing an output. It operates under a single management or entrepreneur. In our model economy, this entrepreneur, whether a single individual or a collectivity, serves as the firm's decision maker. He has committed himself to the firm and he fares as the firm fares. In building our model of the firm, we shall assume that the entrepreneur operates the enterprise so that it will earn the greatest return possible.[2] Because in economics this return is known as profit, we are claiming that the firm is operated to maximize profits; that the criterion of profitability is the firm's sole guide, its sole motivation, in framing decisions.

A. *Profit*

Before constructing our profit maximization model explaining how rational firms behave, let us digress a bit to understand more fully the economist's definition of the term "profit." *Profit* is not a simple concept to comprehend. This is largely true because its popular

---

[2] In the case of the simple, "corner grocery store" type business, the owner and the entrepreneur are the same person. The goal of maximum profits makes sense in this case because the interests of both owner and operator are identical. In the case of the modern corporation, however, ownership and management are separate functions. The stockholders, who legally own the firm, seldom manage it. Instead, managers are hired by the stockholders to run the firm so as to make the most profit for the stockholders. For example, the stockholders of General Motors hire managers to operate the company so as to maximize the firm's profits and thus the returns to the owners. Even though the decision-making function in a corporation is one step removed from the ownership, the use of hired managers as *agents* of the stockholders implies that the profit maximization model which we shall develop also applies in this case. Also see footnote 4.

meaning is different from what the economist finds useful. As commonly used by businessmen and accountants, profit is taken to be a gauge of the condition of the business within the framework of legal forms and taxation practices. The economist, on the other hand, uses the concept of profit to assist him in explaining how the economy functions.

Profit is a residual for both the businessman and the economist, but the character of the residual is different for each. For both groups, profit is the difference between the total revenue and the total cost of a firm (Profit = $TR - TC$). Moreover, for both the economist and the businessman, total revenue (TR) is the total income from the sale of the product. It is calculated by multiplying the price per unit by the quantity sold ($TR = P \times Q$). Thus, the total revenue of the barber who has cut 40 heads of hair at $1.50 per head is $60.

The difference between economist and businessman arises over the definition of total cost (TC). To the businessman, costs arise when the firm makes payments to individuals or other firms for labor, materials, and capital. For the economist, however, this definition is too restrictive. It includes only *explicit costs* and fails to consider *implicit costs*. The definition of the businessman considers costs to be only payments for inputs made to outside suppliers of the firm and ignores the firm's use of valuable resources for which it does not pay.[3] For example, the businessman's concept of costs does not include the contribution of inputs typically provided the firm by an owner-manager. Thus, the economist would claim that the drugstore owner-operator who arrived at his costs by toting up those payments to "outsiders" was underestimating his costs. Because he is interested in measuring the *value of all the resources used* in production, the economist would insist that the value of the labor, land, or capital supplied to the

---

[3] It should be noted that an analogous difference between the economist and the accountant also exists on the revenue side. The accountant includes in total revenue only the dollar in-payments made to the firm for its output. These are *explicit revenues*. What if the owners of the firm provide some of the firm's output to the local professional football team in exchange for season passes? The economist would call these *implicit revenues* and argue that they should also be taken into account in defining *economic profit*. In this discussion, we are ignoring this revenue distinction.

firm by the druggist himself—the implicit costs—be included in the cost calculation.[4] Given these distinctions, the economist states that the firm gains a profit whenever it receives a total revenue (*TR*) which exceeds the sum of its explicit and implicit costs (*TC*).

Perhaps the following example will clarify the economist's definition of these cost, revenue, and profit concepts and their relationship to each other. Consider a two-man barber shop in which one of the barbers is the owner. Assume that during a week the two barbers give 140 haircuts at $2 per haircut, earning a total revenue of $280. The owner of the shop has to pay the other barber a salary of $40—an explicit wage cost. Because he gives as many haircuts as his employee, the owner of the shop charges up a cost of $40 to himself even though it is not paid as a salary. This is an implicit wage cost. Indeed, $40 is as much as he could have earned in any other occupation and is thus his opportunity cost. His rent cost totals another $80. The depreciation on his capital equipment—barber chairs, clippers, etc.—plus a competitive return on his capital (also an implicit cost) totals another $80—depreciation plus interest. His total cost, then, including both explicit and implicit payments to the factors, is $240 ($40 + $40 + $80 + $80). This leaves the owner a profit—a residue— of $40.

But is profit defined in this way merely a residue, a leftover? Is it unrelated to what decisions the firm makes? If profits accrued to firms willy-nilly with no relation to their performance, profits would be of importance only as a residue or a leftover. Although it is sometimes true that profits stem from events over which the firm's decision maker has no control, this is not the way the price system usually works. In general, profit results from change— change in consumer tastes, change in methods of production, change in the markets served or the products sold, or change in

---

[4] The technique for valuing these implicit costs involves the concept of *opportunity costs*. As we have seen, the opportunity cost of choosing something is the value forgone by giving up the chance to choose its alternative. Thus, in our drugstore example, the druggist should have included in his costs the opportunity costs of his labor, capital, or natural resources as determined by the amount of wages, interest, and rent that they could have earned if they had been hired out to someone else.

a million and one other variables. All of these affect the firm's cost and revenue situation. Over some of these changes the firm's decision maker has control; over others he does not. As the decision maker exercises his entrepreneurship by creating or reacting to these changes, profit appears. We shall call profit, then, the return to entrepreneurship. Indeed, it is the firm's decision maker, displaying his creativity and entrepreneurship by seeking to maximize this elusive profit in competition with others, who makes an economy dynamic and responsive.[5]

II. RATIONAL CHOICE AND ITS DETERMINANTS

Given these definitions, let us now investigate how firms choose rationally to maximize their profits. By citing the nature of "rational choice" as the object of our analysis, we again step into the world of theory—the world of abstraction. In taking this step, we do not claim that our theory based on profit maximization completely describes the real-world behavior of businesses. We do not claim that maximum profit exists as the sole objective of firms or, even if it did, that they would pursue this goal with perfect rationality. What we are claiming is that among the many objectives of the real-world firm, profit is the dominant goal. Thus, when the National Biscuit Company builds a new plant in the Midwest, we conclude that the action was approved primarily because the increased revenue from the plant is expected to exceed the cost of building and running it. In substantiating this claim, we need cite only the fact that firms, in making decisions, do measure, weigh, and compare alternatives in an effort to choose the "most profitable" among them. Conscious attempts to choose rationally are in evidence.

In constructing a model of behavior of the firm, let us first treat the business sector in its role as supplier of goods and services and, then, in its role as demander of the factors of production. In considering the business sector as seller, we shall assume that each firm produces only one homogeneous commodity. Moreover, to

[5] Joseph Schumpeter saw that the profit-seeking entrepreneur creates a special and unique kind of force in an economy. His view is discussed in Chapter 8.

simplify our analysis further, we shall assume that each product is produced by a large number of independent firms. By grouping together all of the firms producing a single product, we have an industry. Because each industry comprises a large number of independent single-product firms, the structure of each industry is competitive.

To break into this sector, let us pick at random a single industry, producing a single homogeneous product, say, product x. Then let us pick at random a single firm in this industry. By prying into the workings of this firm, by investigating its nooks and crannies, let us attempt to evolve some basic principles of rational decision making. These principles will deal with the firm's decisions in producing and supplying its product to the market.

The primary question which we ask this firm's entrepreneur is: Given your goal of maximum profits, how do you determine how much output to supply in any period of time? Clearly, the list of factors considered by the entrepreneur is long. We can, however, find the most important ones. Because we have defined maximum profits to be the sole goal of the firm, the factors that are able to modify its profit position clearly affect the firm's behavior. Moreover, because profit equals total revenue minus total cost, the factors that affect either total cost or total revenue also affect profit. Let us attempt to isolate these factors which influence the level of total cost and total revenue.

A. *Product Price*

First, the price of the firm's product (P_x) will have a strong, perhaps dominant, influence on the amount of the product (x) which the firm will produce and supply to the market. This relationship between price and quantity supplied holds because the price directly affects total revenue (TR) which, in turn, directly influences profits. The price of the product times the quantity sold equals the firm's total revenue; and total revenue, together with total cost, determines profitability. In addition to this theoretical linkage between price and profitability, there is substantial real-world evidence of the existence of the relationship of product price to the firm's profits. The briefest encounter with businessmen convinces us of their ultimate concern with the price of their product. When the President of the United States questioned the advisability of an increase in the price of steel in 1962, the ire of the entire industry fell on his shoulders. The battle over aluminum prices and the price of structural steel in more recent years brought on much the same reaction.

Because we are primarily concerned here with how prices are set in an enterprise economy, we shall center our analysis on this determinant of the economic behavior of the firm.

B. *Input-Output Relationship*

The second determinant of the quantity of output supplied by a firm is somewhat trickier to grasp. We have argued that the firm maximizes the difference between its total revenue and total costs—the firm's profits. Ignoring the prices of both inputs and outputs of the firm, the greater the output obtained from a given amount of factor inputs, the greater will be the firm's profits. Conversely, the smaller the amount of inputs required to produce a given output, the greater will be the firm's profits. Thus, the technological relationship between the quantity of inputs and the output—the input-output relationship $(I\text{-}O)$—will affect the profitability of the firm. Like the price of the product (P_x), the input-output relationship $(I\text{-}O)$ will have an important impact on the firm's economic behavior. Put simply, because the input-output relationship determines the profits of a firm by affecting its total revenue relative to total costs (or vice versa), this technological relationship influences how much of its product a firm will choose to sell. If, for example, a new production technique permits a farmer to increase his yield of wheat by 10 bushels per acre, the quantity of wheat he will supply to the market will clearly increase.

C. *Factor Prices*

The final factor which determines how much of its output the firm will supply follows almost directly on the heels of the two already mentioned. Both the price attached to the output (P_x) and the prices attached to the factor inputs (P_f)—the wage rate, the interest rate, and the rent are needed to transform the relationship of inputs and outputs into the relationship of total cost and total revenue. In the same way as the price of the product (P_x) transforms physical output into total revenue (TR), the prices of the inputs transform physical factor inputs into total costs (TC). Hence, just as the price of the firm's product (P_x) and the input-output relationship (I-O) serve as determinants of its economic behavior, so do the prices of the inputs (P_f). Because factor prices directly affect the firm's costs and therefore its profits, they also form an important determinant of the quantity of output which the firm will produce and attempt to sell.

III. THE SUPPLY FUNCTION FOR A SINGLE FIRM

We have seen that there is a functional relationship between the quantity of x supplied (S_x) and the determinants of this quantity —the price of x (P_x), the input-output relationship (I-O), and the prices of the factors (P_f). This relationship may be written

$$S_x = f(P_x, I\text{-}O, P_f).$$

In this functional relationship, S_x is the dependent variable and P_x, I-O, and P_f are the independent variables. From this general function we shall isolate and investigate in great detail the relationship between the price of the good (P_x) and the quantity of output a firm desires to supply (S_x). By holding the other independent variables constant, we can write this relationship as

$$S_x = f(P_x) \text{ ceteris paribus.}$$

With this general function as a basis for our model of the firm, let us analyze each of the independent variables asking how changes in them influence the willingness of the firm to supply its product. We shall then be able to explain the behavior of the firm in supplying its product to the market. First, we shall discuss the input-output relationship (I-O) and then the prices of the factors (P_f) and the price of the product (P_x).

QUESTIONS

1. Consider a small business owned and operated by Mr. A, who is a horse fancier. In his business, Mr. A breeds horses and races them. In fact, he has a stable of over 20 horses. Mr. A oversees the business, serving as accountant, veterinarian, breeder, trainer, horse trailer puller, and general foreman. Mr. A is a trained accountant who could earn $8000 per year in that activity if he

devoted full time to it. Having obtained his veterinarian degree, he could also set up a full-time practice and earn about $12,000 per year. Rather than pursue either of these occupations, he prefers his present business. His wife also spends all of her time working at the stables. In addition, Mr. A has two hired hands who assist him in the operation. The income to Mr. A's business derives from the success of his horses on the race track and the winning purses which they bring home. The costs of the business are, among other things, the wages paid to the hired hands, the feed costs, the rent paid on the stable, and so on. The 1969 income statement for Mr. A's business is shown in the following table.

Income Statement—Mr. A's Stables

Horse Race Earnings (*Income*)		$65,000
Outlays		
Depreciation expense	$ 5,000	
Wages paid to two hired hands	10,000	
Stable and track rent	5,000	
Transportation costs	8,000	
Feed costs	10,000	
Equipment costs	5,000	
Medicine and veterinarian supplies	2,000	
Miscellaneous expenses	10,000	
Total		55,000
Profits		$10,000

(a) The accounting statement shows that Mr. A's stables have been a profitable venture—after expenses were subtracted from income, there was $10,000 left over. Do you think that the income statement gives an accurate picture of how profitable—in an economic sense—Mr. A's stables were? Why or why not?

(b) If you answered No to the above question, you probably think that there are some items which should be added to the cost concept to give a better estimate of economic profit. What items would you add? How would you find values for these items so that you could include them in the *economic* accounting statement? How would you define the concept which would give you a basis for valuing these cost items?

(c) In the text, the discrepancy between accounting profits and real economic profits is attributed to implicit costs which the accountant does not place in the income statement. Could not the discrepancy also be due to implicit revenue or income (see footnote 3)? In the case of Mr. A's stables, can you think of any implicit revenues or incomes which should be taken into account in calculating the economic profit of the enterprise? How would you define these items? How would you value them? Is there any principle which would guide you in valuing them?

(d) Mr. A often tells the story of how some of his friends were kidding him about running the stable. They said, "Mr. A, running the stable is child's play for you. Why, you get as much satisfaction out of running that stable as we do out of playing poker." "I admitted it," said Mr. A. "I told them that I get as much fun out of running that stable each year as I would get out of having a no-strings attached bundle of $50,000 to spend as I please." Does this give you any assistance in answering question (c)? How?

(e) On the basis of the information given, do you think that Mr. A's stables are yielding an *economic profit?* Defend your answer.

(f) In the text, the determinants of a firm's supply were discussed. How would you define the output of Mr. A's stables? How would you measure the supply of output? Discuss the meaning of the input-output relationship in the case of Mr. A's stables. Make a list of the prices of the inputs and outputs which would influence the willingness of Mr. A to supply output. Describe some technological change which might alter the input-output relationship of Mr. A's stables.

2. Costs, we have stated, refer to the value of opportunities which have been foregone. For each of the following decisions which a firm might make, describe the possible nature of the "costs" involved and discuss how you would value each cost.

(a) The decision of a grocery store owner to fire one of his stockboys.

(b) The decision of a grocery store owner *not* to advertise this week in a local newspaper.

(c) The decision of a grocery store owner to advertise this week in a local newspaper.

(d) The decision of a grocery store owner to renovate the interior of the store.

IV. THE INPUT-OUTPUT RELATIONSHIP OF THE FIRM

As we have said, the relationship between the quantity of inputs and the quantity of output is an important determinant of the firm's willingness to supply its product to the market. It should be emphasized that this relationship between inputs and outputs ties together physical units. So many units of labor plus so many

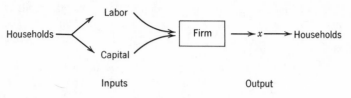

Figure 4-1

units of capital produces so many units of output. It follows, then, that this input-output relationship is a *technological* relationship and not an economic relationship.

How does this variable fit into the decision-making framework of the firm? Consider a simple model of a firm that produces one kind of output, x. Assume that this firm produces its product by using two kinds of inputs, l and c (standing for labor and capital). Figure 4-1 presents a simplified picture of the firm and its "fit" into the circular economic process. The firm buys its factor services (inputs) from the household sector and, after transforming them into product, sells its output back to the household sector.

In analyzing the relationship between inputs and output, we shall concentrate on a period of time that economists call the *short run*. This is a period which is insufficient for the firm to vary all of its inputs. Stated another way, we shall assume that the input-output relationship refers to a period of time in which at least one input must remain fixed or constant in amount. In our model, we shall assume that the firm can vary the amount of input l, while the amount of input c remains fixed. This assumption is a reasonable one. Indeed, real-world firms produce under just such conditions. Within short periods of time (say, up to a year) firms are forced to produce with physical facilities, plants, and equipment that are fixed in amount. It is only in the long run that such inputs to the production process can be varied. Only over a long period of time can the capital facilities of a firm be added to or subtracted from.

If, for example, the demand for steel should fall by 50% next month, the U. S. Steel Corporation could not and would not dispose of some of its furnaces, mills, or other capital facilities. The same situation occurs in a small business like a barber shop. It too has inputs which are fixed in the short run. If business were to increase by a third next month, the owner of the shop could not immediately add to his building in order to create room for an additional chair.

On the basis of this assumption, two important propositions hold true. First, even if the firm were to produce zero units of output (x), the input of capital would remain unchanged and would be greater than zero. That is, the firm's plant and equipment would stay in place and not be affected. Second, this assumption means that increases in the output of x result only from the application of additional amounts of the variable input, labor. Let us, then, investigate this relationship between the quantity of inputs—one variable (l) and one fixed (c)—and the quantity of output (x).[6]

A. *The Total Product Curve*

The uniquely shaped curve in Figure 4-2 displays this input-output relationship for our model firm. It is a basic curve in understanding the economic behavior of a firm. We shall call this a *total product curve,* since it relates the total output produced (x) to the quantity of inputs entering into production—input l being variable and input c fixed.

From the curve of Figure 4-2, it is clear that some amount of both labor (l) and capital (c) is necessary for production to take place at all. There would be no haircuts given in a shop having no barber but only barber chairs. This property appears in the diagram at the origin; with a zero amount of labor input, even though capital is on hand, nothing is produced. The amount of capital used, it should be noted, is specified in the diagram.

A second property of the input-output relationship is also seen in Figure 4-2. From the total product curve, it is clear that the more labor that is employed, the higher will be the total output of x. Note that the total product curve slopes upward and to the right throughout.[7]

---

[6] This relationship is often referred to as the firm's *production function* and written as $x = f(l, c)$. Output is a function of (is dependent on) the inputs, labor and capital.

[7] It is likely that the curve will turn down at some point so that additions of input l will lead to decreases in output rather than increases. However, because this phenomenon will not influence the remainder of our analysis, we shall ignore it here.

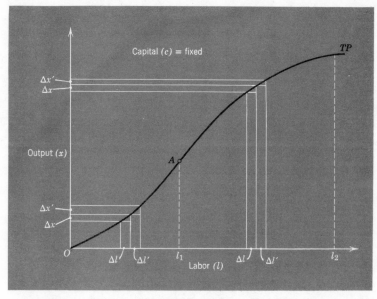

Figure 4-2

Finally, the curve as drawn possesses a peculiar _____ shape. For any amount of labor input from O to l_1, each additional unit of labor (Δl) yields an increase in output (Δx) *greater* than the increase generated by the preceding unit of labor; for any amount of labor from l_1 to l_2, each additional unit of labor (Δl) yields an increase in output (Δx) *smaller* than the increase induced by the preceding unit.[8]

Each of these three properties of the input-output relationship forms an essential element in our analysis of the behavior of the firm. Consequently, we would do well to pause briefly to gain a clearer understanding of them. The first two are intuitively obvious. Taken together, they claim that (1) the input-output relationship—the total product curve—begins at the origin and (2)

[8] The conditions for such a shape could be stated symbolically.

$$\Delta l = \Delta l'$$

If $\qquad\qquad 0 < l < l_1 \qquad \Delta x' > \Delta x.$

but if $\qquad\qquad l_1 < l < l_2 \qquad \Delta x' < \Delta x.$

it slopes upward and to the right. The third property is substantially more difficult to understand. More importantly, it rests on a basic economic law whose meaning we must comprehend. This law determines the peculiar ⟋ shape of the total product curve. It is known by economists as the *Law of Diminishing Marginal Returns.*

B. *The Law of Diminishing Marginal Returns*

First hinted at by Thomas R. Malthus in his *Essay on Population* in 1798, this law was formulated by other famous economists, among them David Ricardo (1817), Nassau Senior (1836), and Alfred Marshall (1890). None other than John Stuart Mill pronounced it to be "the most important proposition in political economy," whereas Marshall went so far as to claim it as "the cause of Abraham's parting from Lot."[9] In verbiage characteristic of his era and profession, Senior stated the law as follows:

Additional labor employed on the land within a given district produces in general a less proportionate return, or in other words, that though, with every increase in labor bestowed, the aggregate return is increased, the increase of the return is not in proportion to the increase of the labor.

Senior was referring to a situation similar to ours—a situation in which additional units of a variable input (labor) are added to a fixed input (land). The law which he presented described an inexorable and unavoidable relationship between inputs (one of which is fixed) and output. Although Senior made his point, perhaps we can restate the law somewhat more clearly.

If equal *additional* increments of a variable input, say, labor, are added to a constant amount of a fixed input, say, capital, the resulting *additional* increments to output (Δx) will, after some point, *decrease*. In Figure 4-2, this point is shown as A. This proposition is true even though the additional units of the variable input generate *increasing* additional increments to output before A is reached.

[9] "The land was not able to bear them, that they might dwell together: for their substance was great, so that they could not dwell together." Genesis 13:6.

For a better grasp of the meaning of this law, consider the following example. A small shoe manufacturing business possesses a plant, an appropriate set of shoe-making equipment, and a stock of leather and other materials. The plant, equipment, and material form the fixed input necessary for production to occur. However, with this fixed input alone, there will be no production —shoes will not be produced if no one runs the machines. Labor must be added if there is to be output. Labor becomes both the variable input and the input essential for production. (See characteristics 1 and 2 of the total product curve.)

Let us now assume that the businessman begins adding equal additional units of labor to the fixed input, and observes the rate of output after each addition. The result is recorded in Table 4-1 and pictured in Figure 4-3. In Figure 4-3, the shaded rectangles represent the marginal or additional output.

As Table 4-1 shows, nothing is or can be produced with zero units of variable input. Total output is zero. However, if one unit of labor is added to the fixed factor, 20 pairs of shoes are turned out. The addition to output (Δx) or the marginal return is 20 pairs of shoes. With two units of labor, the total output rises to 50. Total output is increased by 30 pairs of shoes owing to the additional unit of variable input. This represents an increased marginal return; one man no longer has to run *all* of the machines. However, as still more units of the variable input are added to the fixed input, the additional, or marginal, increments to output begin to decrease—from 30 to 15 to 13 to 10, and so on. Indeed, if enough laborers become added to the fixed plant, the

Table 4-1

Plant, Equipment and Materials	Units of Labor	Total Output	Marginal Output
Fixed	0	0	
Fixed	1	20	20
Fixed	2	50	30
Fixed	3	65	15
Fixed	4	78	13
Fixed	5	88	10
Fixed	6	95	7
Fixed	7	100	5

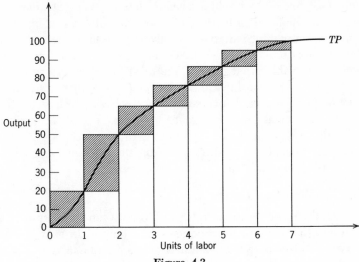

Figure 4-3

marginal returns would not only diminish but would even become negative. After some point, additional laborers would simply find themselves in one another's way.

This example, then, illustrates the *Law of Diminishing Marginal Returns*. As equal additional increments of a variable factor are added to a fixed factor, a point is reached where the *additions* to output decrease. As with the law of gravity, there are many who would defy the law but none who have succeeded.[10] Because of the law, the total product curve is shaped as we have drawn it. Up to point *A* in Figure 4-2, additional equal increments of labor yield increasing increments of output; after point *A*, the increments to output become smaller as additional equal increments of labor are added.

V. THE PRICES OF INPUTS AND
THE COST OF OUTPUT

As we have seen, the firm's total cost of production results from multiplying the quantity of factor inputs by their prices (P_f).

---

[10] If the law could be defied, enough wheat to feed the world could be grown in Yankee Stadium simply by adding enough labor, seed, and fertilizer.

Total cost, together with total revenue, determines profits. Because profits are the firm's primary motivation, the total cost of production is an important variable in analyzing the firm's behavior. In deriving this total cost concept we begin by attaching prices to both the variable input (l) and the fixed input (c). In so doing we derive a relationship called the *total cost curve*. The introduction of the concepts of marginal and average costs gives rise to both marginal and average cost curves. These are derived from the total cost curve. By uniting these concepts with the final determinant of the firm's behavior, the price of the product (P_x), we shall obtain the firm's *supply curve*.

A. *The Total Cost Curve*

The total cost curve is the relationship between the output of a firm and the total cost of producing that output. In drawing the curve, we place output on one axis of the graph and the costs of production on the other. Because costs are simply physical inputs measured in dollar terms, the shape of the total cost curve will be similar to the shape of the total product curve. To clarify the relationship between these two curves, we shall redraw the total product curve in a slightly different way. From this, we shall construct the total cost curve.

Figure 4-4 is the redrawn version of the total product curve.

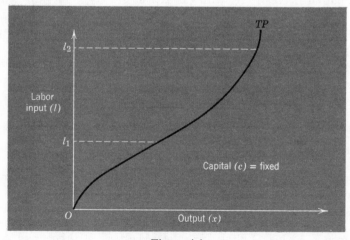

Figure 4-4

It will be noticed that although the relation of inputs to output in Figure 4-4 is identical to the one in Figure 4-2, the axes on the diagram have been reversed. Now, instead of having output (x) on the vertical axis and labor input (l) on the horizontal axis, we have plotted output (x) horizontally and labor input (l) vertically.

As we have seen, the total product curve combines information on two kinds of physical inputs—fixed (c) and variable (l)—and relates this information to the physical volume of the resulting output. By extending the distinction between fixed and variable inputs, we can distinguish two kinds of costs to the firm. We shall call these fixed and variable costs.

Fixed costs are those expenses borne by the firm to pay for fixed inputs (c). These costs include depreciation expense on plant and equipment, interest payments, rental payments on the land used, and taxes. A prime characteristic of fixed costs is that they do not change when output changes. They neither rise when output rises nor fall when output falls: they are fixed. Even if output should fall to zero, the firm would, in the short run, incur these costs. Total fixed cost (TFC) can be thought of as the sum of the products of the fixed inputs and their prices. $TFC = P_{c_1} c_1 + P_{c_2} c_2 + \ldots + P_{c_n} c_n$. Since our model contains only one fixed input, capital, fixed cost is equal to the product of the number of units of capital and the price per unit. If both the price of the fixed input and its quantity are fixed regardless of the level of output, total fixed cost always remains constant. The total fixed cost curve, therefore, appears as a straight, horizontal line in Figure 4-5.

To derive the curve which describes *variable cost*, we proceed in much the same manner. In the case of fixed costs, we have seen that neither the quantity nor the price of the input changes as output changes. This is not so with variable costs. As the total product curve in Figures 4-2 and 4-4 shows, the quantity of the variable input is directly related to the output. As one increases, so does the other. Only the price of the input remains constant. The variability in quantity, however, is not a substantial complication because the total product curve defines precisely how output and variable input relate to each other. By measuring the amount of the variable input (l) in value terms instead of in

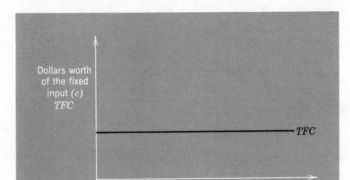

Figure 4-5

physical terms, the total product curve is transformed into a total *variable* cost curve. This is accomplished by changing the vertical axis of Figure 4-4 from physical units of labor to dollars worth of labor. Figure 4-6 pictures this change.

The total variable cost curve has the same shape as the total product curve pictured in Figure 4-4. At first, total variable costs increase slowly as output increases. Then, after the production of *OA* units of output, the Law of Diminishing Marginal Returns

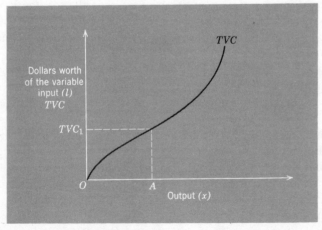

Figure 4-6

begins to apply. Costs now increase much more rapidly as output increases. Whereas the Law of Diminishing Marginal Returns causes diminishing increments to output after some level of input (observed in the total product curve), it causes increasing increments in cost after some level of output (observed in the total variable cost curve). This follows logically. In the one case we add labor unit by unit and find that increments to output diminish. In the other case we add output unit by unit and find more and more labor is required per unit of output. Costs are increasing. Decreasing returns transformed into value terms imply increasing costs.

In Figures 4-5 and 4-6, we see the two kinds of cost-output relationships which confront the firm—the total fixed cost curve and the total variable cost curve. By combining these curves, we derive a still more important cost-output relationship—one between the firm's total cost and its output. To derive this, let us ask: What is the total cost required to produce each of all possible outputs; that is, what is the relationship between total cost and output?

The answer is easily obtained. The total cost of producing any level of output (TC) is equal to the sum of the total variable costs at that output (TVC) and the total fixed cost (TFC). This may be written as

$$TC = TVC + TFC.$$

Figure 4-7 reproduces the total fixed cost relationship of Figure 4-5 and the total variable cost relationship of Figure 4-6—the two dotted lines. Following the definition of total cost, we add these two curves at each output to form the total cost curve. This is shown as the heavy curve in Figure 4-7. As can be seen, the *vertical* distance between TC and TVC is a constant amount equal to TFC. To see how variable and fixed costs are added to obtain total costs, consider the costs of producing output x_4. At output x_4, distance ab represents TFC and the vertical distance ac represents TVC; added together they equal the vertical distance ad which represents TC at output x_4.

The total cost curve is of great importance in analyzing the behavior of the firm. It will be recalled that the total cost of production is one of the two determinants of the volume of profits,

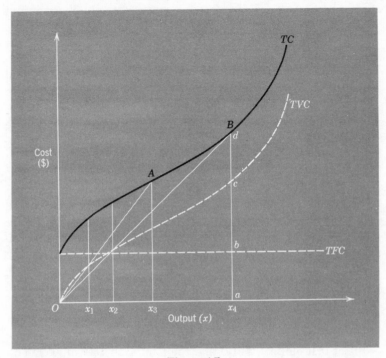

Figure 4-7

the primary motivation of the firm. By combining the input-output relationship (*I-O*) with the prices of the inputs (P_l and P_c), then, we have obtained one of the two primary determinants of the willingness of a firm to supply its product to the market. However, before introducing the price of the output (P_x) and hence total revenue, which is the other determinant of firm behavior, let us place the cost concept in a form which will be more helpful to our analysis.

B. *Marginal and Average Cost*

Marginal and average costs are derived directly from the total cost concept. In order to derive these concepts graphically, we must fully understand their meaning and their relationship to the total cost concept. First, we shall define them. Then, we shall illustrate the definitions by means of an arithmetic example. Finally, we shall derive average and marginal cost curves from the total curve.

How do we define average cost and marginal cost? First let us take *average cost*, which is the firm's per unit cost of producing the output. If, for example, a firm were to produce 100 units of output at a total cost of $200, the average cost—the cost per unit —would be $2. In our previous example, when the barber shop gave 140 haircuts and incurred a total explicit and implicit cost of $240, the cost per haircut—the average cost—was about $1.71; that is, $240 divided by 140 haircuts. In symbols, average cost is the ratio of total cost (TC) to the level of output (x):

$$AC = TC/x.$$

With this definition, average cost can be computed if the total cost of producing any given output level is known.

Marginal cost is a basically different, and ultimately more important, concept. Rather than referring to a single level of output —a single total cost corresponding to a given output—marginal cost deals with the relationship of the *change* in total cost to the *change* in output. Whereas the average cost concept answers the question: "What is the cost per unit of producing x units?" the marginal cost concept answers the question: "Given that we are producing so many units of output (x), what is the *additional* cost of producing an *additional* unit?" Indeed, just as the *marginal* product referred to changes in the amount of output relative to changes in the amount of input, the marginal cost concept refers to changes in total cost relative to changes in output. If the total cost to the barber shop of producing 140 haircuts is $240 and the total cost of producing 141 haircuts is $241.80, the marginal cost of producing the last haircut is $1.80. Marginal cost then, is the additional cost incurred by increasing output one unit:

$$MC = \Delta TC/\Delta x.$$

In the barber shop example,

$$MC = \frac{\$241.80 - \$240}{141 - 140} = \frac{\$1.80}{1} = \$1.80.$$

Both the marginal cost and average cost concepts are closely related to the total cost curve of Figure 4-7. By selecting any output, say x_4, average cost can be computed by dividing total cost (ad) by the number of units of output (Ox_4). Marginal cost is obtained by observing movements along the curve. By definition, marginal cost equals the *slope* of the total cost curve in the output range under consideration. As we have seen, the slope of a curve is the change in the magnitude plotted on the vertical axis divided by the change in the magnitude plotted on the horizontal axis— $\Delta y/\Delta x$. Because total cost is plotted on the Y axis and output (or units of x) is plotted on the X axis of Figure 4-7, the slope of that curve is $\Delta TC/\Delta x$, which is precisely the definition of marginal cost.

C. *The Marginal-Average Relationship*

Although the average and marginal cost concepts relate to different characteristics of the total cost curve, they are not unrelated to each other. Indeed, the relationship between them is intimate

Table 4-2

Games (1)	Points (2)	Total Season Points (3)	Marginal Points (4)	Average Points per Game Column 3 ÷ Column 1 (5)
0	0	0		0
1	22	22	22	22
2	20	42	20	21
3	15	57	15	19
4	3	60	3	15
5	15	75	15	15
6	21	96	21	16
7	23	119	23	17

and fixed. This relationship is described as follows. Whenever the marginal value lies above the average value, the average is rising; whenever the marginal value lies below the average value, the average is falling. Thus, the marginal concept can be thought of as pulling the average along with it. If it is above the average, it pulls the average up; if it is below the average, it pulls the average down. This relationship can be seen clearly by considering the season record of a basketball player. It is shown in Table 4-2.

The source of all of the numbers in the table is clear and the format is a familiar one.[11] We are interested in the relationship between columns 4 and 5—marginal points and average points. Both of these columns are derived from the total point concept in column 3.

From columns 1 and 2, we see that the basketball player started the season with a great first game—22 points. However, in succeeding games, his performance failed to live up to this first game expectation. In the second game he scored 20 points, in the third he scored 15 points, and in the fourth he was held to 3 points. This deteriorating performance is reflected in his average point record, which decreased from 22 at the end of the first game to 15 at the end of the fourth game. Indeed, not until the end of the season was he able to reverse the downward trend in his average.

It was clearly his game-by-game performance which caused this movement in the player's average point record. More precisely, his "points per game" record was determined by the number of points he added to his total season point record in each additional game—his marginal point record. Whenever the additional or marginal points scored in a game were less than his previous average point record, the average fell (games 1 to 4). Whenever the additional points scored in a game were the same as his previous average, the average remained constant (game 5). Whenever the marginal points scored in a game exceeded his previous point record, the average rose (games 6 and 7).

With this understanding of the "marginal" and "average" concepts, how can they be related to the total cost curve pictured in Figure 4-7? As was mentioned earlier, the marginal cost concept is represented in Figure 4-7 by the *slope* of the total cost curve. As we can see by looking at the curve, the slope—marginal cost —first falls as output rises. However, after a certain point, as output continues to rise, the slope reverses its course and begins to rise. The point at which marginal cost changes from "decreasing" to "increasing" is called the *inflection point* and is repre-

---

[11] By changing the first two columns of Table 4-2 to "course hours" and "total grade points," respectively, one obtains the kind of table that must be set up to compute a record of one's cumulative grade-point average during his college career.

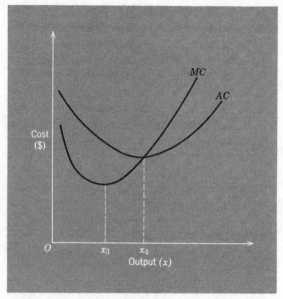

Figure 4-8

sented by A in Figure 4-7. Stated alternatively, the slope of the total cost curve switches from decreasing to increasing as output grows beyond x_3.

The marginal cost relationship is shown in Figure 4-8 as curve MC. It has been derived from the total cost curve of Figure 4-7. That diagram shows marginal cost decreasing up to output x_3, where it reaches its minimum point. Beyond x_3 it increases.

Derivation of the average cost curve from the total cost curve is not as easily accomplished. However, by introducing a crutch, this relationship can also be obtained. As we have seen, average cost is found at any level of output by dividing the total cost by the quantity of output—$AC = TC/x$. Therefore, in Figure 4-7, the average cost at output x_3 is equal to the distance x_3A (total cost) divided by Ox_3 (the output of x). This ratio, it is important to note, is equal to the *slope* of the straight line OA which connects the origin (O) with point A. Drawing the implication of this, we can state: *The average cost at any output level is derived by drawing a line from the level of total cost at that output to the origin and then measuring the line's slope.* Following this process, we can obtain the average cost curve.

From inspecting the diagram it is clear that the straight line from the origin to the curve is very steep at low levels of output; average cost is high. As output increases, the slope of the line (and average cost) falls until a minimum is reached. Then average cost rises again. Clearly, the output at which the slope of the straight line from the origin is least steep represents mimimum average cost. In Figure 4-7, this occurs at output level x_4. At this output level the straight line from the origin (in this case, OB) is as flat as is possible. At x_4, both the slope of the straight line and average cost are at a minimum.

By combining this information with our understanding of the relationship between marginal and average concepts, the average cost curve can be immediately drawn (Figure 4-8). Thus, (1) at output x_4, AC is a minimum and (2) whenever the MC lies below AC, AC is falling; whenever MC lies above AC, AC is rising; whenever $MC = AC$, AC is constant or horizontal. The marginal cost curve, therefore, intersects the average cost curve at its minimum point.[12]

D. *The Nature of Average Costs*

Before proceeding to develop the model of firm behavior, let us look somewhat closer at the shape of the average cost curve. Must average cost curves always be U-shaped and, if so, why? In the short run, as long as some inputs (and therefore costs) are fixed, the average cost-output relationship will be U-shaped. There are two reasons for this.

First, the downward portion of the curve occurs because of the influence of *fixed costs*. As Figure 4-7 demonstrated, total cost is the sum of the total fixed costs and the total variable costs. By definition, total fixed costs are constant even though the firm's level of output changes. It follows from this fact that the share of the fixed costs borne by each unit of output (average fixed

---

[12] This last characteristic follows logically. At point B in Figure 4-7, it will be noticed that the slope of the total cost curve (marginal cost) is equal to the slope of the straight line from the origin to that point (average cost). This is so because the straight line is tangent to the total cost curve at point B.

costs) becomes smaller as the output of the firm increases. For example, if the fixed costs of a barber shop are, say, $50, the *average fixed cost* is $2 if the shop turns out only 25 haircuts. Average fixed costs, however, decrease to 50¢ if the shop turns out 100 haircuts. As output increases, the fixed costs are spread over an increasing number of units of output, thereby decreasing the fixed cost absorbed by each unit. Decreasing average fixed costs tends to pull down average total cost as output increases. Falling average fixed costs, therefore, contribute to the downward sloping portion of the average cost curve.

A second factor explains the upward portion of the average cost curve. This factor is one already encountered—the *Law of Diminishing Marginal Returns*. As will be recalled, this law states that, if there is a fixed input, additional equal increments of a variable input will yield decreasing additional increments of output after some point. By measuring the inputs in dollars so that we can speak of costs, the law can be revised to read: if there are fixed costs, after some point the production of equal additional increments of output will require *increasing increments* of cost. Increasing marginal costs will pull average costs up as well.

For these two reasons, the average cost curve is, as we have drawn it, U-shaped. It slopes downward because of the existence of fixed costs[13] and slopes upward because of the effect of the Law of Diminishing Marginal Returns.

With this derivation of the marginal and average cost curves, the second determinant of supply—the prices of the factor inputs (P_f)—has been incorporated into our model. What remains is to introduce the final determinant, the price of the output (P_x).

VI. $S_x = f(P_x)$ *CETERIS PARIBUS*—THE PRICE OF THE OUTPUT AND THE SUPPLY CURVE OF THE FIRM

Given the average and marginal cost curves, it is relatively easy to determine the quantity of product that the firm wishes to supply (S_x). It has been accepted that the force motivating firm behavior is the desire to maximize profits—the difference between total cost (as the economist defines it) and total revenue. Conse-

---

[13] Note that even if there were no fixed costs, the average cost curve would be downward sloping if there were *increasing* returns to the variable input at low levels of output.

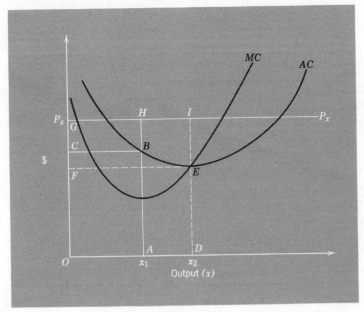

Figure 4-9

quently, in deciding how much of his product to supply to the market, the rational businessman will choose that output which yields him the greatest profit.

Figure 4-9 reproduces the average and marginal cost relationships derived in Figure 4-8. Before introducing the price of the product into our model, we should notice that the *total* cost of producing any output can be represented on this diagram. At any output, total cost is equal to the average cost (AC) times the level of output (x). $TC = AC \times x$. In Figure 4-9, the total cost of producing x_1 units is represented by the rectangle $OABC$—the average cost of producing x_1 units (AB) times the number of units produced (OA). Similarly, for output x_2 the total cost is represented by the rectangle $ODEF$—the average cost (DE) times the number of units (OD).

Total revenue can be represented in much the same manner, and here the price of the product (P_x) enters the analysis. The total revenue of a firm is found by multiplying its output (x) by the price of the output (P_x). $TR = P_x \times x$. Referring to Figure 4-9, if the price of a firm's product equals OG and if the firm sells

x_1 units (OA), the total sales revenue will be $OG \times OA$ or the area of the rectangle $OAHG$.

If total cost and total revenue can be determined graphically, so too can the size of the firm's profit. Because profit is defined as total revenue minus total cost (profit = $TR - TC$), the profit accruing to the firm from producing x_1 units is equal to the rectangle $CBHG$. This is the amount by which total revenue ($OAHG$) exceeds total cost ($OABC$). By the same reasoning, if the price remains at OG but x_2 units of output are produced and sold, the profit retained by the firm is $FEIG$. This is equal to total revenue ($ODIG$) minus total cost ($ODEF$). Clearly, if these two outputs —x_1 and x_2—were the only alternatives open to the firm, it would, without question, choose output x_2. Total profit at x_2 exceeds total profit at output x_1 ($FEIG > CBHG$).

Now the crucial question can be put: How much output will the firm produce and supply at all possible prices? Stated another way, given the input-output relationship (I-O) and the prices of the factors of production (P_f), what is the relationship between the price of the firm's output (P_x) and the quantity it will decide to supply (S_x)?

To help in answering this question, the firm's cost curves are again reproduced in Figure 4-10. It should once more be emphasized that these average and marginal cost curves embody the input-output relationship (I-O) and the prices of the inputs (P_f). Let us assume that the market price confronting the firm is, say, P_x. This price is also shown in Figure 4-10. At that price, the firm can sell as much of its output as it desires. The question then is: How much output will the firm decide to produce if it can sell any quantity at price P_x? Immediately, we can exclude some outputs from consideration—for example, any level of output which is either less than x_1 or greater than x_5. Any output in either of these ranges leads to a total cost for the firm which exceeds the total revenue.[14] This means a negative profit, an inability to cover costs, a loss.

On the other hand, any output between x_1 and x_5 appears to be fair game. For any output in this range, total revenue exceeds

[14] This is easily seen by comparing the cost per unit (average cost) and the revenue per unit (price) for any output level above x_5 and below x_1. For each and every output level in these ranges, cost per unit exceeds revenue per unit.

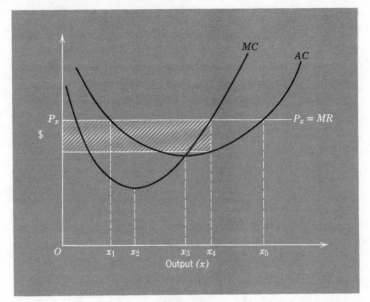

Figure 4-10

total cost and the firm receives a profit. However, some outputs are clearly superior to others. Which output between x_1 and x_5, then, is optimum; which output level will lead to maximum profit?

As will be recalled, the marginal cost (MC) curve is a curve which relates "the cost of producing one more unit" to the level of output. For example, at output x_1 the cost of producing the next unit is seen to be less than the cost of producing the previous unit—the MC curve is decreasing. Similarly, the curve representing the going market price can be called the marginal revenue (MR) curve. If each unit is sold at price P_x, the revenue obtained from selling one more unit—the marginal revenue—is P_x. With the two concepts of marginal revenue and marginal cost in mind, we can determine the optimum output.

Let us experiment. The firm's entrepreneur is asked: "If you are producing and selling x_1 units, would it be worth your while to produce and sell one more unit of output?" After checking the cost and revenue situation, the manager answers, "Yes." His reasoning is not hard to follow. It is based on the *marginal principle*, a basic concept in economics. Because $MR > MC$ at output x_1, the firm will add more to its total revenue than it will to its total cost by producing one more unit. And, if total revenue rises more than total cost, the profit of the firm grows. A rational firm would produce the additional unit. "If you were producing x_2 units," the manager is asked, "would it still be worth your while to produce and sell one more unit?" He again checks his cost and revenue situation and again, proceeding on the marginal principle, answers affirmatively. Again, $MR > MC$. Indeed, the manager will answer "Yes" to the question at any output lower than x_4, for in each case $MR > MC$. Beyond output x_4, however, the situation changes. For any output greater than x_4, the next unit of output will cost more to produce than the additional revenue it will bring in—$MR < MC$. Thus, profits will fall if an additional unit is produced. Consequently, at any output beyond x_4, a rational firm would *not* produce any additional units. In fact, if the firm is producing at a rate greater than x_4, it would pay the firm to cut back production toward x_4.

The principles of firm behavior thus become clear. At any output level at which $MR > MC$, it would pay the firm to increase its output. At any output level at which $MR < MC$, it would pay the firm to reduce output. At output x_4, there is no motivation to change. The optimum level of output for the firm is the unique output at which $MC = MR$. At that level of output the profits of the firm are maximized.

The application of these principles to the firm with the cost curves of Figure 4-10 is a simple matter. Given the going price, P_x, the quantity that the firm will supply is x_4. At that output, $MC = MR$ and the profits of the firm are maximized. At any output level below x_4, the firm has incentive to increase its output; at any output level above x_4, it has incentive to decrease it. In Figure 4-10, the shaded rectangle describes the profits which the firm receives by producing and selling x_4 units. It is the maximum-sized profit rectangle which it is possible to draw in the diagram given the price of x (P_x). The equation $MC = MR$ is consequently the *equilibrium condition* which rational firms seek. $MC = MR$ *is the most basic maximizing condition in all of economics.*[15]

---

[15] Note that the profit-maximizing output for the firm is not where average

A. *The Firm Supply Curve*

In the analysis of the preceding section, the equilibrium quantity supplied at a particular price of x was derived. This same analysis can now be extended, with little trouble, to other prices of x. Because the horizontal line drawn at the price of the output, P_x, is the marginal revenue curve at that price and because the firm, as a rational profit maximizer, will choose to produce where $MC = MR$, the equilibrium output of the firm will depend on the marginal cost (MC) curve. This is easily verified by drawing a horizontal line at several different possible prices in Figure 4-10. In each case the point at which $MC = MR$ lies on the MC curve. In effect, the marginal cost curve becomes the supply curve of the firm.[16] Thus, in Figure 4-11, at a price of $P_x{}'$, the firm will supply x_1; at a price of $P_x{}''$, the firm will supply x_2, and so on.

This supply curve is what we have sought from the very beginning of our analysis of firm behavior. It signifies the relationship between the quantity of output which the firm is willing to supply (S_x) and the price at which the firm can sell the output (P_x). The important thing to notice about this relationship is its general form—upward sloping to the right. This shape explains a most basic behavioral pattern of the individual, competitive firm. Because of the technological and economic forces under which such firms operate, they are willing to supply more output at high

---

cost is the lowest and profit per unit of output is maximized, that is, at x_3. The firm is interested in maximum *total* profits and not maximum profit per unit. Maximum total profit occurs only at x_4—where $MC = MR$.

[16] It would be more accurate to say that the *positively sloped portion of the marginal cost curve* is the firm's supply curve, and still more accurate to state that the positively sloped portion of the marginal cost curve *above average variable costs* is the supply curve of the firm. The first of these modifications arises because the negatively sloped portion of the MC curve presents an unstable equilibrium with the MR curve. An additional unit of output at such an intersection causes MR to exceed MC and output would move away from the "equilibrium" instead of toward it. The second modification arises because the firm would not even be able to cover all of its variable costs, to say nothing of meeting its fixed costs, if the price of the output falls below average variable cost. By producing *zero* in this situation the firm can avoid all variable costs and therefore absorb a loss of only fixed costs—a better situation for the firm, although still not a good one.

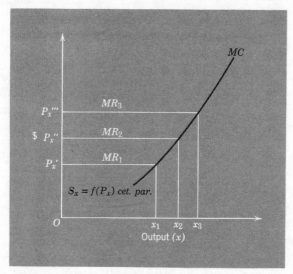

Figure 4-11

prices than at low prices. This is a natural and not unexpected result. Indeed, in the case of the competitive business firm, this behavior can be described as the *Law of Upward Sloping Supply*. Moreover, the basic root of this relationship is not difficult to find. We have run into it before—the Law of Diminishing Marginal Returns. If additional units of input yield diminishing increments to output, it seems only reasonable to expect the firm to require a higher price per unit in order to produce and supply additional units. Or, to put it the other way around, a higher price will induce the firm to supply more output because it will compensate the firm for the higher additional costs which it will incur as output is increased.

B. *The Market Supply Curve*

Having come this far, we have almost—but not quite—completed the analysis. Just as we had to derive the market demand curve from the individual household demand curves, so must we go from the parts to the whole in deriving the market supply curve. The question we must ask is: How will the *total* supply of good x respond to changes in the price of x? Again the process is one of *horizontally* summing the curves of each of the individual units.

In the household sector each individual unit demanded a multitude of goods and services. We had to ferret out the individual demand curves for good x from each household before we could add them together. In the business sector, however, each firm supplies but one commodity. Each firm presents only one supply curve to the market. Because all of the firms producing the same product form an industry, we are deriving the *industry* supply curve for that product.

By horizontally adding the supply curves (marginal cost curves) of each member of industry x in the same way as we added demand curves in the last chapter, we obtain the market or industry supply curve for good x. This curve relates the various quantities of a particular good which suppliers are willing to offer for sale at different prices. By repeating the analysis for each of commodities $a, \ldots, z$, we can determine the industry (market) supply curves for all commodities produced in the economy. Because the individual firm supply curves are upward sloping, the market or industry supply curve will also slope upward.

QUESTIONS

1. Consider the following short-run production data for a firm producing standardized power lawnmowers. Assume that the plant and equipment possessed by the firm cannot be altered in the short run. Only labor and materials are variable. These latter inputs are used in a constant relationship to each other—1 man-year of labor to 200 units of material. We will call each of these combinations a "bundle" of variable inputs.

Variable Inputs per Year	Capital Goods	Output of Lawnmowers per Year
0 bundles	Fixed	0
1 bundles	Fixed	20
2 bundles	Fixed	50
3 bundles	Fixed	100
4 bundles	Fixed	140
5 bundles	Fixed	170
6 bundles	Fixed	185
7 bundles	Fixed	195
8 bundles	Fixed	200
9 bundles	Fixed	203
10 bundles	Fixed	204
11 bundles	Fixed	204

(a) Plot the relationship of inputs to output on a sheet of graph paper. If all of the points are connected by straight lines, at what input level does the point of inflection appear to occur?

(b) Construct a table in which you display the marginal and average output data. Plot these data on another diagram. (A question often arises as to where to plot the marginal output and cost data. Because the marginal concept refers to a change in some variable, it cannot be tied to any one point on the scale. As a convention, plot the marginal numbers at the *midpoint* of the interval to which they refer.)

(c) Does this input-output relationship satisfy the Law of Diminishing Marginal Returns? Explain.

(d) What pieces of information do you need in order to derive the total cost curve?

(e) Assume that each bundle of labor and materials costs $7000 and that the annual cost for capital is $10,000. Form a table showing (1) marginal and average fixed costs for each output level, (2) marginal and average variable costs for each output level, and (3) total marginal and average costs for each output level. Plot all of these costs on the same diagram. For each pair of curves demonstrate that the average-marginal relationship described in the text holds.

(f) Which of the six curves plotted in question (e) would you inspect to determine the output level at which the Law of Diminishing Marginal Returns begins to take hold? Does this output level have any relationship to the output level at which the inflection point occurred?

(g) Using the curves plotted in question (e), defend the proposition that fixed costs contribute to the downward sloping portion of the average cost curve.

(h) Using the curves plotted in question (e), discuss why the propositions stated in footnote 16 are true.

(i) What level of output will the firm produce if the market price of lawnmowers is $280? Why? For what reason would the firm not produce one more lawnmower? or one less?

(j) What is the total profit earned by the firm when it is in equilibrium? Demonstrate that the equilibrium output level is superior to the output level at which average costs are at a minimum.

(k) What would happen to the supply curve of the firm if the annual cost for capital rises to $15,000? If the cost of each bundle of labor and materials rises to $8000? If the level of output for each of the input levels shown in the above table rises by 10 percent? What would be the equilibrium output in each of these cases if the price of lawnmowers is $280?

2. "The Law of Diminishing Marginal Returns implies a Law of Increasing Costs." Discuss.

3. "Marginal costs help the firm to decide how much to produce; average costs help the firm to decide whether or not to produce the good at all." Discuss.

4. Why is the marginal revenue curve for the *competitive* firm a horizontal straight line drawn at the level of the price? Where is the average revenue curve?

5. Consider the following expenses of a firm. Classify them as fixed or variable and state why you so classified them.

    (a) Maintenance expense on a large computer which the firm owns.

    (b) Rental expense on a large computer.

    (c) Rental payments on a building which the firm occupies on five-year lease.

    (d) Electric utility costs.

    (e) Depreciation expense on machinery.

    (f) Gasoline for delivery trucks.

    (g) Insurance on factory and machines.

    (h) Costs for night watchmen.

    (i) Costs for cardboard boxes in which output is shipped.

VII. $D_f = f(P_f, I\text{-}O, P_x)$—A MODEL OF BEHAVIOR FOR THE COMPETITIVE FACTOR DEMANDER

It was stated at the beginning of this chapter that there are two dimensions of firm behavior which are particularly relevant for analyzing how a market system works. We have so far explained the process of rational choice for the firm as a supplier of output. Now we must observe the firm in its role as a buyer or demander of inputs. We must analyze how the firm decides which and how much of the available inputs it will purchase. Again we shall isolate the factors that determine firm behavior and then single out one of them, the price of the inputs (P_f), for particular scrutiny.

What, then, are the forces that determine firm behavior as it purchases factors of production? Surprisingly (although perhaps, on second thought, not so surprisingly), these forces are the same as those that interact to determine the firm's supply decisions. For example, it can hardly be questioned that the input-output relationship (I-O) is a relevant consideration. Without doubt a change in this relationship would lead to a change in the quantity of inputs demanded to produce any given output. Similarly, because the price of the firm's product (P_x) is a prime determinant of the level of its output, product price must also influence the quantity of inputs demanded. If a higher P_x elicits an increased output (as the Law of Upward Sloping Supply maintains), it will also elicit changes in the demand for inputs. Finally, few would deny the influence of the price of the factor itself (P_f) as a determinant of the amount of it which the firm will demand.

Given these determinants of factor demand we can write the following demand function:

$$D_f = f(P_f, I\text{-}O, P_x).$$

Because we are again primarily interested in the impact of only one of these forces on the demand for a factor—namely, its price (P_f)—we can hold the other determinants constant and isolate the influence of price alone. The function then becomes

$$D_f = f(P_f) \text{ ceteris paribus.}$$

While each firm has a demand curve for each of the inputs which it uses, we shall concentrate on only one factor—labor. In so doing, we can modify the functional relationship to refer to this one factor. Because the price of labor is the wage rate (W), we can write

$$D_l = f(W) \text{ ceteris paribus.}$$

In analyzing the demand for labor, we shall assume a firm that produces one kind of output (x) by combining two inputs, labor (l) and capital (c). Again, let us consider capital (c) to be fixed and labor (l) to be variable. This, it will be recalled, is the same simplified model analyzed in deriving the supply curve for the product. With these assumptions, the input-output relationship (I-O) pictured in Figure 4-2 will again serve us in dealing with the demand for factor inputs. It is reproduced in Figure 4-12. As before, this total product (TP) curve increases throughout, with

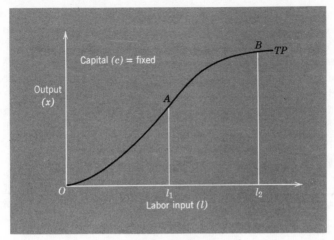

Figure 4-12

a section displaying increasing marginal returns (*OA*) and a section displaying diminishing marginal returns (*AB*).

A. *The Total Revenue Product Curve*

We can now incorporate into this relationship (*I-O*) a second determinant of the firm's demand for factors, the price of the output (P_x).[17] By multiplying each output level on the total product curve in Figure 4-12 by the price of the output, the relationship between input of labor and total revenue is obtained. This multiplication transforms the physical relationship between the quantity of labor (*l*) and the quantity of output (*x*) into a relationship between the quantity of *l* and the *value* of the output of *x*. For example, if the barber shop turns out 15 haircuts with 10 hours of labor, a physical relationship, and if the price of haircuts is $2, we can say that the 10 hours of labor produces $30 worth of haircuts, a relationship of physical input to value of output. Because total revenue is defined as the quantity of output which the firm sells (*x*) multiplied by the price at which it is sold (P_x), we shall call this transformed total product curve the *total revenue product* curve.

---

[17] It will be noted that the price of *x* (P_x) is held constant throughout this analysis as is the input-output relationship (*I-0*).

Thus, in Figure 4-13, we display a *total revenue product (TRP)* curve relating the value of the output ($P_x \times x$) to the number of units of labor employed (l). As seen in the diagram, the *TRP* curve has the same general shape as the total product curve in Figure 4-12. Indeed, by multiplying each output level by a constant number of dollars—the price of x (P_x)—the only thing that changes on the diagram is the concept plotted on the vertical axis. Instead of plotting output in physical units on the vertical axis as in Figure 4-12, we now have the value of the output measured in dollars—the total revenue product.

Embodied in this total revenue product curve (*TRP*) are two of the three determinants of the demand for the input labor, namely, P_x and *I-O*. Only the final (and primary) independent variable—the wage rate (*W*)—remains to be incorporated.

B. *The Marginal Revenue Product Curve*

In order to simplify introduction of the wage rate into the model, we must make a familiar kind of adjustment in the total revenue product curve (*TRP*). In much the same way as we secured the marginal cost (*MC*) curve from the total cost (*TC*) curve, we shall now derive the *marginal revenue product (MRP)* curve from the total revenue product (*TRP*) curve. This is done to show the relationship between the number of units of labor employed and the *addition* to the firm's revenue resulting from employing one more unit. For example, if the barber shop produces 15 haircuts with 10 hours of labor and earns $30, and if by employing one more hour of labor it could turn out two additional haircuts and earn a total of $34, the marginal revenue product at that level of labor use would be $4. In mathematical symbols:

$$MRP = \Delta TRP / \Delta l.$$

As was emphasized in the marginal cost-total cost relationship, the marginal curve is equal to the *slope* of the total curve. Therefore, when *TRP* slopes upward at an *increasing rate* (from *O* to *A*), the *MRP* will be *increasing*. Where *TRP* slopes upward at a *decreasing rate* (from *A* to *B*), the *MRP* will be *decreasing*. Figure 4-14 shows the *MRP* curve as derived from the *TRP* curve of Figure 4-13. Up to l_1 units of labor input, *MRP* increases. From l_1 to l_2 units of labor input, the *MRP* decreases. With this adjust-

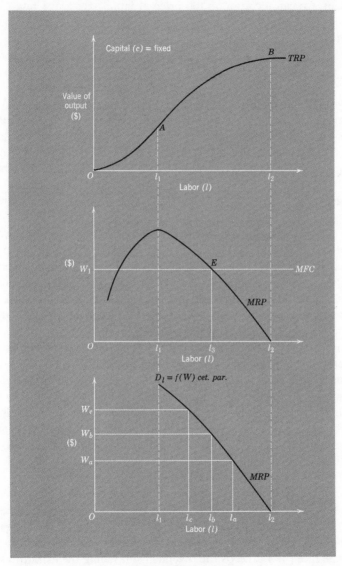

Figure 4-13 (*top*)

Figure 4-14 (*center*)

Figure 4-15 (*bottom*)

ment, we can incorporate the price of labor—the wage rate (W) —into the model. It is the final step in deriving the firm's demand for labor.

In Figure 4-14, let us assume that the going market wage rate is W_1—that the firm must incur a cost of W_1 for each additional unit of labor it hires. Given the input-output relationship (I-O), the price of the firm's product (P_x), and the price of labor (W), how much labor will the firm decide to hire? How many labor hours will the firm demand? Again using the principle of marginal comparisons, the firm is able to answer the question and easily explain its decision. At a wage of W_1, the firm will hire l_3 units of labor, for at this level of labor input profits are maximized. Let us examine this decision as well as the marginal principle underlying it.

Why does the firm choose to demand l_3 units of labor at a wage rate of W_1? Why is point E in Figure 4-14 an *equilibrium* position for the firm? We can best answer this question by demonstrating why no amount of labor other than l_3 could be considered optimum. Take, for example, a quantity less than l_3, say, l_1. At l_1, the wage rate (W_1) is substantially less than the marginal revenue product of labor (MRP). Therefore, by hiring an additional unit of labor, the firm earns additional revenue (from selling the additional output which is produced) which exceeds the additional cost from hiring the extra unit of labor. The marginal revenue product exceeds the *marginal factor cost* (MFC) or the wage rate (W). Because $MRP > MFC$, the addition to the firm's total revenue (TR) exceeds the addition to total cost (TC) and, consequently, profits ($TR - TC$) are increased by the hiring of the additional unit of labor. Therefore, input l_1—and, indeed, any amount of labor less than l_3—is less than optimum. The firm can increase its profits by hiring additional amounts of the factor at any input level below l_3.

The reverse situation occurs for any level of labor input greater than l_3. In this range, the marginal factor cost (MFC) or the wage rate (W) exceeds the revenue from selling the extra product (MRP). Thus, for amounts of labor in excess of l_3, not only would the firm decrease its profits if it hired an additional unit of the input but, more important, total profits could be increased if fewer units of labor were hired. By decreasing the use of labor, total revenue would decrease more slowly than total cost and profits would rise.

By exploring levels of labor input which are both less than and greater than l_3, we have concluded that, at a wage rate of W_1, the firm would increase its use of labor up to l_3, but not beyond. At l_3 there is no tendency to change. An equilibrium results as profits are maximized. *For the competitive firm in the factor market, the equilibrium condition is MRP = MFC.*

C. *The Demand Curve for Factors*

By extending this analysis, we can derive the firm's demand curve for labor. Given that the firm maximizes profits where $MRP = MFC$ and given that the price of labor (W) to the competitive firm equals MFC, the firm will equate the wage rate with the marginal revenue product no matter what the wage rate. Thus, as pictured in Figure 4-15, the negatively sloped portion of the MRP curve becomes the firm's demand curve for labor.[18] It relates the quantity of labor demanded (D_l) at all possible wage rates (W), holding all other determinants of demand constant. This is the basic concept which we set out to derive.

As we have derived it, the firm's demand curve for factors of production slopes downward to the right. This is the same general shape as the household's demand curve for goods and services. Although the reasons lying behind the shape are substantially different in each of the two sectors, the result is the same—more is demanded at lower prices and less is demanded at higher prices. Again, we call this the *Law of Downward Sloping Demand.*[19]

To complete our analysis, we must go from the single firm's demand for a single factor to the market demand for all three

[18] Just as the negatively sloped portion of the MC curve formed an unstable equilibrium with the price of the output and thus could not be a part of the supply curve for the firm (see footnote 16), so too the positively sloped portion of the MRP curve is disqualified from being part of the firm's demand curve for a factor.

[19] The demand for factors is often referred to as a "derived demand." Firms demand inputs only because they can sell the output produced from the inputs, that is, because there exists a demand for their output. Therefore, the firm's demand for inputs is *derived from* the demand for the firm's product.

factors. The process of getting there is the same as before. By repeating this analysis of the labor demand curve for natural resources and capital for this firm and every other factor demander, and horizontally summing the individual firm demand curves for each of the factors, the market demand curve for each factor can be obtained. Because the firm demand curves slope downward to the right, the market demand curve for each of the factors will also show a negative slope. These market curves describe the behavior of the business sector in demanding factor inputs. They yield the relationships which we need to analyze the market system—the relationships between the price of factors (P_f) and the quantity demanded by business firms (D_f) holding all other determinants constant. At higher factor prices, the business sector demands fewer units of any factor than at lower prices.

QUESTIONS

1. Consider the table in question 1 of the previous set of questions (p. 127) and the information in part (e) of that question. Assume that lawnmowers are selling for $280 each.
   (a) Construct a table showing the total, marginal, and average revenue product for each level of variable inputs.
   (b) Plot the total and marginal revenue product curves. (Again, plot the marginal variables at the midpoint of the interval over which they are measured.)
   (c) At what level of variable inputs does the Law of Diminishing Marginal Returns take effect?
   (d) How many bundles of variable inputs will the firm purchase?
   (e) Show *graphically* the effect on the quantity of variable inputs demanded of a $20 increase in the price of lawnmowers. Of a $500 increase in the price of a bundle of variable inputs. Of a 10 percent increase in the level of output at each input level. Of an increase of $1000 in the cost for capital.
2. Assume that you are operating a factory and discover that some input used is generating *increasing* marginal revenue product. What would you do? Why?
3. "If a producer uses his inputs efficiently, an increase in the price of one of them will alter the amount of it which is used." What force causes this change? A central planning agency memo? Pressure from some government agency?

4. "The basis for the Law of Downward Sloping Demand for factors of production is identical to that for the Law of Upward Sloping Supply of output." Do you believe this? If so, why? If not, why not?

5. It has been noted that a competitive business firm operates between two horizontal lines—one on the demand for inputs side and one on the supply of outputs side. Identify the two lines and explain why the firm is so constrained.

6. In all of our discussion in this chapter, we have failed to introduce the notion of "input substitutability." In the text we assumed that there was only one variable factor—labor. In the questions dealing with the lawnmower factory, we did so by assuming that the *two* variable inputs—labor and materials—had to be used in a fixed relationship. Obviously, however, firms can substitute inputs for each other. In nearly all production processes, machines can be substituted for some workers with no change in the level of output, or vice versa. For example, as motor vehicles became cheaper relative to horses, milk companies substituted trucks for horses on home delivery routes. Clearly it is the relative prices of the inputs which determines how factors will be substituted for each other. In this question, we shall use some of the concepts developed in the appendixes to Chapters 1 and 3 to illustrate "input substitutability."

   (a) On a piece of graph paper, reproduce Figure A3-6. Instead of plotting goods on the axes, plot inputs, say, labor on the *x* axis and machines on the *y* axis.

   (b) Whereas on the indifference map each of the curves represents a constant amount of satisfaction, in this diagram each of the curves represents a constant level of output. If you choose, you can label the curves 100 units, 200 units, and so on. Because we are dealing with output quantities, let us call these curves *isoquants*. By definition, each curve shows the combinations of inputs which can be used to produce any quantity of output. By referring back to the discussion in the appendixes to Chapters 1 and 3, explain why the isoquants slope downward and to the right. Why do they not intersect? Why are they bowed in toward the origin?

   (c) Draw a straight line on your diagram tangent to one of the isoquants like the line of obtainable combinations *AB* in Figure A3-6. This line is called an *isocost* (or equal cost) line. Why? Why should it be a straight line? Just as the line of attainable combinations in Figure A3-6 depends on a certain number of dollars (total income) and two prices, so too does the isocost curve. What is the dollar value on which any

isocost line depends? What are the two prices on which it
depends? How is the slope of any isocost curve defined? What
values would you have to know in order to calculate the slope?

(d) The tangency of any isocost and isoquant curve is called an
equilibrium. Describe what any such tangency or equilibrium
tells you. Why should a point of tangency be an equilibrium?

(e) In the appendix to Chapter 3, consumer equilibrium was
stated in terms of the ratios of marginal utilities and prices.
Here, however, we are dealing with outputs, not utilities. How
would you state the equilibrium condition of the firm in allocating his costs among various inputs?

(f) On your diagram, show what will happen to the isocost line
and the equilibrium inputs and outputs if you were to double
the level of total cost.

(g) Is the result of doubling the price of labor consistent with the
Law of Downward Sloping Factor Demand? Discuss.

(h) "If the price of machines falls, the marginal product of
machines will be adjusted downward by increasing the number of machines used, both to substitute some machines for
labor and to increase the output, which at lower cost can
profitably be sold in greater amounts." Discuss this statement,
making use of a diagram.

VIII. CONCLUSION AND SUMMARY

By following much the same type of logical analysis as we developed in the chapter on the household sector, we have come to
an understanding of the nature of decision making in the business
firm. Whereas in the household sector, utility maximization served
as the primary motivating force, the goal of maximum profits has
been taken to the prime mover of the firm. In this chapter we
have sought the logical implications of this objective in both the
product (or supplying) market and the factor (or buying) market. We first isolated the relevant determining factors in each
case and then, putting these factors together in a model, logically
derived both a *product supply curve* and a *factor demand curve*
for the firm. In each case the variable quantity (the quantity supplied or demanded) was related to a price and, in each, the impact of the price on the quantity was stated as a functional
relationship. Through this approach, we were able to explain

rational firm behavior in both the sale of its output and the purchase of inputs.

In the following chapter we shall extend this elementary understanding of decision making in both the household and business sectors by permitting these two key economic sectors to interact in the marketplace. In so doing, our goal will be to understand how a market *system*, through the interactions of independent buyers and sellers, establishes prices, determines incomes, rations consumption, and organizes output—that is, how a market system answers the basic economic questions of what, how, and for whom.

5

The Organization and Functioning
of Competitive Markets

The household and the business sectors are the principal elements of the economy. In Chapters 3 and 4 we dissected and studied these elements in an attempt to understand their internal operation. We analyzed how these sectors confront certain basic data, incorporate them into their decision-making framework, and make decisions which satisfy certain objectives.

Now our task changes. Rather than observe individual parts of the economy in isolation, we wish to put together functioning members of the economy so as to create a model of how they interact. The task is now one of amalgamation. To achieve this, we shall first establish a mechanism through which these constituent parts of the economy can interact. We call this mechanism a "market." It is an arena in which the household sector meets the business sector, where demanders meet suppliers, where goods are exchanged for money, where prices are made. We shall analyze both the structure of markets and their functioning, emphasizing the mechanics of their operation.

I. THE STRUCTURE OF AN IDEAL MARKET

A market is a collection of individual decision-making units, some of which desire to buy (demand) and some of which desire to sell (supply) a particular good or service. In our model of a com-

140

petitive economy, there is a market for shoes, a market for toma-
toes, a labor market and, indeed, a market for every good and
service which is bought or sold. In the words of one economist, a
market in a money economy has the function of "bring[ing] together buyers and sellers who wish to exchange goods and money
. . . ; individuals who together play the primary role in determining prices and quantities."[1] This statement puts the spotlight
on the prime characteristic of a market; some people give up
money and get goods or services while other people give up goods
and services and get money. The demanders (buyers) exchange
money for commodities, and the suppliers (sellers) exchange commodities for money.

Although markets are often found in a single location as, for
example, the New York Stock Exchange, they need not be so
restricted. We can talk about the market for haircuts in South St.
Louis, the market for steel on the West Coast, or the market for
automobiles in the United States. Nor is it necessary for the
buyers and sellers to confront one another face-to-face in the
marketplace. For example, if we were to decide to buy 15 shares
of Fruehauf Trailer Co. stock on the New York Stock Exchange,
the transaction would be handled by specialized intermediaries
known as brokers. We would have no idea from whom we bought
the stock, and the person who sold the stock would have no
knowledge of the purchaser. As long as buyers can make their
desires known *in some way* to sellers (and sellers to buyers), a
market can exist.

In analyzing the structure and functioning of markets, we shall
deal with a special kind of theoretical market model. It is a market
that is both *perfect* and *competitive*. In discussing theory, we
should again point out that we are not presenting an exhaustive
description of the real world. Rather, we are attempting to understand a few aspects of real-world behavior by examining some
fundamental cause-and-effect relationships which exist in the
world. Our aim is to explain some elemental facets of economic
behavior in the real world through the use of logical concepts and
relationships. The function of economic theory is to enable us to

[1] George Stigler, *The Theory of Price*, The Macmillan Co., New York, 1952,
pp. 55-56.

understand what goes on in real-world markets without having to completely describe them and without having to know each of the buyers and sellers. By understanding the nature of some strategic economic relationships, we can construct models to predict market outcomes.

A. A Perfect Market

What, then, is meant by a *perfect* market? Basically, we refer to an attribute of the participants in the market. We assume that both the buyers and the sellers have complete knowledge of market conditions; that any change in market conditions will be immediately known and acted on. When, for example, the price of cola goes from 5¢ to 10¢ and the price of all other sodas remains unchanged, we assume that all consumers learn of it immediately and are free to react as they please. Such perfect knowledge possessed by buyers and sellers causes the market itself to be perfect. Because the participants are aware of each change in market conditions and can react to these changes without delay, the market itself adjusts instantaneously to any disturbance. Unlike real-world markets in which ignorance of market conditions is widespread, there is no adjustment lag in perfect markets. In an economy with perfect markets, there is no need for advertising or other supplemental market information services.

B. A Competitive Market

The concept of a *competitive* market, like that of a perfect market, is an abstraction. Like other concepts which we have discussed, competition means something quite different to the economist than it does to the businessman. Whereas the businessman tends to equate competition with the idea of personal rivalry ("Football is a competitive sport."), the economist speaks of competition as a situation in which there is no rivalry. Rather, *a competitive market possesses a multitude of participants with each participant so small relative to the entire market that he has no significant influence on the market or on the other competitors.* Instead of a kind of hand-to-hand combat situation, competition in economics is an impersonal phenomenon. To the economist, then, the market for, say, corn is substantially more competitive than the market for steel. Several hundred thousand farmers enter the corn market as sellers, whereas there are but a dozen or two sellers of steel. Ironically, while no corn farmer considers another to be his competitor, each steel producer considers himself in hard competition with his rivals.

The most important characteristic of a competitive market is that no single participant has the power to affect the market outcome in any significant way. If he pulls out of the market, a rather strong action for an individual trader, the market and other traders fail to notice or react to his absence. Likewise, if he doubles his demand or his supply nothing happens. Because of the impersonal character of the market, all of the participants in a competitive market are price takers, not price makers. No buyer or seller has control over the price at which he buys or sells. A competitive price is determined by purely impersonal forces at work in an impersonal market. They are forces which no single participant can control.

A second characteristic of a competitive market is that there is no obstruction or restriction placed on supply, demand, or the level of the price. Any demander or supplier is perfectly free to enter or leave a market at his own discretion. For example, in a competitive market a baker can sell cakes or cookies and use his revenue to buy labor or capital or flour at his own discretion. He can make this decision with regard only to how he will gain or lose because of it. Similarly, a laborer can leave one job market and enter another as he wishes. Such absence of restriction signifies that there is nothing in the economy, other than the market forces generated by individual choice, that can set prices. Governmental price supports or minimum-wage legislation or electrical equipment price fixers are absent. Because of the perfect mobility of resources and the absence of restriction, no single individual, firm, or institution has what the economist calls "market power."

The final characteristic of a competitive market is that only one homogeneous commodity is sold in any given market. One man's grade A corn is sold in the same market as all other men's grade A corn; every pair of shoes sold in a particular shoe market is identical to every other pair of shoes sold in that market.

II. THE LAW OF SUPPLY AND DEMAND

A. *Market Forces—Supply and Demand*

The prime movers in our model market are the forces of supply and demand. They determine the price of the good and the quantity exchanged in any given market. To analyze how prices are formed, let us select one of the multitude of perfect and competitive markets in our theoretical system, say, the market for shoes. This market, like all markets, is established to permit an exchange of goods (or services) for money. Two kinds of participants operate in it: those with money who want shoes (demanders) and those with shoes who want money (suppliers). We already know the traders in this market. The households are the demanders and the business firms in the shoe industry are the suppliers.

The demand and supply relationships presented to this market by these groups are also known.[2] For the demanders of shoes there is an inverse relationship between the price of shoes and the quantity demanded. Buyers will take more shoes at $12.95 per pair than at $15.95 per pair. Such a relationship is described by curve *DD* in Figure 5-1. This curve is a market demand curve and, as such, it incorporates the individual demands of all the households. Its negative slope reflects the Law of Downward Sloping Demand.

For the suppliers of shoes the relationship is somewhat different. Because of the Law of Diminishing Marginal Returns, a higher price induces a greater output than does a lower price. Consequently, a direct relationship exists between the price of shoes and the quantity that potential sellers are willing to supply to the market. This relationship, SS in Figure 5-1, reflects the Law of Upward Sloping Supply. At a price of $15.95 per pair, suppliers will offer to sell a larger quantity of shoes than at $12.95 per pair.

In representing the forces of supply and demand as a supply curve (*SS*) and a demand curve (*DD*), the quantities demanded and supplied are pictured as being dependent *only* on the price

---

[2] It will be recalled that a cursory discussion of supply and demand relationships was presented in Chapter 2.

	D↑	D=	D↓
S↑	*A* $P?Q↑$	*B* $P↓Q↑$	*C* $P↓Q?$
S=	*D* $P↑Q↑$	*E* $P=Q=$	*F* $P↓Q↓$
S↓	*G* $P↑Q?$	*H* $P↑Q↓$	*I* $P?Q↓$

Figure 5-1

of the commodity. Many other factors, it will be recalled, are hidden in such a simplification. In drawing the demand curve we have made the *ceteris paribus* assumption. *The tastes and preferences of the household sector, its income level, the prices of other goods, and the number of demanders are all held constant in deriving the demand curve* for, say, shoes. If any one of these variables should change, the demand curve for shoes would be altered. If everyone's income, for example, doubled some night, the number of shoes demanded the next morning *at any given price* would increase.

The same *ceteris paribus* assumption applies to supply. *The prices of the inputs, the input-output relationship, and the number of sellers are all assumed to be constant in drawing a single supply curve.* As with the demand curve, if one of these variables changes, the supply curve itself changes. But let us save the analysis of these changes for later.

The demand and the supply curves are tools necessary for us to discover how prices and quantities in any given market are determined—why the price of shoes is $14.95 and not $20.95 or $12.50; why 5000 pairs of shoes were sold last month and not 7000 or 20,000.

B. *Competitive Bidding and Equilibrium*

In the establishment of any given market price, either demanders or suppliers will adjust to an undesirable situation by engaging in a process called *competitive bidding*. This process occurs as traders raise or lower the prices at which they offer to buy or sell. Consider the supply and demand relationship pictured in Figure 5-1 and reproduced in Figure 5-2. Assume that the going price of shoes is $20. At that price the demanders in the market want to buy *OA* pairs of shoes. This follows directly from the meaning of the demand relationship—a curve which relates the quantities of a good which demanders stand ready to buy at all possible prices. For the same reason, the firms in the shoe industry want to sell *OB* pairs of shoes at a price of $20. Consequently, at the price of $20, the quantity of shoes supplied (Q_S) exceeds the quantity of shoes demanded (Q_D). Suppliers want to sell more shoes at a price of $20 than demanders wish to buy. The quantity *OB–OA* exists as a *surplus* on the market; a situation clearly undesirable to some members of one of the two groups.

As a group, demanders are not the dissatisfied ones. At a price of $20 they desire to buy *OA* pairs of shoes and, because at least that many are available, they leave the market satisfied although

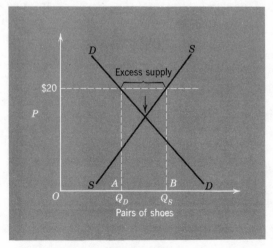

Figure 5-2

perhaps grumbling about the high price of shoes. The suppliers of shoes react differently, however. At a price of $20, they desire to sell *OB* pairs, but can only dispose of *OA*. Those sellers who are unable to sell their goods are the unhappy traders. It is these would-be sellers, unable to find buyers for their commodities, who inaugurate the process of competitive bidding.

Rather than sell nothing at all, these suppliers begin to shave their price. They recognize that they can woo some buyers by charging a price slightly lower than $20. It is here that the process of competitive bidding starts. Suppliers, unhappy with the going price, begin to competitively bid it down. As long as quantity supplied exceeds the quantity demanded ($Q_S > Q_D$), competitive price bidding on the part of sellers will continue. Such a situation is a *buyers' market*. The suppliers scramble to search out buyers, and in their search they bid down the price, all of which is in the buyers' interest.

The reverse situation occurs if the going price of shoes is, say, $10, as in Figure 5-3. Now the quantity demanded exceeds the quantity supplied ($Q_D > Q_S$). There are some would-be buyers in the market who desire to buy but can find no available supply.

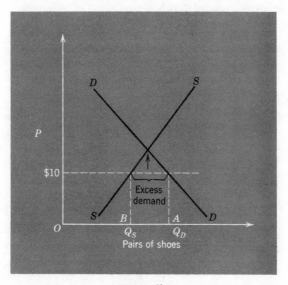

Figure 5-3

The excess of demand over supply in this case is equal to the quantity *OA–OB*. In this situation, it is the would-be buyers who are the unhappy ones. In an attempt to attract some of the insufficient supply, these buyers will offer to pay more than $10 for a pair of shoes. They will bid up the price. This competitive bidding by demanders will continue so long as $Q_D > Q_S$. This is called a *sellers' market*. Buyers are the ones now scrambling and in the process the price is being bid up—a situation favorable to sellers.

From this analysis we can draw a firm conclusion. Whenever the price of a commodity is above the intersection of the supply and demand curves, competition among sellers tends to force it down; whenever the price is below the intersection, the competitive bidding of buyers forces it up. At the intersection, the quantity which suppliers are willing to offer (Q_S) equals the quantity which demanders desire to buy (Q_D). At this price $Q_D = Q_S$ and there is no reason whatever for it to change. This price is shown in Figure 5-4 as $14.

At the price at which $Q_S = Q_D$, all of the buyers of shoes are happy. They can acquire just the amount that they desire at this price. Sellers are also happy at this price, since they can dispose of the amount that they want to sell. This price, therefore, balances the force of supply with the force of demand: it causes *OA*

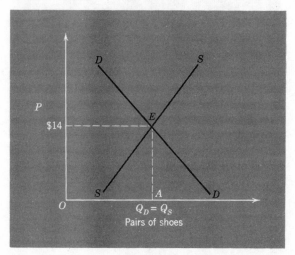

Figure 5-4

pairs of shoes to be traded at the single and uniform price of $14. Point *E*, representing this price and quantity, is the supply and demand *equilibrium*. It is called an equilibrium because neither the price of shoes nor the number of pairs exchanged has a tendency to change. There is no one to upset the market because the quantity supplied at this price equals the quantity demanded. $Q_S = Q_D$ *is the equilibrium condition.* This balancing of forces, this perpetual tendency toward equilibrium, is the *Law of Supply and Demand*.

C. Changes in Equilibrium

We have demonstrated that with a single pair of supply and demand curves in a market, the price and quantity will always tend toward equilibrium. In fact, in perfect, competitive markets, this "tendency" becomes an accomplished fact. Any deviation from equilibrium is instantaneously corrected by the process of competitive bidding. However, an equilibrium will remain unchanged only under certain conditions. If any one of the many factors which have been held constant in drawing the supply and demand curves should change, either or both of the curves will shift. If, for example, all consumers should awake one morning to find their income to be twice that of the previous day, the original demand curve for shoes would no longer be appropriate. Each consumer would allocate some additional income to the available products which give him utility and, because shoes fall into that category, more shoes would be demanded at any given price than before the change in income. That is, the entire demand curve would shift to the right.

Thus, changes in tastes and preferences, in the income level of the households, in the prices of other goods, and in the number of consumers all cause the demand curve to shift its position. Depending on the impact of the changes in these variables, the demand curve may shift either up or down. It may increase as from *DD* to D_1D_1 in Figure 5-5 or decrease as from *DD* to D_2D_2.

The same type of *ceteris paribus*-related mechanism is present in the supply curve. If any of those variables assumed constant in drawing a single market curve—the price of the inputs, the input-output relationship, the number of firms in the industry—should

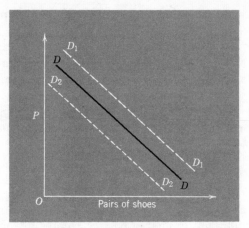

Figure 5-5

change, the supply curve will also shift. Again, depending on the impact of the change, the curve will either increase (shift to the right) or decrease (shift to the left). For example, if the number of firms selling shoes should increase, the supply curve—being the sum of the firms' marginal cost curves—will shift to the right. It will increase from, say, SS to S_1S_1 in Figure 5-6. Or, conversely, if something should happen to decrease the output per unit of input for the firms in an industry, as a moldblight in Florida would

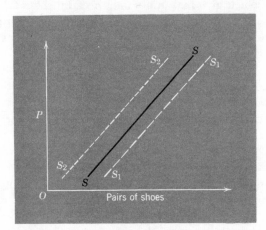

Figure 5-6

affect orange producers, the marginal cost curves of all the firms will rise causing the industry supply curve to shift to the left—to decrease from, say, SS to S_2S_2.[3]

D. *An Example of Changing Equilibria*

The question presented by these supply and demand shifts is clear: How will they affect the market equilibrium? To answer this question, let us consider the recent history of the market for agricultural products in the United States. During the past few decades, enormous changes have occurred in this market, which have affected the supply and demand functions for agricultural products. Consequently, we should be able to trace these market changes by working with the supply and demand model.

On the demand side, two major changes must be accounted for. First, the United States has experienced a substantial increase in population and with it an increase in the number of buyers of food. Second, the real income of the average consumer has risen as the economy has grown. For both reasons, the entire market demand curve for food has increased markedly in the past decades. Because of the increase in the number of consumers, the number of individual household demand curves included in the market curve has increased. Because of the increase in consumer income, the individual household demand curves themselves have shifted to the right. If DD and SS in Figure 5-7 are considered the demand and supply curves for agricultural products in, say, 1920, this change in the determinants of demand could be said to have caused DD to shift to the right—to, say, $D'D'$.

If we assume that this shift in demand was the only change in the market since 1920 (which, as we shall see, has clearly not been the case), we can evaluate its influence on the equilibrium price and quantity. With the changed demand, the 1920 equilibrium (E_1) would not be sustained over time. Given the new demand curve $D'D'$, a price of P_1 would yield a situation of substantial excess demand. With excess demand, competition among demanders would force the price to rise. Indeed, a new equilibrium would occur when the price was bid up to P_2 inducing an increase in the

---

[3] If this is not directly obvious, the reader should go back to the cost curves of Chapter 4 and ask: What will happen to the firm's marginal cost curve if the total product curve of the firm is shifted downward?

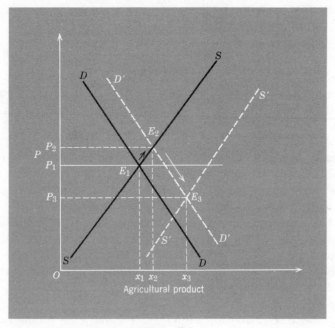

Figure 5-7

quantity supplied from x_1 to x_2. A new equilibrium would then result at E_2 where once again $Q_D = Q_S$.

In the market for agricultural products, however, supply conditions did not remain unchanged during this period. Since the 1920's, there has occurred a "technological revolution" in agriculture. Improved seeds, fertilizers, and equipment and the development of superior methods of cultivating, planting, and harvesting have significantly altered the input-output relationship on the individual farm. In order to produce any given output, fewer inputs are now required. Consequently, the average and marginal costs of the individual farm have fallen substantially. The marginal cost curve has shifted far to the right. In fact, even though there are far fewer farms today than in 1920, the marginal cost curves of the remaining farms have shifted so far to the right that the market supply curve has increased far more than the market demand curve. This is pictured in Figure 5-7 as a shift of the supply curve from SS to S'S'.

With this new supply curve (S'S'), neither E_1 nor E_2 can serve as equilibria. Assuming that $S'S'$ and $D'D'$ describe the current market conditions, a going price of either P_1 or P_2 would leave a substantial excess supply—a substantial number of sellers who could not find buyers. In either case, competition among suppliers would create a buyer's market. The price would be bid down to a new equilibrium, an equilibrium where $Q_D = Q_S$. This equilibrium is pictured as E_3 with the price equal to P_3 and the quantity exchanged equal to x_3.

Understanding these changes in the supply and demand curves, we are able to gain insight into the changes which have occurred in agriculture since 1920. Owing to the increase in both supply and demand, the quantity of agricultural products exchanged has increased substantially over the past few decades. Because the supply curve has shifted far more than the demand curve, the market price of agricultural commodities has fallen. Through the application of theory, understanding of real-world behavior is obtained.[4]

With shifts in supply or demand, new equilibrium positions replace old, prices rise or fall, and the quantity exchanged increases or decreases. Changes in the forces of supply and demand produce concurrent changes in prices and quantities—changes in observable market data. Moreover, underlying the changes in supply and demand are a multitude of changes in other variables—some economic, some psychological, some sociological, and some technological. That is, changes in the *determinants* of demand and supply cause the demand and supply curves to shift as described. These shifts, in turn, cause the observable changes in the prices and quantities seen in the marketplace. When, for example, the wholesale price of steel scrap first rises by 50% and then falls by more than 30% in less than 12 months, as it has done in recent years, we can be sure that either supply or demand, or both, were shifting substantially and rather irregularly.

In Table 5-1, the direction of the changes in the equilibrium

---

[4] In this analysis we have dealt with only a few of the changes in the determinants of supply or demand. For example, we said nothing about the changes in the household's tastes and preferences for food relative to other commodities or the changes in the prices of other consumption goods or of the inputs into the agricultural industry. These changes would have the effect of further shifting the supply and demand curves and further altering the equilibrium.

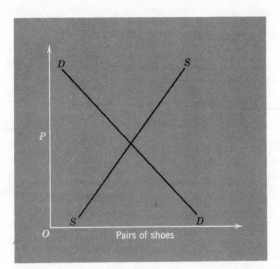

Table 5-1

price and quantity of various combinations of demand and supply shifts is summarized. For example, in Box *A* it is seen that if both demand and supply increase—shift to the right—the quantity exchanged will also increase while the price may go up or down or may remain constant. In attempting to understand fully the market mechanics involved in supply and demand analysis, the reader would do well to attempt independently to derive the many changes in the characteristics of the equilibrium as summarized in Table 5-1.

III.   THE ELASTICITY OF SUPPLY AND DEMAND

Before concluding this discussion of market mechanics, we must deal with one final concept. This is the responsiveness of the quantity of a good which is supplied or demanded to a change in its price. In previous sections, we have seen how shifts in demand (with supply held constant) and shifts in supply (with demand held constant) change the equilibrium price and quantity. In analyzing an increase in the supply of agricultural commodities, we discovered that the equilibrium slid down the demand curve;

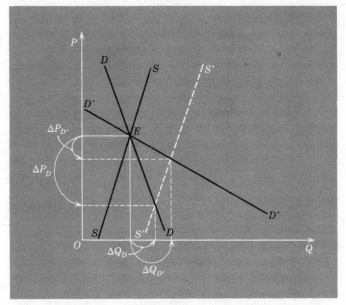

Figure 5-8

the price decreased and the quantity increased. When the demand curve shifted to the right, the equilibrium slid up the supply curve causing both price and quantity to increase. In analyzing the effect of these shifts, the degree to which the price and quantity change is an important consideration.

When, for example, the equilibrium changes by sliding down a demand curve, it is the shape of the demand curve which determines the extent of the price-quantity change. Thus, in Figure 5-8, the shift of supply from SS to $S'S'$ elicits a much bigger price change with demand curve DD than with $D'D'$. This is due to the different shapes of the two curves. Conversely, the change in quantity is larger in $D'D'$ than in DD. Because $D'D'$ is flatter than DD, the quantity variable responds more to the changed supply than does the price.

A. *Elasticity Defined*

The concept used to analyze these differing degrees of responsiveness is called *price elasticity*. It is defined as *the degree to which*

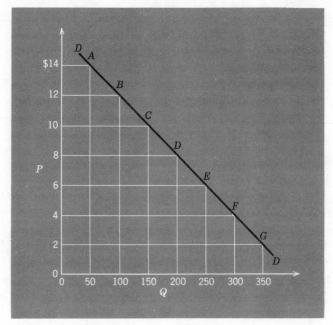

Figure 5-9

the quantity demanded (or supplied) changes in response to a change in price along a single curve. In the case of demand curves, this concept is referred to as price elasticity of demand; in the case of supply curves, it is known as price elasticity of supply. To evaluate the elasticity of a demand curve, the extent to which quantity demanded changes in response to a price change must be compared to the extent of the price change; to evaluate the elasticity of a supply curve, the response of quantity supplied to a price change is compared to the extent of the price change. Thus, in Figure 5-9, the price elasticity of demand describes the degree of responsiveness of *quantity demanded* to a change in price from, say, $12 to $10.

The degree of elasticity is measured by an *elasticity coefficient.* According to this measurement device, price elasticity is the ratio of the *percentage change* in quantity demanded (or supplied) to the *percentage change* in price.[5]

---

[5] At first glance it would appear that the use of "percentage change" is

That is,

$$\text{Elasticity} = \frac{\% \text{ change in quantity}}{\% \text{ change in price}}$$

or, in mathematical terms,

$$E = \frac{\Delta Q/Q}{\Delta P/P}.$$

On the basis of this definition, we can compute elasticity if we know the change in quantity (ΔQ), the change in price (ΔP), a base quantity (Q), and a base price (P).[6]

Employing this coefficient, let us run through a computation of the elasticity of a demand curve segment. We shall calculate the elasticity of the demand curve segment BC in Figure 5-9. First, we must find the change in quantity (ΔQ) for this segment. By

---

merely excess baggage; that "absolute change" or the inverse of the slope of the demand curve $(\Delta Q/\Delta P)$ would work fully as well. For two reasons this concept is unsatisfactory. First, if absolute change were used, the measurement of responsiveness would change whenever one changed the units in which either quantity or price was measured (for example, tons to bushels or dollars to cents). If percentage changes are used, the elasticity measurement is not altered when the price or quantity units are changed. Second, the concept of percentage (or relative) change permits the comparison of the responsiveness of the demand curves of different commodities. The measure of responsiveness using absolute quantities does not. For example, if we would use absolute change as a measurement of responsiveness, we would have to compare tons of steel and tubes of toothpaste if we were talking about these two products—a meaningless comparison.

[6] There is some confusion over which P and Q to use for the base when a discrete change occurs—the higher or the lower price involved in the change or the higher or the lower quantity involved in the change. To eliminate this confusion we shall take the average of the higher and lower price and quantity: $(P_1 + P_2) \div 2$ and $(Q_1 + Q_2) \div 2$. With this definition of the P and Q in the equation, we can rewrite it as follows:

$$E = \frac{\dfrac{\Delta Q}{\dfrac{Q_1 + Q_2}{2}}}{\dfrac{\Delta P}{\dfrac{P_1 + P_2}{2}}}.$$

inspecting the diagram, it is discovered that from B to C, quantity demanded changes from 100 to 150. Hence, ΔQ in the formula is 50. Next, we have to determine a base quantity to be used in calculating the percentage change in quantity. Following the rule of footnote 6, we shall take the average of the higher and lower quantities, or the midpoint of 100 and 150. Hence, Q in the formula is 125. It follows that the percentage change in quantity is 50/125 or .4. By identical reasoning, the percentage change in price is found to be .182. From this procedure we calculate the elasticity of demand from B to C as

$$E = \frac{\dfrac{150 - 100}{\dfrac{150 + 100}{2}}}{\dfrac{12 - 10}{\dfrac{12 + 10}{2}}} = \frac{\dfrac{50}{125}}{\dfrac{2}{11}} = \frac{0.4}{0.182} = 2.2.$$

Following the same procedure, the elasticity of the segment CD is

$$E = \frac{\dfrac{200 - 150}{\dfrac{200 + 150}{2}}}{\dfrac{10 - 8}{\dfrac{10 + 8}{2}}} = \frac{\dfrac{50}{175}}{\dfrac{2}{9}} = \frac{0.29}{0.22} = 1.3.$$

From this calculation, we conclude that the first segment of the demand curve (BC) is therefore more elastic than the second segment (CD). In percentage terms, the responsiveness of quantity demanded to a price change in the first case exceeds the responsiveness in the second case.[7] This is so even though the *slope* of the two segments—the absolute response—is the same.

---

[7] One might object, quite legitimately, that our computation here is not correct—that, rather than 2.2 and 1.3, the numbers should be -2.2 and -1.3. By convention, however, economists have decided to consider the

B. *Degrees of Elasticity*

Three distinct classes of elasticity measurement can be distinguished: elastic, inelastic, and unit elastic. They are exhaustive classes so that every demand or supply curve segment must fall into one of them. Each class is defined by its relationship to the elasticity measurement of unity ($E = 1$). As is clear from the elasticity formula, *unit elasticity* occurs where the percentage change in quantity just equals the percentage change in price. Similarly, all demand or supply curve segments in which the percentage change in quantity exceeds the percentage change in price possess an elasticity measurement greater than unity ($E > 1$). Such segments are called *elastic*. All demand or supply curve segments in which the percentage change in quantity is less than the percentage change in price possess an elasticity measurement less than unity ($E < 1$) and are called *inelastic*. In Figure 5-9, both segments *BC* and *CD* are elastic demand curve segments even though one is more elastic than the other.

In addition to these three classes, we should notice two special cases of elasticity: *infinite elasticity* and *zero elasticity*. In the first case, the elasticity measurement equals ∞ and the demand or supply curve is a horizontal line as displayed by *DD* in Figure 5-10. Here, if the price changes from P_1 to any other price, the percentage change in quantity is infinite. The opposite situation occurs when a demand or supply curve has zero elasticity. This is pictured as the vertical line in *D'D'* in Figure 5-10. Now, no matter what the price change, the demanders or suppliers of the commodity are willing to demand or supply only Q_1. Thus, the numerator of the elasticity coefficient in this case is zero and, consequently, so is the entire coefficient.

---

absolute value to be the appropriate measurement of elasticity. This makes good sense. We are only interested in measuring the degree of responsiveness and not whether the response is positive or negative. Depending on the market curve with which we are dealing, we already know the direction of the response. If it is a demand curve the quantity response will be in the opposite direction of the price change, giving a negative value; if it is a supply curve the two variables will move in the same direction giving a positive value.

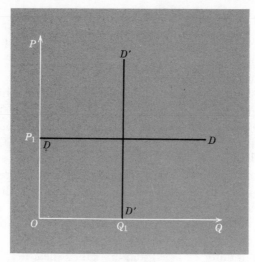

Figure 5-10

C. *Elasticity and Total Revenue*

The elasticity concept is more than a neat theoretical gadget with which economic theorists toy, although it is that too. A solid grasp of this concept is necessary if one is to understand how parts or sectors of an economy function and how the operation of some sectors of the economy affect behavior in other sectors. This is so because of the relationship of the *price elasticity of demand* to another concept with which we are already familiar, the concept of *total revenue*.

Until this point in our discussion we have considered total revenue to be the total sales income of a firm. We have defined it as the quantity of its product which a firm has sold times the price at which the sale was made ($TR = P \times Q$). The total revenue of a shoe firm that sells 10,000 pair of shoes at $20 per pair would therefore be $200,000. The total revenue concept, however, can be applied to an industry as well as to a firm. Indeed, an industry is simply a number of firms producing the same product. Thus, given a market price and a market demand curve, both the quantity demanded and the total revenue of the industry can be determined. In Figure 5-9, for example, given a price of $12 and the demand curve *DD*, 100 units can be sold yielding a total market revenue of $1200. Or, at a price of $10, 150 units can be sold yielding a total revenue of $1500. For an industry as well as a firm, $TR = P \times Q$.

What, then, is the relationship of total industry revenue and the elasticity of demand? Because both total revenue and elasticity depend on the interaction of the price and the quantity variables, it is not surprising that this relationship is a firm one. It can be stated as follows. *If demand is elastic, a decrease in price will increase total revenue; if demand is inelastic, a decrease in price will decrease total revenue; if demand is of unit elasticity, a change in price will not affect total revenue.* To verify this relationship, the reader would do well to compute the elasticity for each of the segments of the demand curve in Figure 5-9 and compare these measurements with the changes in total revenue over each of the segments.[8]

The importance of this relationship between the elasticity of demand and total industry revenue must be stressed. We have seen that shifts in the supply curve alter the price-quantity equilibrium. We have not yet seen that shifts in the supply curve also have an impact on the sales revenue of the industry and therefore on the firms in the industry. An industry facing an inelastic demand, for example, would find that an increase in its supply curve would *decrease* its total sales revenue—a case of selling more units but earning less revenue. For the buyers of the industry's products, however, the impact is reversed. They obtain more units but give up less of their income for them. The opposite situation occurs for industries facing an elastic demand curve. Here, increases in the supply curve swell total revenue and decreases

---

[8] It will be noticed that on this straight-line demand curve, the elasticity measurement is different in each segment even though the slope is the same throughout. Moreover, it will be noticed that the curve is elastic in all segments above the midpoint and inelastic in all segments below the midpoint. This phenomenon is true in the case of every straight-line demand curve. Thus, in Figure 5-9, demand is elastic from a price of $16 to a price of $8 and inelastic at any price less than $8. From this it follows that at the price of $8, total revenue must be at a maximum. If this last statement is not clear, one would be well advised to review the relationship between elasticity and total revenue.

in supply trim total revenue in any given market. This relationship forms an important consideration in analyzing the behavior of both sellers and buyers.

D. *Determinants of Elasticity*

We are left with one final question about elasticity. Why do different commodities display different demand and supply elasticities? Let us consider demand first, since it is the most troublesome. One of the most notorious cases of demand inelasticity is that of agricultural commodities. Perhaps by seeing why the quantity demanded of these commodities is not responsive to changes in their price we can get a clue to the factors that cause differing degrees of elasticity.

Without question, a primary characteristic of farm products is that they are necessities. If life is to be sustained, food must be consumed. Consequently, even if the price of food changes a great deal, the quantity of food that people demand will remain relatively constant. If the price of food rises, people cut down on other things but keep their food intake about the same. If the price falls they will not generally consume a great deal more; the stomach, in this case, is a limiting factor. But necessity and limits to consumption are not the only reasons for the inelasticity of the demand for agricultural products.

Another consideration is that any given farm product accounts for a relatively small portion of a consumer's budget. For such small items price changes are absorbed and go largely unnoticed. The case of salt is a classic example. Even if the price of salt would double, few people would decrease their use of it.

The clear lack of substitutes for farm products is still another contributing factor. If there were a multitude of things that one could substitute for food intake, the elasticity of demand for food would undoubtedly be much greater—people would switch from food to other commodities if the price of food rose.

In general, then, *price inelasticity of demand* results when a good (1) has no close substitutes, (2) is a necessity, (3) has a physical limit on the amount of its consumption, and (4) is only a small item in the consumer's budget.

In discussing the determinants of demand elasticity, one must be very careful. The way in which a good is defined has a great deal to do with the elasticity of its demand. Liquid beverage, as a commodity, has a very inelastic demand. There are no good substitutes for drinking. The demand for soda, on the other hand, is much more elastic—a number of close substitutes come directly to mind. For the same reason, the demand for cola is still more elastic, and the demand for Pepsi-Cola is extremely elastic. If the price of Pepsi-Cola rose by two pennies while the price of Coca-Cola remained unchanged, a large shift of patronage would occur. They are rather close substitutes.

The reasons for differences in the elasticity of supply are easier to handle than the reasons for differences in demand elasticity. Essentially, supply elasticity is synonymous with the flexibility of an industry's output, that is, the ease with which output can be adjusted to changes in price. This flexibility is related to the cost structure of the firms in an industry and, in particular, to the shape of their marginal cost curves. If the marginal cost curves are steep, the industry supply will be inelastic; if they are flat, the industry supply will be elastic. As one observer put it: "The supply of genuine paintings by a dead artist is highly inelastic, but the supply of copies is likely to be highly elastic."

IV. CONCLUSION AND SUMMARY

The objective of this chapter has been to develop a framework for thinking about the process of exchange in a market economy. Obviously, exchange can take place only if buyers and sellers confront each other and it is this confrontation that the institution of the market makes possible. In the market, prices are established and the quantity of the good to be traded is determined by the interaction of buyers and sellers.

In analyzing this process of exchange, we developed several basic concepts. These included the supply and demand curves, equilibrium, supply and demand shifts, and elasticity. All of these concepts aided us in thinking precisely about the mechanism of the market. They enable any two people to discuss meaningfully the process of exchange and to analyze with consistency the effect of changes within the household and business sector on the price and quantity exchanged of particular goods and services.

Having analyzed the details of market mechanics, we must not lose sight of the larger role played by the tool of market analysis. Indeed, the primary functions of the market concepts developed in this chapter are that of integration or synthesis. For example, knowledge of the Law of Supply and Demand allows one to trace the effect of a change in consumers' income on the profits of shoe manufacturers. It allows one to trace a change in the input-output relationship of producing, say, gasoline, to the quantity of cars which will be purchased by consumers. Similarly, knowledge of elasticity enables the analyst to discover how the sales revenue of an industry becomes altered as the willingness of producers to supply increases or decreases. In short, knowledge of market mechanics is necessary to discover how economic changes in the household sector affect the business sector and *vice versa*, and how changes in either sector influence the prices of goods and services and the quantity of them which is bought and sold.

QUESTIONS

1. The following two equations describe a market demand relationship and a market supply relationship for a particular good, say, breakfast cereal. The price is measured in cents per package and the quantity is measured in hundreds of packages per unit of time:

$$Q_S = -30 + 20\,P,$$

$$Q_D = 400 - 8\,P.$$

   (a) Construct a table which relates the quantity demanded to the price (by 1¢ intervals) from 8¢ to 22¢. (Simply calculate the quantity demanded for each assumed price using the demand equation.) Construct a similar table which relates the quantity supplied to the price (by 1¢ intervals) from 8¢ to 22¢.

   (b) On a piece of graph paper, plot the supply and demand curves which are defined by the two equations.

   (c) From your graph, what is the equilibrium price of breakfast cereal? What quantity will be exchanged per unit of time in equilibrium?

   (d) Assume that the government decreed that the price of breakfast cereal could not rise above 10¢ per package. Describe the market situation in this case. What group(s) of traders would be displeased by this decision? What proportion of the total quantity demanded at this price would be satisfied?

2. Because of an exceptionally good harvest, the price of cereal grains (an input to breakfast cereal producers) falls substantially. This decrease in the input price reduces the marginal costs of cereal producers which ultimately influences the supply curve of breakfast cereals. The new supply curve is defined by

$$Q_S = -10 + 20P.$$

(a) Plot the new supply curve on the same diagram as was used for question 1.

(b) What would happen to the equilibrium price and quantity exchanged of breakfast cereal because of the exceptionally good harvest of cereal grain?

(c) Describe the process by which the price would change from the original equilibrium level to the new equilibrium. What set of traders would initiate the process?

(d) What is the elasticity of demand between the old and new equilibrium prices? On the basis of your calculation, what do you think happened to the total sales revenue of breakfast cereal producers because of the shift in the supply curve? Check your conclusion by calculating total sales revenue at the old and the new prices.

3. Go back to the original equilibrium. Consider the following changes which might occur in the world. Evaluate how each of them would be likely to affect the equilibrium quantity and price. For each change, discuss whether the impact on the equilibrium would occur through a shift in the demand curve or a shift in the supply curve and state which determinant of demand or supply would be the vehicle through which the equilibrium would be affected.

(a) The managers in the breakfast cereal plants become inefficient so that more inputs are required per unit of output than previously.

(b) Research findings demonstrate that the application of a particular kind of fertilizer used on cereal grains has serious adverse health effects through consumption of the grain.

(c) The manufacturers of pancake mixes wage a major nationwide advertising campaign entitled "Pancakes for breakfast mean strength for the whole day."

(d) It is discovered that inhalation of the dust in the cereal plant reduces life expectancy. Because of this the managers of cereal plants find that they have to pay 30¢ more per hour in order to attract a labor force.

(e) The price of milk triples.

4. Describe carefully the difference between "supply" and "quantity supplied" and "demand" and "quantity demanded."

5. "Price is a rationing device." Discuss this statement showing how prices serve as signals in the allocation of spending and resources.

6. "When money is exchanged for goods at the equilibrium price, *both* the buyer and the seller are better off than if the exchange had not taken place." Do you agree with this statement? Can you show graphically (or logically) that this is so.

7. Which of the following are consistent with a perfect and competitive market?

   (a) There is a limit to the number of taxicabs which a city can have and the only way to get to be a taxicab driver is to buy the medallion from an existing cabbie.

   (b) In order to sell drugs, you must have a pharmacist's degree.

   (c) In order to be a plumber you must get the permission of the existing members of the plumbing trade.

   (d) In order to see, test, and get the price of the various automobiles you would consider buying, you must travel 65 miles and take an entire weekend.

   (e) In order to sell used cars, you must sign an affidavit stating that you will deal honestly with your customers and potential customers.

   (f) Sellers of breakfast cereals would like to sell more of their available supply at existing prices than they are able.

   (g) In order to buy circus tickets, you have to send in a filled-in form with your check or money order.

6

The Performance of a Perfect Market System

At this point in our analysis we must link together all of the markets in the economy. A market system, after all, entails more than the behavior of the household sector or the business sector or the market process by which the supply and demand for a particular good or service becomes reconciled. A market system consists of the interactions of all of the component parts and processes in the economy. Because the only purpose of an economic system is to serve the needs of the people, it is this criterion of economic welfare which we shall use to judge performance of the market system.

In this chapter, then, we shall discuss the general equilibrium of the entire market system and investigate how and how well the market system answers the three basic questions: What? How? For Whom? We shall be especially interested in the ways in which these answers are, from society's viewpoint, good or bad, and whether the market system serves or fails to serve the public interest.

I. THE CONCEPT OF GENERAL EQUILIBRIUM

In our study of households, firms, and markets, we have been doing what economists call *partial equilibrium analysis.* That is, we have taken these sectors one at a time and have analyzed their behavior under certain assumed conditions and in isolation from the rest of the economy. In our analysis of each of these parts of the economy, we have employed the *ceteris paribus* assumption and concentrated on the limited number of relationships in which we were most interested. In analyzing household behavior, for example, we obtained the relationship between the price of a good and the quantity demanded. We did this by assuming that all other relevant variables were constant. These included the consumer's tastes and preferences, the prices of other goods, and the consumer's income. It is the application of this *ceteris paribus* assumption in the study of individual sectors that has caused our analysis thus far to be "partial."

The world, however, does not operate on the *ceteris paribus* assumption. There are no real-world mechanisms for holding some variables constant while allowing others to change. In the real world, all variables are in motion simultaneously and, more important, they are all related. Thus, when an early frost destroys one-half of the orange crop and raises the prices of oranges and orange juice, it disturbs the equilibrium in the soft-drink market —the prices of other goods are no longer constant. The soft-drink situation, in turn, disturbs the equilibrium in the beer and ale market and so on, *ad infinitum.* An analogous situation holds in the factor markets; the discovery of a new technology influences the relative demands for labor and capital, the prices of labor and capital, and the incomes of those who supply labor and capital.

Because each market perpetually moves toward an equilibrium, the entire competitive system, being a composite of those markets, moves toward an equilibrium. Because the process of change is never ending, however, this sought-for equilibrium is never achieved. The study of a market system's perpetual tendency toward an equilibrium position is called *general equilibrium* analysis. This concept is of such importance to an understanding of how a price system works that we would be shirking our task if we skimmed over it lightly.

In order to understand the general equilibrium characteristic of a market system, we must grasp the system's quality of extreme interrelatedness, which, we must emphasize, is closely related to the term *economic adjustment.* We have seen that the decision maker in each sector of the economy is able to adjust his choices so as to move toward a partial equilibrium or optimum position —a maximum profit or maximum utility position. Moreover, in the marketplace, prices and quantities exchanged also adjust to form an equilibrium. In each market equilibrium position, there is no consumer who is unable to buy the good at the prevailing price, no seller who is unable to sell his product at this price, no surplus or shortage of any good or factor and, therefore, no tendency for price to change. With all of these conditions met we have what is called a general equilibrium, a situation of complete *economic adjustment*. With all of the goods and services markets in equilibrium, with all of the factor markets in equilibrium, with all of the households and all of the businesses in equilibrium, the economic system itself is in adjustment.

The interrelatedness of the parts of the market system can be further understood by observing the economic effects of a change in one of the economy's basic variables—say, a change in tastes, or a change in an input-output relationship, or a change in any one of the other variables that might shift some demand or supply curve. With such a shift, one market is thrown out of equilibrium and an adjustment in its equilibrium becomes necessary. The adjustment that must take place is clear; both the price and the quantity exchanged in this market will be altered. A new equilibrium will result.

This, however, is only the first step in a long chain of events. We assumed in deriving each demand curve that all prices other than the price to which it is related remain constant. If some price, therefore, is changed, this assumption no longer holds. The demand curves for all goods related to the commodity whose price has changed will shift. Because of these changes, succeeding adjustments are required in all markets and in all sectors—the outputs of various industries change, factor demands change, the prices of factors change, incomes change, and so on. The impact of the original change is ricocheted through the entire circular flow. Surely the statement of Schumpeter cited earlier[1] catches the essence of this elaborate system of linkages.

As a real-world example of this circularity, of this extreme interrelatedness, consider the following brief description of the English Cotton Famine of the 1860s after the disruption caused by the Civil War.

[1] See footnote 14 in Chapter 2.

The Civil War led to a near suspension of English imports of American cotton, which in 1860 had amounted to about four-fifths of the English supply. The price of cotton at Liverpool rose from 8 pence per pound in June of 1860 to a peak of 31½ pence in July of 1864.

The [price rise caused by the] famine led to a great decrease in the demand for cotton fabrication, and hence in the demand for the services of cotton mills and their laborers. Wage . . . rates fell an unknown amount, and workers earnings fell much more when they were forced to work with the inferior Surat cotton.

Of course a large expansion took place in rival fabrics. The production of flax quadrupled between 1861 and 1864 in Ireland, and yarn imports rose greatly; even so prices of linen goods rose about 60 percent between 1862 and 1864. Similarly, the wool industry experienced a great boom: imports of wool rose by a third during the period, and raw wool prices rose more than 40 percent. . . . Some migration of cotton workers and entrepreneurs to Yorkshire (a wool fabricating center), and of weaving of woolens to Lancashire (a cotton fabricating center), helped the latter area.

The unemployment in Lancashire caused great distress. . . . The great decrease in consumer expenditure in the area hit shopkeepers hard, and landlords even harder. . . . By 1863 about one-fourth of the families requiring public assistance were not directly connected with the textile industry.

Of course the effects reached to industries for which cotton textiles was an important customer. The textile machinery industry had a bad slump until 1864, and warehouses of the region suffered also. The Lancashire and Yorkshire Railway . . . had a decline in both passenger and freight traffic in 1862 and 1863.

In Birmingham . . . , the button and needle industries had to discharge many workers, but the edged-tool industry expanded greatly to provide tools for new cotton plantings in India and Egypt.

It does not seem bold to conjecture that everyone in England was somehow affected by the cotton famine: as a consumer, in the price of clothing; as a laborer, in the altered directions of the consumer spending; in the effects on transport, banking, and commerce; as a capitalist, on the return on investments in textiles and other industries.[2]

A. *A Simple Model*

The extreme interrelatedness of the parts of a price system can be described in yet another way—by building a model and observing

[2] George Stigler, *op. cit.* pp. 288-289.

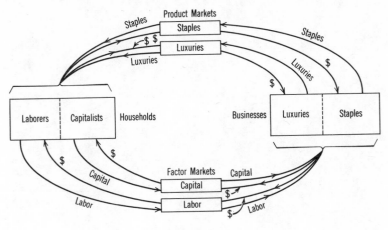

Figure 6-1

its operation. As before, we must make some simplifying assumptions in order to give the model substance and also make it manageable.

First, let us assume that the economy which this model describes is a competitive market economy which produces only two homogeneous goods. We shall call them "luxuries" and "staples." Second, let us assume there are only two factors of production used in producing these two goods, labor and capital. Third, let us assume that the production of luxuries is *capital intensive* (a high ratio of capital to labor in the production process) while the production of staples is *labor intensive* (a low ratio of capital to labor). Fourth, let us assume that the people in this economy can be divided into two groups, each of which earns income. We shall call these two groups labor suppliers (laborers) and capital suppliers (capitalists). Finally, let us assume that the economy is in general equilibrium. Every household and business is in optimum position and the price in every market equates the quantity supplied with the quantity demanded.

Figure 6-1 depicts the structure of this model economy. The household sector is divided into two groups: laborers and capital owners. The group of laborers supplies labor services to the businesses and capital owners supply the services of capital. Both

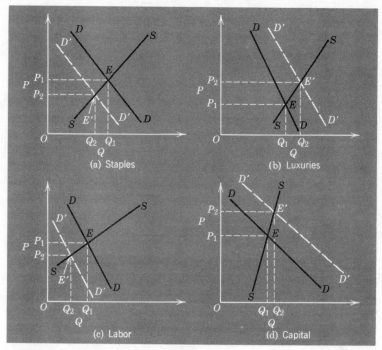

(a) Staples

(b) Luxuries

(c) Labor

(d) Capital

Figure 6-2

groups purchase luxuries and staples with incomes earned from supplying the services of their factors. The business sector, too, is divided into two groups: the luxury-goods industry and the staple-goods industry. Both produce their product by hiring the services of labor and capital. Therefore, there are four competitive markets in this economy—two product markets and two factor markets.

The market conditions conforming to the model's assumptions are indicated in Figure 6-2. Each of the four markets in this economy is seen in equilibrium (E). The equilibrium price in each market is P_1 and the equilibrium quantity is Q_1. In addition, the total revenue in each of the markets is depicted by the rectangle P_1EQ_1O in each diagram. In Figures 6-2a and 6-2b, this rectangle refers to the total sales revenue of the staple and luxury goods industries, respectively. In Figures 6-2c and 6-2d, it refers to the income received by the laborers and capital owners, respectively.

B. *The Effects of a Change in Consumer Tastes*

The best way to grasp the interrelatedness of the parts of our model economy is to watch it in operation. However, to put it into operation some basic change must occur to alter the existing general equilibrium. One of the forces determining the level of one or more of the supply or demand curves must change. To stimulate this change artificially, let us assume that consumers' tastes and preferences shift. In particular, let us assume that the tastes of both laborers and capitalists shift away from staples and toward luxuries. Such shifts in consumer tastes are common in the real world. People's preferences do change—compact cars do replace large sedans, knee-length skirts go out of style, miniskirts come in.

Let us now observe how our model economy adjusts to this disturbance in the general equilibrium. The first impact of this change in tastes is clear; the demand curves for both luxuries and staples shift. In the case of staples, consumers are willing to buy less at each given price after the change in tastes than before the change. The demand curve for staples shifts to the left from *DD* to, say, *D'D'* in Figure 6-2*a*. The opposite result occurs in the market for luxuries. There, because of the change in tastes, consumers desire to increase their purchases at any given price. The demand curve for luxuries shifts to the right from *DD* to, say, *D'D'* in Figure 6-2*b*. These demand shifts now elicit changes in a multitude of other economic variables as the system moves to regain equilibrium. Let us trace some of these changes.

With the shift in demand curves, the change in tastes originating in the household sector makes itself known in the markets for goods and services. As seen in Figure 6-2, the price of staples falls and the price of luxuries rises. From these markets, the shock is then passed along to other sectors. To the business sector, the changed prices represent a modified set of signals for each of the industries. The firms in both the luxury industry and the staple industry react to these price changes by modifying the quantities which they produce and supply to the market.[3] This is so because

---

[3] It should be noted that it is the quantities supplied of luxuries and staples which are altered and not the supply curves.

of the positive slope of the marginal cost curves of the firms in these industries. As each firm seeks its equilibrium where the marginal cost (MC) of producing the last unit equals the marginal revenue (MR) or price realized from selling that unit ($MR = MC$), and as the marginal cost curve slopes upward to the right, greater quantities will be supplied at higher prices than at lower prices. Therefore, the higher price of luxuries will elicit an increase in the quantity of luxury goods supplied and the lower price of staples will lead to a contraction in the quantity of staples supplied. From these changes a new equilibrium evolves in each of these markets. This new equilibrium is depicted as E' in Figure 6-2a and 6-2b. The price and quantity of luxuries increases, and the total revenue of the luxury industry rises. The price and quantity of staple goods decrease, and the total revenue of the staple industry falls.

Clearly, this is not the end of the chain of repercussions. As the output of one industry rises while that of the other falls, the demand for the factors of production, the inputs, is also affected. When output in the staple industry falls, the demand for both labor and capital decreases. However, because the staple industry is labor intensive, the decrease in the demand for labor is substantially greater than the decrease in the demand for capital.

Conversely, when the output of the luxury industry rises, the demand for both labor and capital increases. In this case, the demand for capital increases a great deal while the demand for labor only rises a little. The luxury industry is capital intensive.

In the case of labor, the combination of the large *decrease* in demand from the staple industry and the small *increase* in demand from the luxury industry decrees a *net decrease* in the market demand for labor. This is shown as a decrease in the demand curve for labor from DD to $D'D'$ in Figure 6-2c.

For capital, the reverse occurs. The large *increase* in capital demand from the luxury industry coupled with the small *decrease* in demand from the staple industry decrees a *net increase* in the market demand for capital. The demand curve for capital rises from DD to $D'D'$ in Figure 6-2d. Because of these shifts, the price of labor, the quantity exchanged, and the income of laborers fall, while the price of capital, the quantity exchanged, and the income of capital owners rise.

The impact of the original change in tastes and preferences has gone full circle, arriving back at the household sector. But this is still not the end. The two groups in that sector, the laborers and the capital owners, have experienced a shift in incomes—the incomes of the laborers have decreased and the incomes of the capital owners have increased. Thus, relative to the laborers, the capital suppliers have become more well-to-do.

With this change in the distribution of income, the household sector's demand for goods and services becomes modified a second time. With a new set of incomes, consumers will again reallocate their expenditures between luxuries and staples. The demand curves will shift again. Thus, the original change in tastes has generated a secondary shift in demand which, like the first, is transmitted through the circular flow of the price system. Prices and outputs are again changed in all markets, and again the distribution of income is modified. And so the process continues as the economy adjusts and readjusts in its struggle to regain a new general equilibrium.

In this analysis, we have traced only a few of the many repercussions set in motion by the original change in consumer tastes. There are several lines of impact which we have purposely neglected or assumed away. They complicate our simple model significantly. Each of them, however, is present in the real world. None can be ignored in a complete analysis of the interrelationships of the parts of an economic system. Let us but mention several of these other lines of impact and deal with one longer-run repercussion in some depth.

First, we have seen that the original change in tastes and preferences changes the entire price structure in the economy. This change further modifies one of the independent variables which determines demand for any good or service, namely, the prices of all other goods and services (P_n). When this variable changes in the demand equation of all consumers, it follows that all market demand curves are further jiggled. To analyze this effect, we would have to know the direction and size of the change in the demand for, say, good x because of a change in the price of y.[4] We ignored this entire chain of impacts in our analysis.

---

[4] As we saw in Chapter 3, whether goods are *complements* or *substitutes*

Another example: because of the original change in tastes, the price of luxuries rose from its original level. Consequently, the firms in the luxury industry begin making substantially higher profits than they had previously. The price of luxuries begins to exceed the average cost of producing them. The reverse occurs in the staple industry. The firms in this industry experience losses. In a competitive economic system the factors of production are *mobile*. They can change their location or employment and do so as their self-interest guides them. Consequently, firms will leave the staple industry over time in order to avoid the losses. Because of the higher level of profits, resources will move to the luxury industry. In the long run, with fewer firms in the staple industry, the supply curve of staples would shift to the left and with more firms in the luxury industry, the supply curve of luxuries would shift to the right. The price of staples would tend to rise back toward its original level; the price of luxuries would tend to fall back toward its original level. The quantity of staple goods exchanged would continue to fall; the quantity of luxuries exchanged would continue to rise.

However, these are only the changes in the product markets which would be induced by the entry and exit of firms. The factor markets would also feel the impact. The demand for capital

---

becomes most important in analyzing the impact of changes in the prices of one good on the demand for other goods. A change in the price of one good will have different impacts on the demand curves for other goods, depending on whether they are complements to or substitutes for the good whose price has changed. If the two goods are complements, a change in the price of one will cause the demand curve of the other to shift in the opposite direction of the price change. If the price of good x decreases and good y is a complement of good x, the demand curve of good y will shift to the right (increase). The opposite occurs in the case of substitutes. If two goods are substitutes, an increase in the price of one results in an increase in the demand for the other. Examples of complementary goods are hamburger meat and buns. If the price of hamburger meat rises, people will cut back on their consumption of hamburgers and consequently fewer buns will be needed—the demand curve for buns will *decrease*. On the other hand, hamburger meat and pork chops are substitutes. The demand curve for pork chops will *increase* when the price of hamburger meat rises. The reader would do well to test these relationships with other pairs of goods which appear to be related, for example, candy and chewing gum, soap and water, beer and pretzels.

would show another *net* increase because of the entry of firms into the capital-intensive luxury industry combined with a decline in firms in the staples industry. The demand for labor would show another *net* decrease due to the exit of firms from the labor-intensive staple industry combined with the increase of firms in the luxury industry. With the shift in the number of firms as well as in their size, the price and quantity of labor (and, therefore, the incomes of laborers) would fall still further while the corresponding variables for the capital suppliers would continue to rise. We also ignored this entire long-run process in our original analysis.[5]

Furthermore, we said nothing about the relative use of the factors of production in the two industries. Perhaps as the output of the luxury industry increases, production in each firm would tend to become more labor (or more capital) intensive. This would have a further impact on the factor market and, in turn, on the market for goods and services.

Again, we said nothing about the likelihood that the households would change their willingness to supply labor and capital because of changes in their incomes. If their willingness would change, the supply curve of factors would shift, the prices of factors would change, and the incomes of factor suppliers would be modified. All of these changes would react through the circular flow of the economic system affecting businesses, commodity markets, and again households. We ignored all of these possibilities in analyzing the operation of our simple model.

C. A Change in Technology and the Money Market

The tendency of the market system to adjust to a new equilibrium may be illustrated by yet another example, one which involves both economic growth and the operation of the money market.[6]

---

[5] The reader would be well-advised to work graphically through the analysis presented in the previous two paragraphs. Not only is it a good exercise in market mechanics, but it is also most helpful in gaining an understanding of how changes in market variables lead to succeeding changes in individual firm behavior.

[6] A more extensive treatment of the role of money in economic activity may be found in *National Income and Employment Analysis,* by Arnold Collery, a volume in this series.

Consider the repercussions of a change in technology, a common source of disturbance to the general equilibrium.

Suppose that a new machine is invented which is expected to be much more efficient in processing wheat than the old technology. The new machine requires more resources to produce it than the old type. However, the entrepreneur who will produce the new machine expects that this increase in cost will be more than offset by the value of the increased output of processed wheat. The producer of the new machines, needing money with which to buy the resources to build them, turns to the money market. In this market, too, prices and quantities are determined by supply and demand.

In seeking to borrow money, the firm joins other borrowers in the money market. Some are households who wish to shift their spending from the future to the present, perhaps because of an illness. There are business firms which expect an increased demand for their products. They may wish to buy more machinery and equipment, build a new factory, or merely expand their stock of goods in inventory. In each case borrowers wish to gain control over goods and services now, and are willing to pay for the money to gain that control. Each business firm, including our machine manufacturer, expects that the receipts from its action will be enough to cover the cost of production plus the cost of money, and also provide a residual, a profit.

The price of money, *interest*, usually is expressed as a rate or percent of the sums to be lent or borrowed. The interest rate is a cost for the borrower. The household which borrows will have to reduce future consumption spending more than it increases present spending in order to pay the interest. The business firm must add interest expense to its other costs in calculating its profit. The lower the interest rate, the lower the cost of money and the more that borrowers will want to borrow. The demand for money fits the Law of Downward Sloping Demand.

The suppliers of money are households which are willing to postpone spending for present satisfaction in order to consume in the future if they receive a payment for doing so. There are many reasons why households generally prefer present consumption to postponement of consumption for the future. We each face the uncertainty associated with the unknown—the chance that something may happen to us so that we may not live to enjoy future consumption. There is the further risk that prices of what we buy may rise so that less can be bought in the future with each dollar that we save. If households lend money rather than hoard it in a mattress, there are additional risks. The borrower may be unable or unwilling to pay back the money. If he contracts to pay back the money only after a specified time, there is the risk that the borrower may face an emergency and need the money in the interval but not be able to get it. Then, again, the market price of money may rise before the end of the contract period and the lender would not receive this higher price for his money immediately. Suppliers of money face risk and uncertainty of various sorts and will lend money only if they are paid for it.

The higher the interest rate, the more that lenders receive for accepting the risk of giving up control over their money, and the more they are willing to lend. The higher the price, the greater the quantity of money that will be supplied in this market. The Law of Increasing Supply pertains to the money market just as it does to product markets.

Returning to the invention of the new wheat processing machine, we may now trace the effect of this technological change through the various markets and observe the effect on the circular flow.

Producers enter the money market seeking additional funds needed to produce and install the new machines. These demanders (borrowers) are added to those already in the market so that demand for money has increased. The entire market demand curve shifts to the right. The demand curve now intersects the supply curve at a new higher interest rate (price). The price of money rises as does the quantity of it borrowed or lent. Lenders lend more money, foregoing some consumption and releasing productive resources. Borrowers borrow more money and and, in spending it, attract resources. The decrease in spending by lenders decreases the demand for resources, largely those used to produce consumption goods. Having obtained more money, borrowers increase the demand for capital goods and attract some of these additional resources. Productive resources have shifted from the production of consumption goods to the production of capital goods with the money market serving as the vehicle of this shift. Because of the new technology, a whole series of price changes are recorded, extending through labor, capital, and goods and services markets. Through these changing signals and the responses of businesses and households to them, the market system moves toward a new general equilibrium.

What we have done in this section is to demonstrate how fundamental changes in a competitive economic system are transmitted from sector to sector, from market to market, and from individual to individual in a never-ending process as the economic system moves toward a new general equilibrium. We have shown how changing prices create profits for some and losses for others and how these profits and losses cause a shift in the flow of resources from one sector to another, a reallocation of resources. By isolating the factors leading to changes in the income of laborers and capital suppliers, we have illuminated the process by which society's income is distributed. We have shown how, in a price system, the decisions of consumers make the entire system jump, changing outputs in the direction of the changed demand, changing profits, reallocating resources, and determining incomes. In general, what we have done is to show *how* a market system performs its basic resource allocation and income distribution functions; how it answers the questions of *what* to produce, *how* to produce it, and *how to distribute* it among the people.

II. THE MARKET SYSTEM AND THE WELFARE OF THE PEOPLE

To judge how good an economic system is we must be concerned not only with *how* it does certain basic things but also with *how well* it does them. To make a judgment on the quality of performance, we must have in mind some standard, some criterion, to which a given economic performance may be compared. We shall claim that the primary goal of our economic system, the most important and basic task which a system must accomplish if it is to be a "good" system, is the *efficient production and distribution of the right kinds of goods*. The people of a society are served best if their economic system uses social resources in the most efficient way to satisfy the demands of consumers. We shall label *efficient* a system which performs in this way.

To attain this goal, an economic system must effectively perform three functions. First, it must produce the *right* goods and services. Second, it must produce these goods and services at the *least social cost*. Finally, it must *efficiently* allocate this output among the people. Let us take these tasks and, applying concepts already learned, investigate how a competitive price system stands up.

A. What to Produce

First, how well does a competitive price system determine *what* is to be produced? This question is perhaps the easiest of the three with which to deal. Stated most simply, the price mechanism assures that the corporate body of consumers will get precisely that bundle of commodities that it most wants. It assures that the highest valued bundle of commodities will be the bundle that business firms find it worth their while to produce. How will this occur?

Given their tastes and preferences, their incomes, and the price structure in the economy, consumers make their desires known to the marketplace by offering to exchange their income for goods and services. As often stated, they enter the marketplace and vote for the goods they want using dollars as ballots. If people want a good sufficiently, they will pay enough to make its production worthwhile. Their willingness to pay is reflected in the demand curve presented to the market and, hence, in the price of the product. As long as the price exceeds the marginal cost of production, businesses will earn an additional profit on extra units and will be willing, indeed eager, to produce the extra units. The higher that consumers bid up the price, the more businesses will produce. Output will expand according to consumers' wishes. Surely, if the consumers in contemporary American society decided they wanted *Chateaubriand* at every meal and were willing to pay the price, they could bid the price high enough to persuade businesses to produce the desired supply.

This principle of *price equal to marginal cost* is an important proposition in analyzing the operation of a price system. Not only does this principle demonstrate the process by which consumers' desires become fulfilled, but it also says something important about the effectiveness of the process. Because, in a competitive economy, the price of each good tends to equal its marginal cost, we can say that the production of a dollar's worth of *each* good uses up exactly a dollar's worth of society's productive resources —its labor, capital, and natural resources. That is, *the last dollar's worth produced of any given commodity uses up resources which would never produce more than an extra dollar's worth of another product, no matter where they were shifted.* Consequently, society could not be made better off by allocating its resources any way other than that generated by the price system. Since market prices establish the relative value of different commodities to the society, the resources producing these commodities could never produce anything that consumers would rather have than the goods that a smoothly functioning, competitive market system distributes to them.

Through prices, then, a perfect market economy assures that the production of goods and services will conform to the desires of consumers. It carries out this assurance in the most efficient manner. It allocates resources so that the basket of goods produced is superior in consumers' eyes to any other which could be produced through some other allocation of resources.

B. *How to Produce*

Through our discussion of the "What" question, we have begun to answer the second question: How well does a market economy produce those goods it has decided to produce? That is, how well does it allocate the different factors in the production of these goods? Just as a competitive system regulates what to produce through prices, it also regulates how to produce through the pricing mechanism. In dealing with the problem of what to produce, we saw that the right goods are produced in the right amounts when the price of each good equals the marginal cost of its production. This same relationship must exist if the goods are to be produced properly, that is, if the right combination of inputs is to be used in the production of each of them. Here, however, we must look at this relationship from the other side—from the viewpoint of the producer instead of the consumer.

In our analysis of firm behavior, we built a simple model in which labor was the only variable factor of production. In that model the marginal cost of the firm was the cost of the additional labor necessary to produce an additional unit of product. Conversely, the marginal product of labor was the additional output which the firm obtained from hiring an additional unit of labor. We saw that as long as the marginal revenue product of any input exceeded its price (the wage in our model), the firm continued to hire additional units. The reason for this behavior was that an additional profit was earned by hiring those additional inputs for which the marginal revenue product exceeded the price of the input. In equilibrium, then, each firm in a competitive system uses each input up to the point at which its *marginal revenue product equals the price of the factor.*[7]

The implications of this equality are important for society. What it means is that the society can gain nothing by shifting any factor of production to a use different from the one decreed by the competitive market system. In other words, the allocation of resources resulting from a competitive pricing mechanism is the most efficient possible. It is an optimum allocation. Because of the decreasing marginal revenue product of additional units of a factor employed in any use, the reallocation of resources to a new sector would, *at best,* produce additional output that would match the value of the loss of output in the sector from which the shift was made. There would be no net gain. Thus, *the factor prices determined by the pricing mechanism guide each unit of each factor to produce that output which is of the greatest value to society,* namely, those products consumers most desire. By leading each factor to the use in which the value of its marginal product is the highest possible, the price system, through free markets, efficiently produces each of the goods. The price system must also be judged to be an excellent performer of the *how* task.[8]

---

[7] If this is not clear, the reader can easily review it by referring to pp. 132-135.

[8] In discussing the *how* question, we concluded that the price system allocates the right amount of resources to any particular industry and in the right proportions, and that the industry produces the optimum value of output with these resources. A corollary of this conclusion is that the industry produces its output by using the fewest possible dollars' worth of inputs. That is, the industry produces the output at *least cost.*

C. For Whom to Produce

The final task facing an economic system is the distribution of the goods produced among consumers. How efficiently does the price system answer the question "*For whom?*" As with the previous tasks, the price system makes this allocation in a particular way. It again uses market prices as rationing devices.

In thinking of the allocation of a quantity of goods and services among a number of households each of which possesses unlimited wants, we must have in mind some idea of an optimal or efficient distribution. Such a concept does exist. It was first set out in the late 19th century by an economist named Vilfredo Pareto. According to Pareto's proposition, *a distribution of goods is surely an optimum if it is not possible to find another distribution which would make some households better off without making others worse off.* Thus, if a given number of apples and oranges were distributed between two people and if, after the distribution, the two people were willing to trade some of the apples and oranges with each other, it would be clear that the original distribution was not ideal. By trading, *both* of the parties are benefitted with no one being harmed.

The principle that derives from this is that any given good is properly allocated if it is in the possession of the consumer who wants it more than anyone else *and* whose desire for it is backed up by a willingness to pay more for it than anyone else. *A good is distributed efficiently if the consumer who is willing to give up more of his income for it than anyone else—who is willing to "pay the price"—gets it.* Let us see if a price system secures such a distribution and if it does, how.

We have already discovered that there exists only one equilibrium market price for each good and service in a competitive system. Given these prices, any consumer is free to choose whatever quantity of any given good he desires. This choice is made by each consumer according to the dictates of his tastes and his income. Given an income, his tastes and preferences, and the prices of the goods in the market, *a consumer will increase the purchase of any good as long as the loss of utility from the other goods which he has to forego is less than the gain in utility from the additional unit of the good.* This will be recognized as the opportunity cost concept, which we considered earlier.

Put another way, the consumer will continue buying additional amounts of an item as long as the value of an additional unit exceeds the value of the other things he could buy with the same money—his other opportunities. Operating in this way the consumer will maximize his utility.[9] Because prices come from the interaction of market supply and demand and because the demand comes from consumers' operating according to the maximizing principle just mentioned, market prices regulate the allocation of supply so that those who are willing to pay the price, who are willing to give up more of their incomes than anyone else, acquire the goods. This, according to Pareto's principle, describes an efficient allocation of the goods which society has produced.

How a society finally divides up the goods and services that it has produced among its members is a most crucial question. It should be emphasized that other important considerations besides efficiency are used to judge the merits of any particular income distribution. Equity or justice come immediately to mind.

In a market system, the distribution of the society's output depends ultimately on (1) how the ownership of the factors of production is distributed among the people and (2) the prices of the services of these factors. From this, it follows that if all of the capital in society were held by just a few people, their incomes would be exceedingly high; they would bring to the product market a very great willingness to pay for the goods and services which society has produced and, consequently, they would go home with the lion's share of the output. In our discussion of the allocating power of the price system, we have taken this distribution of the ownership of the factors of production as a given. We have only asked if a price system allocates its current output *efficiently* among the people given their original endowment of factors; we have not asked if it allocates this out-

[9] As we have seen in the indifference curve approach, the optimum occurs when the consumer equates the marginal rates of substitution of the goods in question to the ratio of their prices. If this is not clear, the reader can easily review it by referring to the appendix to Chapter 3.

put *equitably*. Hence, when we judge the distribution to be an efficient one, we must realize that it might also be an inequitable (some would say unjust) one. Because the already wealthy have the ability to secure a large share of society's current output, while the existing poor, possessing but few factors of production, obtain little, an equity standard may well not be satisfied by the price system.

In economics, the equity problem has traditionally been divorced from the operation of the market system. Economists have, for decades, argued that if efficiency is to be attained, equity will have to be achieved outside of the pricing mechanism. They claim that, if society should object to a particular distribution of its current output (income), a *public* decision to rearrange the existing pattern of factor ownership (or the rewards earned from selling the services of particular factors) could be made through taxes and subsidies. Then, given the rearranged income pattern, the price system, through its multitude of *private* decisions, could again proceed to the *efficient* answering of the "what," how," and "for whom" questions.[10]

III. CONCLUSION AND SUMMARY

In this brief chapter, we have attempted to place the spotlight on the market system as a whole. It has been argued that markets are the cement which binds the various sectors of the economy together. Markets take the demands and supplies of businesses and households and convey prices—market signals—to each sector. As the system adjusts to any basic change in tastes or technologies, it is the complex of markets which conveys the impact of these changes to every household and business. Because of the extreme interrelatedness of the parts of an economy that is made possible by markets, the economy as a whole tends to a general equilibrium as each household, business, and market seeks its equilibrium.

In our discussion, we have shown that a competitive, free market system does answer all three of the questions which each and

[10] This equity problem will be discussed further in Chapter 8. See also *The Economics of Poverty*, by Alan B. Batchelder, in this series.

every society faces. Moreover, we have demonstrated that the answers to each of these questions lead a society to an efficient and optimum position, given its unlimited wants, its limited resources and a particular distribution of income. The answers to all of the questions are determined by the preferences of individual and free consumers as these preferences are made known by the willingness of people to spend their money—to cast dollar ballots—on alternative goods and services. As one writer has stated:

> The market performs the democratic task of bringing about a distribution or allocation of goods that takes into consideration the preferences of all the individuals. . . . It is as if it allowed each individual to vote, with dollars, as to which of the available goods and services he wanted to have, and then fulfilled all of the election promises— giving him the things he voted for. The market also permits each individual to vote in different degrees for different items, and in different degrees for additional amounts, in a way which is as much beyond the possibilities of the [political] ballot as a modern skyscraper is beyond a simple mud hut. . . . This is called *consumers' sovereignty,* and forms an essential part of economic democracy.[11]

However, while the market system does promote efficiency, it does not necessarily promote equity or justice in the distribution of the social income. Indeed, many have argued that it sustains —or even promotes—inequity and injustice. This is the most serious charge which has been leveled at the market system, and will be evaluated later.

QUESTIONS

1. Assume a perfect and competitive market system with all markets in equilibrium except the market for, say, shoes. In the market for shoes, the price is above equilibrium for some unexplained reason.
   (a) Without someone or something to artificially hold the price of shoes above equilibrium, what will tend to happen to it? Why?
   (b) Because of the change taking place in question (a), what would you expect to happen to the demand for shoe repair services? Why? How about the demand for bread? Why?

[11] Abba P. Lerner, *Everybody's Business,* Harper and Row, New York, 1964, pp. 62-63.

    (c) What would you expect to happen to the demand for labor and its price as the system adjusts? How about the demand for capital and its price? Why? What kind of additional information would help you to answer this question?

    (d) What would you expect to happen to the income of the households? Why?

    (e) What would you expect to happen to the number of shoe manufacturing businesses? Why?

2. Consider the following sentences from this chapter. In each case, present the reasoning on which the statement rests and list the assumptions implicit in the reasoning.

    (a) "It is the application of this *ceteris paribus* assumption in the study of individual sectors that has caused our analysis thus far to be 'partial' " p. 168.

    (b) "Thus, the original change in tastes has generated a secondary shift in demand which, like the first, is transmitted through the circular flow of the price system" p. 175.

    (c) "The demand for labor would show another *net* decrease due to the exit of firms from the labor intensive staple industry" p. 177.

    (d) "Output will expand according to consumers' wishes" p. 181.

    (e) "[T]he production of a dollar's worth of *each* good uses up exactly a dollar's worth of society's productive resources . . . ." p. 182.

    (f) "[S]ociety could not be made better off by allocating its resources any way other than that generated by the price system" p. 182.

    (g) "Market prices regulate the allocation of supply so that those . . . who are willing to give up more of their incomes than anyone else acquire the goods" p. 185.

3. "The Pareto proposition argues that a society has not achieved maximum welfare as long as there are two people in society who would be willing to trade some goods or services with each other." Do you agree? Why?

4. Distinguish between equity and efficiency in the distribution of income. Why is it impossible to argue that the market system performs well on the "equity of distribution" question. Does it necessarily perform badly?

5. Discuss why the $P = MC$ condition implies that the right answer to the "What?" question is being given by the market system?

6. Why is mobility of factors necessary for a general equilibrium to occur?

7

Interference in the Adjustment Process—
The Problem of Economic Power

If supplies and demands were not artificially manipulated, if the quantities of goods and services exchanged and their prices were free to vary according to the dictates of market forces, if consumers were free to choose among these goods and services as they please, if businesses were free to react to market conditions as they please, we should truly have a competitive economic system. But few things in life possess such freedom, few things run so smoothly and without obstruction. These are no exception. The real world simply does not work in the unconstrained fashion described by the model we have analyzed. Real-world market economies are often obstructed to some degree. Something or someone often interferes in the process of economic adjustment.

This interference is an exertion of *economic power*. When a group of firms in the electrical equipment industry conspires to fix the price of their machinery, they are exercising economic power. When Alcoa sets the price of aluminum where it pleases, as it did earlier in this century, it exerts market power. When labor unions create a situation in which wages can only rise, market power is being exercised. When the Federal government fixes the price of farm products, it is exercising economic power. In each of these cases the circular flow is obstructed; in each case, the competitive price system's optimum allocation of social resources is subverted. The impact of these obstructions on the operation of a competitive price system is the concern of this chapter.

I. TYPES OF MARKET POWER

Before discussing the influence of market power on the price system, we must distinguish the different kinds of such power. Although market power takes on many guises, there are three basic types. Two of them deal with control over the supply or demand of a product. The third deals with control over its price.

A. *Monopoly and Monopsony Power*

To control the supply or demand of a good or service is to possess market power. Free markets are rigged and the market system obstructed when either or both of these forces are controlled. Those who control *supply*, who determine how much of a good or service is to be brought into the market, possess *monopoly power*. Those who control *demand*, who determine how much of a good or service will be taken off the market, possess *monopsony power*.

To possess either is to possess much more than that power alone. Given a market demand curve, control over the supply curve automatically conveys the power to determine the market outcome—the quantity exchanged, the price and, perhaps most important, the total revenue which accrues to the sellers. Similarly, given a market supply curve, the power to manipulate the demand curve conveys this same power. Indeed, if the competitive system can be called economic democracy in which individuals choose freely by casting dollar ballots, the power over either market demand or market supply is equivalent to stuffing the ballot box.

Just as the outcome of a fixed political election benefits the fixers, so does this occur in economic elections. By violating the principle of consumer sovereignty, by interfering with the operation of the pricing mechanism, the exercise of market power yields a gain to a private interest at the expense of the rest of society. Monopoly and monopsony power, therefore, have both a resource allocation (efficiency) impact and an equity impact.

B. *Power of Price Control*

Both monopoly and monopsony power derive from a deficiency within the structure of a market. The third kind of market power, however, is imposed on the market by an outside force. Monopoly and monopsony power control price through control of either supply or demand, but this kind of market power controls the price directly, irrespective of the forces of supply and demand. Of its many names, we prefer to call it simply the *power of price control*. In the real world, its pervasiveness and importance may well exceed that of monopoly or monopsony power.

C. *Market Structure and Market Power*

Monopoly and monopsony power result from a particular kind of market structure. The existence of either monopoly or monopsony implies the absence of competition.

Competitive markets, we have seen, have a unique set of buying and selling conditions. There are so many independent buyers and sellers that no one can affect the price; the commodity exchanged is homogeneous; businesses and households can enter and leave markets at will. Indeed, a competitive market can be defined as one in which monopoly or monopsony power is nonexistent. Each firm and each household is so minute compared to the market that no such power is possible.

If a market does not possess all of these characteristics, if there is one supplier instead of many, if the product is differentiated instead of homogeneous, if entry is blocked and not free, it is not a competitive market. It follows that there are many different market structures possessing many degrees of monopoly or monopsony power. It further follows that each structure generates a different market outcome. In the following sections, we shall investigate a number of these structures, each of which possesses some degree of monopoly power.[1] We shall first analyze the ex-

---

[1] We shall only deal with the effects of monopoly power. Because monopsony power has the same impact as monopoly power—it being the same force operating on the demand instead of the supply side of the market—the general conclusions which we derive in analyzing monopoly also apply to it.

treme case of pure monopoly and then proceed to intermediate market structures called oligopoly and monopolistic competition.

II. THE PURE MONOPOLY MODEL

Pure monopoly lies at the opposite end of the spectrum from pure competition. Indeed, it implies the absence of everything for which pure competition stands. Whereas a competitive industry has a large number of firms producing the identical product, a monopolistic industry has but *one*. Consequently, while a single competitive firm cannot influence the supply of goods coming onto a market, a monopolist can. Firms move into and out of a competitive industry with ease, but entry into the monopolistic industry is effectively blocked. The competitive firm sees only the market price, is unable to affect it and, consequently, seeks an optimum position by adjusting its output to that price. The monopolistic firm, on the other hand, sees the entire market demand curve and is able to pick and choose the price and quantity that best serve its interests. The distinction between what the monopolist and the competitor see when they look at the market is clarified in Figures 7-1 and 7-2.

Figure 7-1 shows the position of the pure competitor and the market in which he operates. The price of the commodity in the competitive market is determined by the forces of supply and

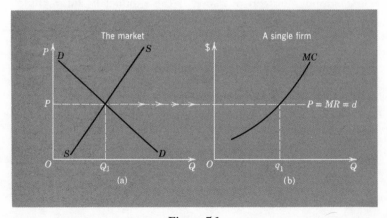

Figure 7-1

demand. Figure 7-1a depicts such a market with its supply and demand curves. The equilibrium price in this market is automatically transmitted to the individual competitive firm pictured in Figure 7-1b. Indeed, this price is the only communication which the individual competitor receives from the market. Because his actions have a negligible effect on the market, the individual competitor views the market price as the demand curve for his output. The market demand curve does not appear relevant to him. The demand curve he faces is the horizontal line at the market price illustrated in Figure 7-1b. Any quantity that he might decide to sell would be taken at the market price; that is, the market will "demand" any quantity from him at that price. Because the firm earns an additional revenue equal to the price for each additional unit supplied to the market, the market price is also the firm's marginal revenue. To reach an optimal position the competitor equates marginal cost and marginal revenue (the market price) and supplies a quantity equal to q_1. As a *price taker*, he operates by adjusting his rate of output to the going market price. His own output is the only thing over which the pure competitor has control.

Figure 7-2 represents a pure monopoly. Because the monopolist is the only firm in the market, there is only one diagram. The marginal cost curve of the monopolist is labeled *MC*. In monopoly, the forces of supply and demand are not the impersonal

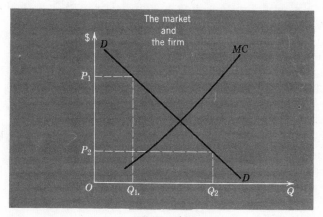

Figure 7-2

forces that establish competitive equilibrium. Market supply is now controlled by one firm. As the only firm in the market, the monopolist faces the entire market demand curve and is free to choose any point on it. The monopolistic firm can charge any price or supply any quantity which would be in its interest— which would maximize its profits. If the monopolist charges P_1, consumers stand ready to buy Q_1; at P_2, consumers stand ready to buy Q_2. Conversely, if it supplies Q_1 units, a price of P_1 will clear the market; when the quantity supplied is Q_2 units, a price of P_2 will clear the market.

A. *Marginal Revenue and Monopoly*

The monopolist is a *price maker,* not a price taker. In view of this freedom of choice, we must develop a model which will explain how much the monopolistic firm will supply and the price it will charge. These are the same variables that the competitive model explained for that market structure. In developing a monopoly model, we shall again adopt the assumption of profit maximization. We shall observe the same marginal principle in action. In the competitive situation, we found that the individual competitor is required to accept that price which is determined in the free market and to choose that output which maximizes his profits. To find this output, the competitor equated his marginal cost and marginal revenue (which was also equal to the price). Applying the same marginal principle, the monopolist also maximizes his profits by equating marginal cost with marginal revenue. Here, however, an additional complication arises; *the monopolist's marginal revenue does not equal the price of the product.*

Marginal revenue diverges from the price in a monopoly situation because of the kind of signals the firm receives from the market. The monopolist is not given a single price; he faces the entire demand curve. For this reason, the price of the output does not remain stationary when a monopolist alters the amount which he supplies. If he sells a larger quantity, the price falls; if he decreases the quantity supplied, the price rises. Moreover, no matter what output the monopolistic firm is producing, it will have to lower its price to sell an additional unit.

Here, then, is the clue. When the monopolist increases his output, he must lower his price to sell it and this lower price is attached not only to the *additional* unit but also *to all of the previous units* of output which the firm was producing.[2] Thus, in selling the additional unit, the monopolistic firm *gains* additional revenue equal to the price at which that unit is sold but *loses* revenue because of the decrease in the price attached to the previous units. This revenue loss is equal to the number of previous units sold multiplied by the decrease in price necessary to sell the

Table 7-1

P	Q	TR	MR
$1.00	0	$ 0	$
			0.90
0.90	1	0.90	
			0.70
0.80	2	1.60	
			0.50
0.70	3	2.10	
			0.30
0.60	4	2.40	
			0.10
0.50	5	2.50	
			−0.10
0.40	6	2.40	
			−0.30
0.30	7	2.10	
			−0.50
0.20	8	1.60	
			−0.70
0.10	9	0.90	

additional unit. Consequently, *the marginal revenue gained from the sale of the additional unit is the additional revenue from the sale of that unit minus the loss in revenue owing to the sale of the previous units at a lower price.* Marginal revenue to a monopolist is, therefore, less than the price. This is illustrated in Table 7-1.

The first two columns of Table 7-1 produce the demand curve shown in Figure 7-3. At a price of $1, 0 units are demanded; at a price of 90¢, 1 unit is demanded; and so on. The monopolist's total revenue at each price is found by multiplying each pair of items

[2] This is true because the firm expects to continue producing at the new rate.

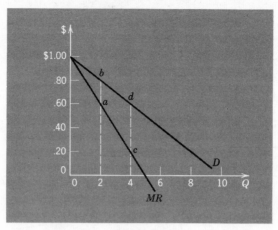

Figure 7-3

in the first two columns. This is displayed in column 3. Thus, as the monopolist moves down his demand curve, total revenue rises, reaches a maximum of $2.50, and then falls. From the total revenue schedule of columns 1 and 3, the *change in total revenue* owing to the sale of additional units can be found. It is the marginal revenue and is represented in column 4. In going from 0 to 1 unit of output, the marginal revenue is 90¢, in going from 1 to 2 units, the marginal revenue is 70¢, and so on. The information in the marginal revenue schedule is also depicted as *MR* in Figure 7-3. From this schedule and the *MR* curve, it is seen that the marginal revenue at each level of output lies below the price and, in fact, deviates farther and farther from the price as the output level rises. At two units of output, for example, the graphic deviation is *ab;* at four units of output, the deviation is *cd*, a substantial increase.

Let us derive this marginal revenue concept more concretely. Assume that the monopolist facing the demand curve of Figure 7-3 is currently selling two units of output at a price of 80¢ and earning a total revenue of $1.60. Assume further that he decides to increase output by one unit—from two units to three. From the shape of the demand curve, he will clearly have to decrease his price from 80¢ to 70¢ to sell the additional unit. What, then, is the marginal revenue? From the sale of the third unit, the monopolist receives 70¢ as an addition to his revenue. However, to obtain this additional 70¢, he must reduce the price on the original two units from 80¢ to 70¢. The firm, therefore, loses 10¢ on each of the first two units or a total of 20¢. What now is the monopolist's *net gain* or *net marginal revenue* from selling the next unit? Considering both the gain in revenue from selling the additional unit and the loss in revenue from selling the previous units at a lower price, the *net* marginal revenue to the monopolist from selling three instead of two units is 50¢, that is, 70¢ minus 20¢.

From this example, the *increasing* divergence of the marginal revenue curve from the demand curve can be readily understood. This increasing divergence phenomenon occurs for two reasons. First, because of the shape of the demand curve, the price charged decreases as output increases. Therefore, the gross marginal revenue from the sale of the additional unit of output is greater at low levels of output than it is at larger. Second, because the price reduction necessary to sell an additional unit affects more units when output is large, the revenue loss is greater when output is large than when it is small. This revenue loss, it will be recalled, is subtracted from *gross marginal revenue* in order to obtain net marginal revenue. For both reasons, marginal revenue drifts farther and farther away from price as output increases. Graphically, the marginal revenue curve displays a steeper slope than the demand curve. Moreover, after the output level at which total revenue begins to fall, the marginal revenue curve becomes negative, a phenomenon never observed in a demand curve.

On the basis of this relationship, let us redraw the demand and marginal revenue curves of Figure 7-3 and add the marginal cost curve of Figure 7-2. These are shown in Figure 7-4.

B. *Rational Choice and Monopoly*

The questions which we asked earlier can now be repeated: "What is the quantity of output which the monopolist will produce, and at what price will he sell it?" Remembering the marginal principle, the answer follows directly. The monopolist facing the demand and cost situation of Figure 7-4 will produce that level of output at which marginal cost equals marginal revenue —output Q_1. Having chosen this output, he will sell it at the highest price he can get for it—P_1 in Figure 7-4. P_1 and Q_1 are the

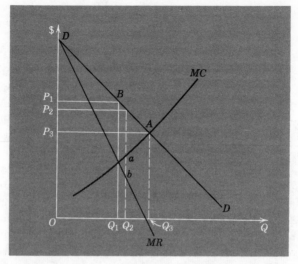

Figure 7-4

equilibrium price and quantity for the monopolist. There is no tendency for him to change either; they are the best attainable.

Why is this true? Why should not the monopolist attempt to increase output to, say, Q_2? In answering this question, the effect of such a change on profits must be considered. If the change increases total revenue more than total costs, it would clearly be worthwhile for the monopolist to increase his output to, say, Q_2. Let us observe the impact on profits from producing beyond Q_1. By increasing output to Q_2, the monopolist sees that total revenue would rise; marginal revenue is positive. This is so even though he has to sell his output at a lower price. But costs would also rise. The firm's decision, therefore, can be reached only after considering how these two variables move in relation to each other. If the additional revenue exceeds the additional cost, profits will rise and the monopolist will produce the additional unit; if the additional revenue is less than the additional cost, profits will fall and the additional unit will not be produced.

As can be seen in Figure 7-4, marginal cost equals marginal revenue at output Q_1. As output increases beyond Q_1, marginal cost rises and marginal revenue falls. Consequently, for any additional output beyond Q_1, say, Q_2, marginal cost exceeds marginal revenue and the firm would add more to its total cost than to its total revenue. A decision to produce that unit would be most unwise. For example, if the firm produced Q_2 in Figure 7-4, his marginal cost on the last unit would exceed marginal revenue by *ab*. By the same reasoning, a reduction in output from Q_1 would decrease total revenue more than total costs and profits would again decrease. Since either an increase or a decrease in output from Q_1 would decrease the monopolist's profits, output Q_1 sold at a price of P_1 is the optimum position. It is the *monopoly equilibrium*.

C. *Monopoly, Competition, and Social Welfare*

With $MC = MR$ established as the equilibrium position of both monopoly and competition, how does the price and output solution of a monopolistic industry differ from that of a competitive industry? What is the impact of monopoly power on the process of economic adjustment and hence on the level of well-being of the citizens of the economy? The first of these two questions will be answered in two steps covering two periods of time—the short run and the long run. Later, we shall analyze the impact of monopoly power on the adjustment process in the entire economy.

The difference between the *long run* and the *short run* must be distinguished before the two market structures can be compared. In economics, neither the short run nor the long run is a definite period of time. Rather, both are distinguished by whether certain events have time to occur. We shall define the short run as *a period which is insufficient for new firms to enter an industry or for existing firms to expand or contract their capacity*. It is a period of time in which only the existing firms with their existing sizes are analyzed. The long run is a period of time which is sufficient to permit existing firms to change their size or additional firms to enter an industry.

D. *A Short-Run Comparison*

In the short run, then, how does the competitive market equilibrium differ from the monopolist's? In competition, we have seen, the price of a commodity and the quantity exchanged are determined in the market by the forces of supply and demand. Competitive equilibrium is established where the supply curve, being the sum of the firms' marginal cost curves, intersects the demand curve. Hence, were the situation in Figure 7-4 a picture of a competitive market, the curve labeled *MC* would be the supply curve and an equilibrium would be achieved where it intersects the market demand curve.[3] An equilibrium price of P_3 would be observed and a quantity of Q_3 would be the equilibrium quantity exchanged.

In monopoly, however, the equilibrium is not established in the market by impersonal forces. The monopolist has the power to regulate the flow of output coming onto the market and, with this power, he can set its price. He has the power to pick an equilibrium which is more beneficial to his private interests than the competitive equilibrium. As a rational producer, he chooses an equilibrium which maximizes his profits. By restricting the amount which he supplies, the monopolist can raise the price of the commodity. He secures a greater profit by producing a *smaller output* and selling it at a *higher price* than does a competitive industry. As we have seen, the monopolist produces Q_1 and sells it at a price of P_1.

In Figure 7-4, the short-run price-quantity solution of the two market structures can be analyzed by comparing point *A*, the competitive solution, and point *B*, the monopolistic solution. First, a greater quantity is exchanged in the competitive industry than in the monopolistic industry. Q_3 exceeds Q_1. This reflects an important facet of the monopolist's behavior; he restricts output. Second, the price charged in the competitive case is a lower price than the price charged by a monopoly. P_1 exceeds P_3. Because the monopolist restricts output, he is able to sell it at a higher price. Third, because of the restricted output and the higher price, the quantity of resources or inputs which are used in the monopoly is smaller than the quantity used in the competitive industry. Production in the competitive industry is carried up to the point at which the price of the product equals the marginal cost of production ($P = MC$), while production in the monopoly case is halted before this equality is attained. Equilibrium in the monopoly is achieved where the price of the commodity exceeds the

[3] Recall that the demand to the individual producer in competition would appear to be P_3A in Figure 7-4. No matter how much or how little he produces and places on the market, the price remains the same.

marginal cost of producing it $(P > MC)$. As we shall see later, this results in either the unemployment or the misallocation of society's resources or both.

Strangely, we have not yet mentioned profitability. Surely, this is a relevant consideration. If the monopolist possesses market power and the competitive firm does not, the monopolist should be more profitable than the competitor. However, this is a long-run rather than a short-run question. Because industry profits may be eroded over a period of time by entering firms striving for a slice of the high profits, abnormal profits in the short run are not relevant. In the short run, even competitive firms may make abnormal profits.

To discuss the profits of either a monopolist or a competitor requires a familiar concept but one which we have not yet introduced into this discussion—the average cost curve. In Figures 7-5 and 7-6, the average cost curve is drawn on the graphs of both the competitive and monopoly models.

Let us assume that both Figures 7-5 and 7-6 show hypothetical short-run equilibrium positions in the two models. The total profit of the firm in each case is equal to *the difference between the price and the average cost times the number of units sold* $[TP = (P \cdot x) - (AC \cdot x)]$. Thus, in Figure 7-5$b$, the shaded area represents the total profit of a single firm among many in a competitive

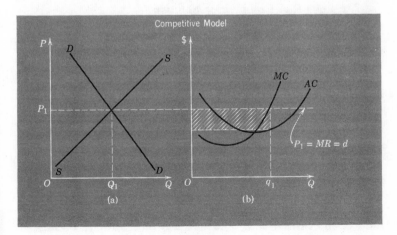

Figure 7-5

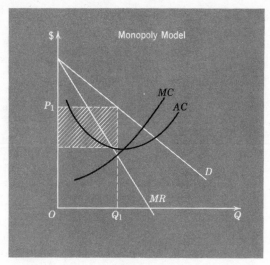

Figure 7-6

industry. The shaded area in Figure 7-6 represents the total profit of the monopolist. In both cases the shaded area equals the amount by which price exceeds average cost multiplied by the output. In both models large profits are being made; not an unusual short-run situation in either case.

E.   *The Long-Run Competitive Solution*

How will these short-run equilibria be modified in the long run? It will be recalled that we have defined the long run to be a period of time sufficient for both the entry and the exit of additional firms and for existing firms to expand or contract. Let us first consider the competitive model. One of the primary characteristics of a competitive industry is that there is free movement of resources and firms into and out of the industry. Clearly, the desire to earn a profit or avoid a loss provides the motive for such movement. Thus, when the firms in a competitive industry are earning a large profit, as in Figure 7-5, additional resources and firms will be attracted into the industry. On the other hand, if the firms were losing money—average cost greater than price—resources and firms would tend to leave the industry. Because of this entry and exit, the long-run equilibrium in a competitive industry will be quite different from the industry's short-run equilibrium.

If, because of large profits, additional firms enter the industry, the number of marginal cost curves will increase and the supply curve will expand. This is so because the supply of a competitive industry is the summation of the marginal cost curves of all of the firms in the industry. The opposite occurs if firms leave the industry. With substantial profits existing in our model (Figure 7-5), additional firms and resources will enter the industry and the supply curve will shift to the right. As it shifts, the market equilibrium slides down the demand curve, the price falls, and the quantity demanded and exchanged rises. In fact, additional firms will be attracted to the industry and the supply will continue to shift to the right until the price falls to equality with the average cost of the firms in the industry. At this point abnormally large profits become eliminated from the industry. Figure 7-7 shows this process of long-run adjustment.

In Figure 7-7a, the additional firms and resources entering the industry because of large profits increase the supply curve from S_1S_1 to S_2S_2 to S_3S_3. Because of the increasing supply the equilibrium moves from A—the original position—to B to C. The price of the product decreases from P_1 to P_2 to P_3 and the quantity exchanged expands from Q_1 to Q_2 to Q_3.

In this process, the individual competitor (Figure 7-7b) is also

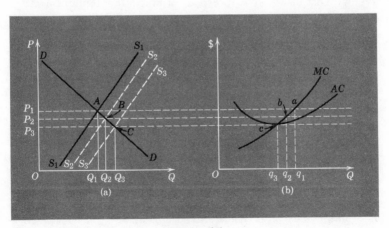

Figure 7-7

affected. As the price falls, he continues to equate his marginal cost with the price (marginal revenue). His equilibrium changes from a to b to c and his output decreases from q_1 to q_2 to q_3. The level of his profits is also affected by the influx of resources into the industry. Because the price is forced downward by the increased supply, the margin between the price of the product and the average cost of producing it decreases. When the price has fallen to P_3, average cost equals price. Profits have withered away through competition. At this point, there is no motive for additional resources to enter the industry. Nor will existing firms be forced out. Point C in Figure 7-7a and point c in Figure 7-7b represent the long-run equilibrium for the competitive industry and firm.

Two things stand out from this analysis. First, in long-run competitive equilibrium there tend to be neither profits nor losses. If such profits or losses existed, firms would be entering or leaving the industry, a sign that long-run equilibrium had not yet been attained. Therefore, *in long-run competitive equilibrium, price equals average cost* ($P = AC$).[4]

The efficiency at which an individual competitive firm is forced to operate in the long run must also be mentioned. As additional firms, attracted by large profits, enter the industry; as the price of the product falls because of the increased supply; and as abnormal profits are eroded, the firm is driven to the minimum point on its average cost curve. It is forced to produce at minimum average cost in order to survive. As can be seen in Figure 7-7, long-run equilibrium finds the firm producing at minimum average cost— at maximum efficiency for the firm.

F. *The Long-Run Monopoly Solution*

But what about the process of long-run change in a monopoly? Indeed, because of the very nature and definition of a monopoly market, there need be no long-run change of the type we observed

[4] This no-profit equilibrium should not be interpreted as zero return to either entrepreneurship or capital. Returns to these factors are normal competitive profits and are already counted and included in the average cost curve. After all, returns to these factors do have an opportunity cost. The no-profit equilibrium is to be interpreted as zero *excess* or *abnormal* return.

in competition. In monopoly, there is no free entry or exit of firms and resources—entry is foreclosed. There is, therefore, no tendency for prices or profits to fall or for supply or efficiency to increase. The absence of competitive pressure from entering firms implies that the short-run monopoly equilibrium need not be modified in the long run.

There is, however, one kind of long-run adjustment which can be made. The monopolist can change the size of his plant, expanding or contracting its physical facilities. The drive for maximum profits is again the motivation for such change. If the monopolist changes plant size, both his average and marginal cost curves change. This change may increase output or decrease it; it may increase the price charged or decrease it; it may increase average costs or decrease them—it is impossible to say. What can be said, however, is that the profits of the monopolist will increase because of such a change. Were it otherwise, the change would not be undertaken.

For the monopolist, the solution in the long run is not substantially different from that in the short run. The price of the product remains substantially above the competitive price; the output remains restricted; too few resources are channeled into production of the product; large profits remain unchallenged; there is no need for the firm to produce at the lowest average cost. In short, *the misallocation of resources noted in the short-run monopoly equilibrium persists into the long run because of barred entry and the consequent lack of competitive pressure.* Thus, Figure 7-6 pictures both the short- and long-run equilibria for the monopolist.[5]

However, this rather dark story of monopoly performance is not complete. The existence of monopoly power has far broader implications when the impact of monopoly behavior and performance is considered in the context of the entire economic system. We shall discuss this later.

---

[5] While this analysis portrays the outcome of a pure monopoly, it should once again be noted that no such purity exists in the real world. In reality, if the customers of a monopolist have alternative outputs which are not produced by the monopolist, his power may be severely undermined. This "competition of substitutes" is an important form of competition in a real economy. See Chapter 8 for an elaboration of this point.

QUESTIONS

1. Consider the demand curve equation used in the questions of Chapter 5, p. 164, $Q_D = 400 - 8P$. Assume that this demand curve is for a commodity which is sold by only one business firm.
   (a) Plot this curve on a graph and construct a demand schedule (a table) based on this equation. Again, use 1¢ price intervals from 8¢ to 22¢ plus 30¢ and 40¢.
   (b) Calculate a marginal revenue schedule using the demand schedule which you constructed in (a). Plot this marginal revenue schedule as a curve on the demand curve graph. (Again, plot the marginal value at the midpoint of the interval over which it is measured.)
   (c) On this graph, draw the marginal and average cost curves of a monopolist supplying this market. Make sure that these curves have the shape decreed by the Law of Diminishing Marginal Returns and that they relate properly to each other.
   (d) What are the equilibrium price and quantity in this market? Why is this an equilibrium?
   (e) Is the monopolist pictured in your graph making a profit? Can you calculate how much profit he is making? What is the profit per unit of output?
   (f) How would the equilibrium price and quantity for the monopolist compare with the short-run price and quantity if this were a competitive industry meeting the demand?
2. "The difference between monopoly and competition is characterized by the difference between the shapes of the demand curves facing individual sellers in each of these markets." Discuss this assertion, and if you conclude that there is a difference in demand curves, describe it.
3. "The most serious economic impact of monopoly is that there is little or no tendency for abnormally high profits to be eroded over the long run." Do you agree with this assertion? If you do not, how would you describe the most serious economic effect of monopoly?
4. "You can always distinguish a monopolist from a competitor on the basis of their motivations." Do you agree? What questions would you ask to determine whether an industry is competitive or monopolistic?
5. "How in the world can you claim that the monopolist produces 'too little?' Why, consumers are not willing to buy even one more

unit of output at the price at which it is selling." Evaluate this statement.

6. In competitive equilibrium, the following equalities hold for the individual firm: $MC = MR$, $P = MC$. How would you have to amend these to describe the equilibrium of the monopolist? Describe the significance of the amendment in evaluating the economic performance of a monopoly.

7. "The trouble with a monopoly in an otherwise competitive full employment economy is that it makes the quantity produced of all other commodities excessive." Do you agree? Why or why not?

8. "It is not possible for a monopolist to be in equilibrium when the price it charges is at a point on the demand curve which is inelastic." Is this statement true? Why or why not?

9. "A monopoly is like a government—it has the power to levy taxes." In what sense is this a true statement? If there is a sense in which it is true, what distinguishes a monopolist from a government?

III. OLIGOPOLY

To find any real-world industry with the characteristics of either pure monopoly or pure competition is no easy task. The agriculture industry is as close to the competitive norm as any but, for reasons which we shall see later, it fails to function competitively. The aluminum industry of a few decades ago was an example of a pure monopoly with effectively barred entry. It is no longer. To be sure, the vast majority of contemporary industries lie somewhere between pure competition and pure monopoly, possessing elements of both. The term *oligopoly* applies to a large number of these real-world industry structures. Indeed, several economists have claimed oligopoly to be the prevailing market structure in the American economy, and one economist has gone so far as to call it "ubiquitous."

The primary characteristic of oligopoly is described by the word *fewness*. Instead of a multitude of firms producing and selling a product as in competition or a single firm as in monopoly, there is an intermediate number—a few. Moreover, the product which oligopolists sell need not be homogeneous as in competition and monopoly; it may be *differentiated*. Both kinds are common. The steel of any firm in the steel industry is identical to the steel of any other steel producer. As one economist put it: "Steel bought from stock is standardized. . . . One man's steel is as good as another's." The steel industry, therefore, is a *homogeneous oligopoly*—a small group of firms producing an identical product.

The automobile industry is another oligopoly. However, its output is not homogeneous. Although a Ford and a Chevrolet sell for much the same price, perform much the same service, and have a similar appearance, they are not identical. Rather, they are differentiated. Nevertheless, they are closely substitutable commodities. Most people are relatively indifferent between them and a few dollars either way will sway their buying decision. Therefore, the automobile industry is a *differentiated oligopoly*—a small group of firms producing a differentiated though highly substitutable product.

A. The Causes of Oligopoly

Before we investigate oligopoly performance and compare it with that of monopoly or pure competition, we must ask: If oligopolies are so prevalent, how did they come to be? What caused their development in the United States?

Many reasons have been given for the development of oligopoly in the American economy. Because many of the prominent oligopolistic industries also contain the nation's largest firms, these reasons explain the growth of big business as well as oligopoly. A close relationship between the growth of oligopoly and changes in certain explanatory variables can be observed in data. Other reasons are not empirical, but logical. It makes sense that oligopoly should result from these factors even though the relationship between them cannot be demonstrated by data. Of the many causes of oligopoly, let us discuss two: *economies of scale* and *mergers*.

B. Economies of Scale

Economies of scale (sometimes called economies of large scale) occur when the average costs of a firm decrease as it grows larger. This may occur when the firm finds that it can utilize new technologies which will make it more efficient only if it expands. Consider, for example, the firm pictured in Figure 7-8. Assume that this firm possesses average cost curve AC_1. The firm produces at lowest cost with AC_1 when it produces output A. AC_1 is a familiar

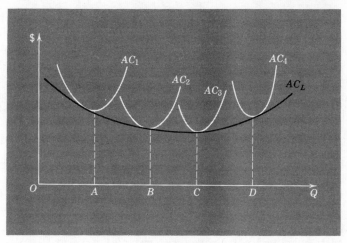

Figure 7-8

kind of curve. It relates the average cost of producing different outputs when the size of the firm does not change—when at least one factor of production is fixed. AC_2, AC_3, and AC_4 are additional fixed-size average cost curves. They refer to the firm's average costs at sizes B, C, and D. All of these curves are *short-run cost curves* because each depicts the average costs of a firm in a period of time too short for the firm to change its size.

By enlarging the size of its plant A to B to C, the firm pictured in Figure 7-8 experiences lower and lower costs of production. Its short-run average cost curve changes from AC_1 to AC_2 to AC_3. These curves, it should be noted, shift down as they move to the right. The firm is able to incorporate the technology of mass production by growing bigger. It gains the economies which go with this technology. However, as expansion proceeds beyond C, the economies of scale become exhausted. AC_4 is higher than AC_3. *Diseconomies* set in. Beyond some size, larger firms may be less efficient than smaller firms because of management and communications problems. The curve AC_L displays the average cost of production for this firm *at different scales*. Because the change of firm scale is a long-run concept, this curve is the *long-run average cost curve*.

Assume now that the firm of Figure 7-8 has the short-run cost curve AC_1. This firm equates its marginal cost and its marginal revenue, determines the output which maximizes its profits, and supplies that quantity to the market. If, by looking at a larger size, the firm sees that its average costs can be decreased to AC_2 or AC_3, it will not be satisfied with its short-run position. It will tend to enlarge, and to attain lower costs, larger output, and consequently higher profits. When economies of scale exist, the profit motive gives incentive to exploit them. By making such a move, the firm absorbs a larger share of the industry's market. It does so at the expense of its competitors. As a result, the output of the industry becomes concentrated in fewer and fewer hands. If carried far enough, oligopoly results.

Two questions arise: Have sufficient economies of scale existed so that large size and fewness can be attributed to them? If they have existed, what factors caused them?

As to whether such economies exist and have existed, there seems to be little doubt. In an important study, an economist investigated 20 prominent manufacturing industries in the United States, ranging from petroleum refining to steel to automobiles.[6] Defining an "optimal firm" as one just big enough to exploit the economies of large-scale production in its industry, he found about one half of the 20 industries able to absorb 10 or fewer such optimal firms. That is, if each firm in these industries were big enough to attain minimum long-run average cost (scale C in Figure 7-8), there would be room for only 10 or fewer firms in each of these industries. In these industries oligopoly is decreed by the existing economies of large scale.

In a fascinating book, Allan Nevins has documented these economies of large scale for a single firm, the Ford Motor Company.[7] From 1907 to 1908, Nevins points out, Ford produced fewer than 6500 cars and sold them at the typical price of $2800 each. By 1910 to 1911, the scale of the company had increased about five times; in that year nearly 35,000 cars came off the assembly line. These sold at a typical price of about $800—less than

[6] Joe S. Bain, "Economies of Scale, Concentration, and the Condition of Entry in Twenty Manufacturing Industries," *American Economic Review*, March 1954. See also Joe S. Bain, *Barriers to New Competition*, Harvard University Press, Cambridge, 1956.

[7] Allan Nevins, *Ford, the Times, the Man, the Company*, Scribner's, New York, 1954.

one third price charged three years before. By 1916 to 1917, the size of the Ford operation was 100 times that of a decade earlier and 20 times its 1910 to 1911 size. In that year, over 700,000 cars were produced and sold at a price of slightly over $350. By increasing its scale a hundredfold, Ford was able to cut the price of the car to one eighth of the price at the smaller scale. Moreover, the lower priced car was a better car. As scale increased, economies of large-scale production were reflected in lower prices for a better product.[8]

Why have such economies of scale occurred? The most straightforward answer is one word—technology. From the beginning of the industrial revolution to a few decades ago, the vast majority of technical innovations and inventions worked in the direction of increasing the economies of large scale—the economies of mass production.[9] The change in the source of power from muscle to steam with its required *in loco* steam plant and assembly line attached to the steam line, the change in materials used for production from wood to iron and steel, the change in processes from labor intensive to large, single-purpose machines, and the change in transportation from the ox cart and the canal to the railroad with its opening up of nationwide markets—all of these technological changes made production substantially more efficient in large firms than in small ones.

These changes did not occur overnight. Rather, they developed over a long period of time, as one innovation succeeded another. As they became known, market structures in industry after industry began to reflect them. Between 1880 and 1900, the changes in technology took their toll in radically transformed market structures. Where there had been many producers of each product, there remained only a few. Highly competitive markets turned into oligopolies. This was the period of the Great Combination Movement in the American economy. Robert L. Heilbroner describes it this way.

In the early 1800's . . . no single plant controlled as much as 10 percent of the output of a manufacturing industry. By 1904, seventy-eight

[8] It should be noted that a portion of these lower prices was due to increased competition which reduced the amount of Ford's profits.
[9] See John M. Blair, "Technology and Size," *American Economic Review*, May 1948.

enterprises controlled over half of the output of their industries, fifty-seven controlled 60 percent or more, and twenty-eight controlled 80 percent or more. . . . By 1904, there were over 300 [$10,000,000 companies in the nation] with a combined capitalization of over $7,-000,000,000. Together these giants controlled over two-fifths of the industrial capital of the nation and affected four-fifths of its important industries.[10]

C. *Merger*

While changed technology is one of the most important causes of oligopoly, other forces have also converted many firms into mass producers, and many industries into oligopolies. The most common of these is the *merger,* the joining together of two existing firms to form a single, larger one. Although merger has undoubtedly resulted in economies of scale, it is not clear that these economies motivated most mergers. In fact, some economists claim that the existence of a merger is evidence that such economies of scale do not exist; the firm would have grown internally if they did. This argument holds that the real reason for the merger is the desire to obtain market power, to achieve the ability to control price and thus overcome a major pressure plaguing firms in competitive markets.

Aside from the motive for merger, the fact remains that the merging of smaller firms to form bigger ones is one of the most significant causes of big business, high industrial concentration, and oligopoly market structure. Indeed, it is estimated that from 1895 to 1929, the period of the most intense merger activity, more than $20 billion dollars of corporate wealth was merged into larger business firms. The industries that were transformed into oligopolies through such merger activity form an impressive list: steel, automobiles, tobacco, petroleum, agricultural equipment, biscuits and crackers, and many more.

In one study of the influence of mergers on industrial structure, 74 large firms in 22 prominent industries were analyzed.[11] It was

---

[10] Robert L. Heilbroner, *The Making of Economic Society,* Prentice-Hall, Inc., Englewood Cliffs, 1962, pp. 118-119.

[11] J. F. Weston, *Role of Mergers in the Growth of Large Firms,* University of California Press, Berkeley, 1953.

found that in 6 of the industries, merger accounted for more than 50% of the total growth of the firms analyzed; in 13 of the 22 industries, merger accounted for more than 30%; and in 18 of the industries, merger accounted for more than 20% of firm growth. Mergers, whether motivated by the desire to take advantage of economies of scale or the desire to secure monopoly power, are important contributors to the creation of oligopolistic industries.

D. *Oligopoly Behavior*

Unfortunately, there is no standard theory of oligopoly behavior such as exists for pure competition and pure monopoly. Each oligopoly operates in a particular milieu, surrounded by a unique set of circumstances. Moreover, each new set of conditions elicits a different pattern of behavior. Consequently, no single model can universally explain oligopoly behavior. For example, in some oligopolistic situations a pattern of *price leadership* arises. In the steel industry, U.S. Steel usually sets the industry price, and the other firms follow it. In other situations, a pattern of *market sharing* evolves, as in the meat packing industry. In still other cases, a tacit understanding not to compete in price exists with the rivals wooing business through advertising, sales effort, and other forms of *nonprice competition*.

One basic pattern of behavior is common to all oligopolies. Noticed by many observers, this pattern has been described in several ways. The Supreme Court has called it "conscious parallelism of action." Others have referred to it as "tacit oligopoly collusion," or "oligopolistic rationale." Because of the size and closeness of the firms in an oligopoly, each is forced to react in some way to any action of its rivals. Thus, any action considered by an oligopolist will be taken only after the expected reaction of its rivals has been weighed and evaluated. If the firm should anticipate a violent response to its action, its decision to go ahead would not be the same as if it expected a quiet acceptance. This process of each firm's weighing its rivals' response to every anticipated action distinguishes oligopoly behavior from that of all other market structures.

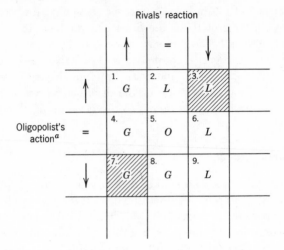

^a Entries in the matrix refer to changes in the *oligopolist's* profits

Figure 7-9

E. *A Simple Oligopoly Scenario*[12]

To demonstrate this "oligopolistic rationale," this mutual inter-dependence, let us analyze two oligopoly situations. We shall call the two situations the *price leadership case* and the *"live and let live"* case. Both are common patterns of oligopoly behavior.

Figure 7-9 contains a three-by-three matrix, which shows all possible combinations of the actions of an oligopolist and his rivals' response to them. The entries on the left-hand side of the matrix describe the three possible actions which any given oligopolist might initiate—he might raise his price ($\uparrow$), keep it the same ($=$), or decrease it ($\downarrow$). The entries along the top refer to the *response* of a rival to any of the oligopolist's actions. The rival can increase his own price ($\uparrow$), decrease his price ($\downarrow$), or keep it unchanged ($=$).

To fill in the boxes of the matrix, we must determine how each of the nine possible combinations of action and reaction influences

---

[12] This analysis draws heavily on one by Tibor Scitovsky. See Tibor Scitovsky, *Welfare and Competition*, George Allen and Unwin, London, 1952, pp. 384-392.

the oligopolist's profits. To do this, we shall make three assumptions about the state of affairs in the market.

(1) Both the oligopolist and his rivals are selling the product at the same price, say, *P*.

(2) If the oligopolist raises his price and all of his rivals raise theirs, the oligopolist's profits will rise. That is, the price at the beginning of the analysis is below the *industry's* profit maximizing price.

(3) If the oligopolist lowers his price and none of his rivals lowers theirs, his profits will rise, but if his rivals follow him down, his profits will fall.

On the basis of the particular situation defined by these assumptions, we can fill in the cells of the matrix. Each entry will display the effect on the oligopolist's profits of any combination of action and reaction—*G* referring to gain, *L* referring to loss, and *O* referring to no change.

Let us begin with the *status quo*. If neither the oligopolist nor his rivals changes price, nothing happens to the oligopolist's profits—no gain, no loss. We place an *O* in the center cell of the matrix. However, if the oligopolist were to keep his price unchanged and his rivals were to react to this by either raising or lowering their price, the situation would be different. Were the rivals to raise their price, sales would shift from them to the oligopolist and his profits would rise. On the other hand, if the rivals lowered their price, they would induce customers to shift from the oligopolist and the oligopolist's profits would fall. We place a *G* in cell number 4 and an *L* in cell number 6.

By the same token, were the oligopolist to raise his price while the rivals kept theirs unchanged, the oligopolist would lose sales and his profits would decrease. Conversely, were the oligopolist to lower his price while the others kept theirs constant, the oligopolist would gain both sales and profits. This latter case follows from assumption 3. Hence, we place an *L* in cell number 2 and a *G* in cell number 8.

This leaves only the four corner cells unfilled. They present no problem. Surely, if the oligopolist's profits rise when his rivals keep their price constant as he lowers his, he will also increase his profit when they raise their price as he lowers his. We place a *G* in the bottom left-hand cell of the matrix. By the same reasoning, if the oligopolist loses when his rivals keep their price unchanged as he raises his price, he will lose even more if they lower their price as he raises his. An *L* is placed in the upper right-hand corner. The entries in the remaining cells 1 and 9 follow directly from assumptions 2 and 3, respectively.

From the matrix, we can already isolate two important and basic characteristics of oligopoly behavior. First, it is obvious that an oligopolist's profit is not determined by his behavior alone but also by the behavior of his rivals—by their reactions to his actions and *vice versa*. Second, because of this interdependence of profit among oligopolists, the action of any rational oligopolist is determined by his rivals' expected reaction. Understanding these characteristics of oligopoly behavior, we can use the matrix to analyze two particular oligopoly patterns—price leadership and "live and let live."

F. *Price Leadership*

Patterns of price leadership often develop in oligopolistic industries—especially those in which a group of smaller firms compete with one very large producer. This is the case in the steel industry. Not anxious to antagonize the giant, the smaller firms permit it to set the industry price and follow its every move. Recognizing this pattern of reaction, the leader behaves on the assumption that every action which it takes will be imitated by the followers.

The price leader, therefore, faces only three of the nine possibilities represented in the matrix. If he raises his price, the others will too; if he keeps it the same, so will his rivals; if he decreases his price, the rest of the firms will follow suit. Only cells 1, 5, and 9 are relevant to this case.

Facing these three choices, a rational price leader has a clear course of action. If he raises his price, the entire industry price will rise and his profits will increase. Either of the other actions will hold his profits constant or reduce them. Recognizing that the other firms will follow, the price leader will raise his price until his profits are maximized. The net result of this behavior could be called *collective monopoly*—the firms in the industry behave as if they had formed a cartel and had agreed to follow a common price policy. They behave like plants of a single firm under a single manager.

As a result of a price leadership pattern, the oligopoly tends to charge monopolistic prices, earn monopolistic profits, and restrict output as does a pure monopolist. This tendency appears even though there is no overt agreement among members of the oligopoly but only a tacit acceptance of one of them as price leader.

In addition, it is clear from the model why such arrangements should exist in the real world and, indeed, feed on themselves. By following the leader, the other oligopolists increase their profits as the price rises toward the monopolistic level. They have incentive to strengthen the relationship rather than weaken it. Attempts to pursue an independent price policy are abandoned with little reluctance. Consequently, many economists have concluded that the "monopolistic solution," with all of its adverse consequences, does not require the existence of a monopolist. It may occur through a tacit agreement of the members of an oligopoly to a policy of price leadership.

G. *"Live and Let Live"*

The second oligopoly situation is characterized by the phrase "live and let live." Although this behavior pattern also arises out of an oligopoly market structure, it holds little resemblance to price leadership. In the case of price leadership, the oligopolist was certain of his rivals' reaction pattern. Every change in price becomes imitated. In this case, however, there is no tacit agreement among the oligopolists and little knowledge of rivals' reaction patterns. The high degree of uncertainty concerning reaction patterns causes the oligopolist to proceed cautiously. He fears the consequences of a bad move.

From the matrix, it is clear that were an oligopolist to keep his price unchanged, he would have no indication at all of his rivals' reaction. They might lower their price, raise their price, or keep it the same. However, if the oligopolist lowered his price, his rivals would either lower their price or keep it unchanged but, in all likelihood, would not raise it. Finally, if an oligopolist raised his price, his rivals would either raise their price or keep it unchanged but, in all likelihood, would not lower it. With these assumptions about rivals' behavior, all of the cells in the matrix in Figure 7-9 become possibilities except the two corner cells that have been shaded.

When an oligopolist is uncertain of rival reactions and wants to play it safe—to live and let live—which price policy will he pursue? Will he raise his price, lower it, or keep it unchanged? From studying the matrix, it is clear that the firm may suffer a loss, regardless of its choice. It all depends on the reaction of its rivals. Likewise, it may gain, no matter which policy is chosen. Assuming that the oligopolist desires to maximize profits and, above all, to avoid losses, what policy should he choose? Let us take the possibilities one at a time.

First, what is likely to happen if the oligopolist keeps his price unchanged? His rivals can raise or lower their price or keep it unchanged. If they lower their price, the oligopolist will clearly incur a loss. His profits will decrease. Even if the oligopolist attempts to remedy this by matching the price cut (moving to cell 9 after the rival cuts price), he will still lose. Thus, a decision to keep price unchanged can result in an irremediable loss of profit.

Second, what will likely happen if the oligopolist lowers his price? This policy can also result in a severe loss. If the oligopolist lowers his price and the rivals follow his action, he will be in the same situation as in the first course of action. Moreover, if the oligopolist attempts to correct his situation by again raising his price, there is no assurance that his rivals will follow him back up. He may simply shift from losing cell 9 to losing cell 6. Again, the loss may be permanent and irremediable.

Third, only if the oligopolist raises his price will the situation be different. Even if he loses in this case (because his rivals keep their prices unchanged), the loss will not be permanent. By cutting his price back to the previous level, the oligopolist could recover his earlier rate of profit.

This same situation can be viewed somewhat differently. From Figure 7-9, it is clear that at all costs the oligopolist must avoid choosing that policy which will cause his rivals to lower their price. As seen in the right-hand column of the matrix, if they should lower their price the oligopolist can only lose. On the other hand, the oligopolist will be best off if he can induce his rivals to raise their price. This can be seen in the left-hand column of the matrix. The question is: What should the oligopolist do to encourage his rivals to raise their price and to discourage them from lowering it?

The best policy for the oligopolist is clearly to raise his own price. Not only does this *prevent* his rivals from lowering their price, but it encourages them to increase it. The worst loss that the oligopolist could sustain in this case would occur if the rivals kept their price unchanged. But even then, the oligopolist can avert a permanent loss by again reducing his price.

Raising his price, therefore, is the safest policy for the oligopolist to adopt. It is the policy least likely to unsettle conditions. Indeed, and this is the importance of this case, if every oligopolist in the market believed in playing it safe, in living and letting live, the result would be the same as in price leadership. Prices and profits would rise and output would be restricted. The solution would again tend toward that of pure monopoly.

Although we have considered only two cases out of a multitude of possibilities, the general pattern of oligopoly behavior is clear. Because the gross interdependence of one rival on another is recognized by all, because any rival's behavior is anticipated, reacted to, and countered by the rest, because each rival desires maximum profits and recognizes that vicious warfare will harm all, the market solution will, in all likelihood, not be the competitive one. It will, in fact, tend toward the monopolistic solution.

IV. MONOPOLISTIC COMPETITION

A. *Market Characteristics*

The final market structure we shall consider is *monopolistic competition.* As the name implies, this form of industry structure possesses characteristics of both competition and monopoly. Although it is characterized by many firms like competition, each firm does not produce and sell a uniform or homogeneous product. Rather, each firm has control over its own unique commodity. However, the product produced by each firm is highly substitutable with the products produced by the other firms in the industry or group. This high degree of product similarity is what distinguishes the monopolistically competitive market from either monopoly or competition. Thus, monopolistic competition occurs where *a large number of firms produce highly substitutable commodities and other firms are free to enter the market with a differentiated or similar product.* While in oligopoly there are a few firms producing a product, here there are many. While in competition the product is homogeneous, here it is not. While in monopoly there are no close substitutes for the product of a firm, here there are many.

The next time you go into a drug store, spend a few moments studying the plethora of cold remedies. Each of the many remedies bears a claim for its own particular effectiveness—the product is differentiated. Nevertheless, all of them presumably perform one primary function—relief from cold symptoms. Thus, they are closely substitutable products and a few cents either way will sway the customer's purchase. Moreover, anyone can develop a new remedy and sell it over the drug counter. The market for cold remedies is, therefore, monopolistically competitive as are the markets for most household items. As a matter of fact, in all likelihood, the drug store is itself a monopolistic competitor. If prices on each item here were a few cents higher than those of other drug stores in the neighborhood, this druggist would lose business. The service he renders is a close substitute for the service rendered by the many other drug stores in the area.

The highly substitutable product characteristic of monopolistic competition is incorporated into the demand curve facing the individual monopolistic competitors. Figure 7-10 pictures two demand curves. The curve labeled *DD* in Figure 7-10*a* is the *market demand curve*. It represents the relationship of total quantity demanded to price in the market. As the market curve, it may be elastic or inelastic depending on the nature of the demand for the product. If the quantity demanded is responsive to changes in the price, the market demand is elastic; if the quantity is not responsive, market demand is inelastic.

In Figure 7-10*b*, the *demand curve facing the individual monopolistic competitor* is labeled *dd*. This curve displays a very high degree of price elasticity. Any individual monopolistic competitor knows that if he changes the price of his product even a little, the quantity that he can sell changes a great deal.

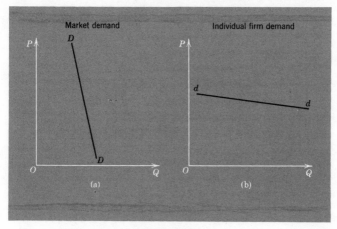

Figure 7-10

This is due to the close substitutability of his product with those of his competitors. While an individual firm has some control over the price of its product, it does not have very much. Were it to raise its price a little, many customers would shift to a competitor; were it to reduce its price slightly, it would gain many of its competitors' sales.

This situation is substantially different from either pure competition or monopoly. Because of product homogeneity, the firm in a competitive market has *no* control over the price that he charges. The demand curve that he faces is an infinitely elastic horizontal line. The monopolist, on the other hand, produces a product with no close substitutes. Being the only firm in the market, he faces the entire market demand curve. His control over price is total.

B. *Behavior and Performance*

To analyze the behavior and performance of monopolistic competition, we shall again build a model. As with our other models, we must make assumptions before we can draw conclusions. First, let us assume that there are a large number of firms producing a differentiated but very similar product. Second, we shall assume that all of these firms are in the position pictured in Figure 7-11: they all have costs represented by *MC* and *AC*; they face an

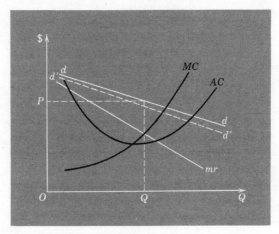

Figure 7-11

extremely elastic demand curve for their product dd; they are in short-run equilibrium $(MC = MR)$; they produce Q units of output and sell them at a price of P; and they are earning a large profit. With these assumptions, the question is: In an industry with this structure, what will happen in the long run—will the equilibrium pictured in Figure 7-11 be modified or will it not?

In monopolistic competition, as in pure competition, ease of entry and exit is a primary characteristic. In each case, it is the presence or absence of expected profits which provides the motivation. If large profits exist, new firms and resources will move into the industry to take their slice; if the industry is experiencing losses, firms and resources will leave the industry.

In our model, large profits are being made $(P > AC)$ and new firms will enter the industry. The short-run equilibrium pictured in Figure 7-11 will be modified. Each of the new entrants, by placing its somewhat differentiated product on the market, will carve out a segment of the market for its own. Significantly, the market segment which is carved out by the new entrants is composed of sales which the other firms in the market would have made if no entry had occurred. By gaining a share of the market for themselves, the new entrants decrease the market for each of the existing competitors.

Figure 7-11 depicts this process of market erosion for one of the existing competitors. Because of the large profits in the industry, new firms enter the market, carve out a part of the market for their own product, and cause the market of the existing firms to be eroded. Whereas the demand for the products of the existing firms was *dd* before the new firms entered, their entrance has the effect of reducing the existing competitors' demand curve to, say, *d'd'*.

As long as profits are being made in this industry, as long as the *dd* curve lies above the average cost curve, entry into the industry will occur. And every time entry takes place, the *dd* curve of the existing firms shifts down toward the average cost curve. The nature of the long-run equilibrium in monopolistic competition now becomes clear. As long as entry takes place, the *dd* curve decreases until profits are eliminated. This situation is pictured in Figure 7-12. The *dd* curve of existing firms has fallen until it is tangent to the average cost curve. Figure 7-12 pictures the long-run equilibrium of the monopolistic competitor.

In moving from short-run to long-run equilibrium, several things happen to the industry. Because of entry there are more firms than before. As the demand curve of the individual competitors is whittled down, the price falls from P to P_1. In long-run equilibrium, profits are forced toward zero.

Having defined the long-run equilibrium, we can compare the performance of a monopolistically competitive industry to that of

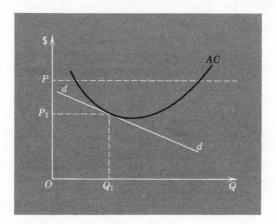

Figure 7-12

pure competition and pure monopoly. It appears that the performance of monopolistic competition lies somewhere between these two extremes. It is not as desirable as competitive performance but not as undesirable as the monopoly solution.

As Figure 7-12 shows, the price charged by a monopolistic competitor in long-run equilibrium is higher than the price charged by a competitor. The competitor's price, it will be recalled, is forced down to the minimum point on the average cost curve in long-run equilibrium. For the same reason, the quantity produced by a monopolistic competitor is smaller than that produced by a competitor. In monopolistic competition, each firm in long-run equilibrium has some excess capacity. We can conclude that because of the small degree of monopoly power present in this market structure, the quantity produced is somewhat smaller and the price somewhat higher than in competition.

However, because of the excess capacity which exists in each firm, a more serious inefficiency rises. To produce a given output, a greater number of firms is required in monopolistic competition than in pure competition. This clearly represents misallocated resources and economic waste.

Finally, it should be noted that the long-run monopolistic competition solution is similar to that of pure competition with respect to profitability. In both cases, profits are eliminated as free entry forces price down to average costs. This is substantially different from the long-run monopoly solution.

C. *Advertising*

The description of the performance of a monopolistically competitive industry (and, in fact, some oligopolies) would be incomplete if we failed to mention the problem of advertising. Clearly, advertising and other forms of *nonprice competition* are the main techniques used by firms to gain entry into monopolistically competitive industries. Advertising is the chisel used to carve out a share of the market.

The reason such nonprice competition is present in this market structure is clear. The existence of differentiated products spawns such expenditures. Because the allegiance of customers can be shifted from one product to a close substitute with little persuasion, the individual firm has incentive to use advertising to gain or maintain a market share.

In a very real sense, such expenditures on advertising—expenditures which support one of the nation's largest service industries—can be considered a *social waste*. Since their primary effect is simply to shift business from one firm to another with the consuming public paying the cost (which is reflected in increased product price), advertising expenditures yield little or no net social gain. Such a result cannot be ignored in evaluating the performance of monopolistic competition as a market structure. This is not to claim, however, that *all* advertising expenditures are wasteful. Those expenditures that inform the consumer of products, prices, and services of which he would otherwise be unaware provide real economic benefit. They increase the mobility of resources in the economy and make markets more perfect by augmenting the knowledge of consumers. This is a benefit which must be compared with the cost of these expenditures. However, those advertising expenditures whose purpose is to shift trade from one firm to another with a slightly differentiated product do not yield such a benefit. Although they may provide a substantial private gain to the firm doing the advertising, their social gain is nonexistent.

QUESTIONS

1. In what sort of market structure do you think four-year, coeducational, liberal arts colleges operate? Why? How about supermarkets, automobile companies, cigarette companies, computer manufacturing companies, tie manufacturing companies, toy retailers?
2. "The key difference between an oligopolist and a monopolistic competitor is that the oligopolist produces a homogeneous product." Do you agree? Why or why not?
3. "In some industries, the Law of Diminishing Marginal Returns does not hold. That is why they have become oligopolistic." Discuss and evaluate.
4. Why is "conscious parallelism of action" or "rivalry" present in oligopoly when it is not present in monopolistic competition?
5. Discuss the relationship between the elasticity of the demand curve facing a firm and the degree to which its product is substitutable

with the product of other firms. Is this relationship positive or negative? Why?

6. What would have to happen to transform a differentiated oligopoly into monopolistic competition? Would the existence of substantial economies of scale have anything to say about the probability of such a transformation occurring?

7. Explain why "excess capacity" is often cited as a characteristic of monopolistic competition. "Excess capacity" in a monopolistically competitive industry often has two components—"excess industry capacity" and "excess firm capacity." Distinguish between these two and describe why both kinds tend to be associated with monopolistic competition.

8. "Collusion" is often thought of as businessmen meeting in hotel rooms to rig the price of an industry's output. Is this the way "tacit oligopoly collusion" works? Describe the basic differences in the two types of collusion. Is there likely to be any difference in the final outcome of the two types?

V. THE POWER OF PRICE CONTROL

Early in this chapter, we noted a type of market power different from monopoly or monopsony power. We called this power the power of *price control*. The distinguishing characteristic of this power is that it is imposed on a market by some outside force.

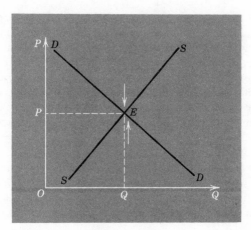

Figure 7-13

This force ignores supply and demand considerations and manipulates the market price directly.

In a free and competitive market, prices are determined by the forces of supply and demand. As in Figure 7-13, the market price of a good or service attains equilibrium where the supply and demand curves intersect. In such a free market, if the price were higher than *P*, excess supply and competitive selling would force it down toward *P*. This is a buyer's market. If the price were lower than *P*, excess demand and competitive buying would force it up toward *P*. This is a seller's market. The price and quantity in such a free situation vary according to the dictates of supply and demand.

A. *Surpluses and Shortages*

Assuming now that an external force enters this free market and, ignoring the forces of supply and demand, decrees with authority that the price at which each unit of a product shall sell is the price which it sets. By chance, this price might be the market equilibrium price. In this case, the price setter might as well have taken no action at all. The free market conforms to his desire. However, the price setter is likely to set a price different from the market price—a price either higher or lower than *P*. In Figures 7-14 and 7-15, these possibilities are presented.

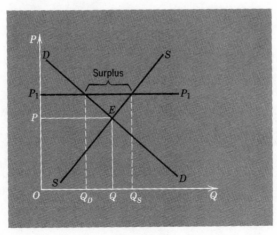

Figure 7-14

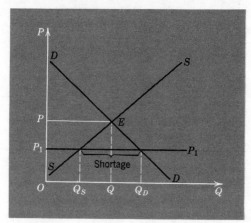

Figure 7-15

Figure 7-14 depicts the first of these possibilities. Whereas the free market would establish a price of P, we shall assume that the external price setter decrees a price higher than P, say, a price of P_1. At this price, the quantity which buyers will take from the market, the quantity demanded (Q_D), is less than the quantity which suppliers will bring to the market, the quantity supplied (Q_S). Because the price is maintained above the equilibrium price, a surplus equal to $OQ_S - OQ_D$ develops. The market simply cannot be cleared at a price of P_1.

Such an externally fixed price affects consumers of the product in two ways. They are not only forced to pay a higher price for the product but, equally serious, they are unable to buy as large a quantity as under the free market equilibrium.

The opposite situation occurs if the external price setter decrees a price lower than the market equilibrium price. This is pictured in Figure 7-15. Again, the market equilibrium is at E yielding an equilibrium price and quantity of P and Q. If the price were set at P_1, a disequilibrium would again occur. The quantity demanded (Q_D) would exceed the quantity supplied (Q_S) and an insufficient supply (or excess demand) would plague the market. A *shortage* equal to the amount that consumers desire to buy at this price (Q_D) minus the amount that sellers are willing to supply (Q_S) would result.

Clearly, the impact of this situation differs from that in Figure

7-14. While consumers had to purchase the product at a price above equilibrium in that case, here they secure the product at a price below the market price. In both cases, however, the quantity exchanged is restricted. Because sellers are willing to bring only Q_s to the market, only that amount will be exchanged at the below-equilibrium price.

B. *Farm Policy*

The exercise of this external power of price control is not uncommon in the real world. Indeed, for certain commodities all of the time and for almost all commodities at some time, this has been an accepted procedure. Farm products are an example. Because of low farm income and deteriorating farm prices, the government has supported the price of certain agricultural products for over two decades. The prices have been inevitably set above the free market price and, as would be expected from Figure 7-14, the market has not cleared—a surplus has accumulated. With the quantity of farm products supplied exceeding the quantity demanded, further measures were necessary to avoid the physical destruction of food. Being responsible for the creation of the surplus, the government did the next best thing. It bought the surplus and placed it in the massive storage bins which can be observed from any highway passing through agricultural areas.

C. *Minimum Wages*

Minimum wage legislation may have much the same impact as farm legislation. For some occupations, the price of labor appears to be set above the wage rate that clears the market. The setting of an above-equilibrium price may again create a surplus. In this case, however, there is no special provision for the purchase (or support) of the surplus labor. Whatever labor is displaced simply enters the ranks of the unemployed. By artificially raising wages, such legislation may, therefore, increase the level of unemployment. Perhaps more important, it will tend to increase the unemployment of those workers who can least afford it—the workers who, when they were employed, earned the lowest wages.

While minimum wage legislation is often defended as helping those workers in the society earning the lowest incomes, our theoretical discussion suggests that it may not do so. And, as is often the case in economics, it is not easy to measure empirically the true impact of such legislation. For example, one study of firms in the Southeast region of the United States indicated no clear tendency for workers to be laid off or unemployment to increase after the passage of the minimum wage bill.

There are many reasons that our theoretical outcome may be modified in the real world. Let us mention just a few. First, because of a lack of precise knowledge in the real world and a reticence to abandon the *status quo,* adjustments to economic change are neither precise nor instantaneous. Rather than crisp response, adjustment has the character of broad, somewhat uncertain tendencies. We should not be surprised if we are unable to get instantaneous readings of the labor market effect of minimum wage legislation. Second, if firms have some market power in purchasing labor, the government price fixing (minimum wage legislation) may merely offset private market power. In this case, the minimum wage law may actually result in resource allocation closer to that which pure competition would provide. This, too, limits our ability to make any certain claims about the effect of the minimum wage legislation. Third, if there are other forces in the economy which are inducing expansion of employment at the same time that the minimum wage legislation works in the opposite direction, the impact of the wage legislation alone may be impossible to siphon off and measure. This is the danger in using partial equilibrium analysis in appraising the impact of public policy on the economy. The *ceteris paribus* assumptions of the partial analysis simply may not hold in the real world.

D. *National Emergencies*

Minimum wage legislation and agriculture price support legislation reflect public dissatisfaction with how the price system allocates income. Price control during war reflects public dissatisfaction with the way the price system allocates resources when social demand must take precedence over private individual demand. In a national emergency, the supply of most consumer goods is cut back to allow for the production of war materials. The cutback in the supply of consumer goods causes the price of these goods to rise. To avoid these rising prices and the accompanying inflation, the government has commonly instituted a system of price control. A ceiling price is set on a broad range of goods above which the price is not permitted to rise. This ceiling is clearly established below the market equilibrium and, hence, results in a situation similar to that pictured in Figure 7-15. The buyers wish to purchase more than the sellers are willing (and, in the case of a national emergency, able) to supply. A shortage results.

In a national emergency, as in the agricultural situation, the government steps in to alleviate the problem caused by the fixed price. In World War II, for example, the government rationed the available supply of consumer goods through a system of coupons and stamps. This rationing program accomplishes what the society desires during wartime. It eliminates the danger of inflation and restricts the use of particular nonessential kinds of goods. In doing this, it frees resources for wartime outputs. It should be noted, however, that this form of social control directly substitutes the judgments of political leaders for the freely expressed tastes of consumers. Consumers are prohibited from using dollars as ballots in buying the goods and services they desire.

E. *"Fair Trade"*

One final form of this external power of price control should be mentioned. Although disguised under the title of "fair trade," it has the same impact as governmental price fixing. Through fair-trade legislation passed by either state or federal governments, individual *producers* are permitted to establish the *retail* price of the goods which they produce but do not sell at retail. For example, the makers of men's shirts would be allowed to determine the price at which the haberdasher must sell the shirts under fair trade legislation. There is only a slim chance that producers will choose the market equilibrium retail price. For obvious reasons, they will set the price in their own interest and above the free market price. Hence, the impact of fair trade is similar to that of the monopoly solution—the price is raised, the quantity exchanged restricted, the price structure distorted, and resources misallocated. Because the producer can restrict his own supply in this case, the problem of the surplus is automatically eliminated.

QUESTIONS

1. Consider the demand and supply functions for breakfast cereal in question 1 of Chapter 5, p. 164. Assume that the government decreed that, because breakfast cereal was such a vital food, it would not be permitted to sell for more than 10¢ per package.

    (a) Presumably the government's objective would be to encourage the consumption of breakfast cereal. Would its decree have that effect?

    (b) What would be the shortage of breakfast cereal?

    (c) What would you expect to happen to the number of firms in the breakfast cereal industry?

    (d) What steps could the government take if it wanted both to encourage the consumption of breakfast cereal and to keep the price below 10¢ per package?

2. Setting prices above and below equilibrium hurts some people and helps others. Assume that the rent of apartments in Chicago was set by the government at a below equilibrium level. How would you feel about this decision if you were:

    (a) A poor apartment dweller.

    (b) A rich apartment dweller.

    (c) A slum landlord.

    (d) A homeowner.

    (e) A newly married couple looking for an apartment.

    (f) A black family moving from Georgia to Chicago.

3. Perhaps the dominant example of price control in the United States economy is the military draft. The maximum price that the Defense Department can pay military personnel is set by law. At the set-in-law price, the quantity of men demanded often exceeds the supply of men willing to work in the service at that price—there is a shortage. Diagram this situation. How does the government resolve this situation? Who would gain and who would lose if the men required for the service were obtained by hiring in the open labor market at the prevailing wage rate? Describe what would happen to: taxes, the prevailing wage rate in the economy, and the defense budget. What are the economic and noneconomic reasons

why you would favor (or disapprove of) this system of meeting the military manpower requirement?

VI. THE IMPACT OF ECONOMIC POWER: CONCLUSION AND SUMMARY

In this chapter, we abandoned our analysis of how a competitive market system works. We were interested in how the efficient performance of the competitive system becomes modified when market power is substituted for competition. The two basic types of market power were discussed in this chapter—market or industry structures in which the requirements of competition were not met and markets in which some external force arbitrarily sets the price. In the first category, we discussed the market structures of monopoly, oligopoly, and monopolistic competition. In the second category, we analyzed the effect of arbitrarily setting a price both above and below the market equilibrium.

In studying the competitive system, we learned that the optimum allocation of national resources requires the free movement of all goods and services, including the factors of production. Any good, service, or factor must be permitted to move freely if prices, including wages, are to perform their resource-allocating duties with efficiency. Indeed, because of the elaborate interdependence of the system's parts, a restriction imposed at one point in the economy is an indirect restriction on the entire mechanism.

Only when businesses have no power over prices or markets is the output of an economy adjusted so that the marginal cost of each commodity is equal to its price ($P = MC$). This adjustment occurs because the single, competitive producer faces a price which is equal to his marginal revenue ($P = MR$) and produces where his marginal cost equals this price.

In each of the market structures observed in this chapter, the $P = MC$ relationship does not hold. Under conditions of imperfect competition (monopoly, oligopoly, monopolistic competition), the single firm has control over price. It faces a demand curve for its product which slopes downward and to the right. For this reason, marginal revenue to the imperfect competitor is less than the price ($MR < P$). By producing where marginal cost equals marginal revenue ($MC = MR$), the imperfect competitor restricts output below what it would be if market power were lacking. It halts production while the cost of producing the next unit—the marginal cost—is less than the value of the next unit to the consumers, as represented in the market price. When market power is present, $MC < P$.[13]

The effect of this market power, whether held by buyers (monopsony power) or sellers (monopoly power), is to restrict output, to reduce the movement of goods, services, and factors, and to cause a misallocation of resources. Much the same result was seen to occur when the market price was arbitrarily set by an external force. This, then, is the most basic result of market power. It results in restricted outputs in the controlled sectors as judged by the preferences of consumers and evidenced by the casting of their dollar ballots.

Such restriction excludes resources from activities in which consumers wish them to be employed and forces them either into alternative employments which are not as desirable in consumers' eyes or into unemployment. Consequently, these resources either produce products which are less urgently desired or produce nothing at all. This results in a reduction in the value of their marginal product, which is synonymous with economic waste.

We conclude, then, that the most important impact of market power is its restrictive ability, its forcing of some sectors of the economy to be too small relative to others as judged by the preferences of consumers. Such restriction has many implications. Prices are no longer determined by the market, resources become misallocated, the productivity of factors is lower than otherwise, and social waste results. The prices of restricted outputs are higher than otherwise, abnormal profits accrue to the firms in the restricted sectors, and society's income is redistributed by those private interests doing the restricting. Moreover, ineffi-

---

[13] This sentence follows directly from the previous sentences: In monopoly, $MR < P$; profit maximizing businesses attain equilibrium where $MC = MR$; therefore, in equilibrium, $MC < P$. From this it follows that production is halted where the value to society of the next unit of output—the price—exceeds the cost of producing it.

ciency and excess capacity are created within individual industries, costs are higher than otherwise, and again social waste results. We have, therefore, studied market power because of its impact on allocative efficiency and the economic welfare of people. In comparing it to competitive performance without market power, it comes off badly.

8

The Models and the Real Economy: Problems and Prospects

The presumption in a market-directed society is that, in pursuing their own self-interest, individuals will act to maximize social welfare if they are subjected to the discipline of competition. The model of competitive markets that we have presented demonstrates the logic of this conclusion. In contrast, the models of noncompetitive markets illustrate how market power, control of supply or demand, leads to misallocation of resources and a consequent failure to achieve maximum social welfare.

I. CONTROL OVER SUPPLY AND DEMAND

If competition serves as a disciplinary force for self-interest, we can expect that market participants will try to escape it; they will attempt to gain control over supply and demand. Adam Smith recognized this tendency when he wrote, "People of the same trade seldom meet together, even for merriment and diversion, but the conversation ends in a conspiracy against the public, or in some contrivance to raise prices."[1] Or, again, "Masters are always and every where in a sort of tacit, but constant and uniform combination, not to raise the wages of labour above their

[1] *The Wealth of Nations,* The Modern Library edition, Random House, New York, 1937, p. 128.

236

actual rate. . . . Masters too sometimes enter into particular combinations to sink the wages of labour even below this rate."[2] In the 185 years since Smith wrote, both workers and employers have constantly sought to combine. Labor unions have developed into strong institutions whose primary purpose has been to raise the price of labor through control of its supply. Oral agreements have been reached among competitors in the electrical equipment industry in recent years as well as among assembled steel industry magnates at the famous Judge Gary dinners earlier in the century. In addition, manufacturers have sought shelter from competition by organizing trusts, cartels, and mergers.

If the only force leading to the control of supply or demand were cupidity, society might merely formulate and enforce rules prohibiting noncompetitive behavior. This is the essence of the common-law tradition which has held conspiracy in restraint of trade to be illegal. It is the spirit of antitrust legislation which aims to maintain competition by forbidding certain kinds of mergers, by outlawing conspiracies for price fixing or division of markets, and by preventing predatory practices that are designed primarily to destroy competitors.

A. *Economies of Scale*

Rule and rule enforcement have become complex because cupidity has an ally in technology. The continuing and accelerating technical revolution has created production units whose minimum efficient size (measured in units of output) is very large. We pointed out in Chapter 7 that economies of scale decree oligopoly in a large number of industries. Sometimes these economies occur because a single key machine, in its smallest efficient size, will produce an enormous output. In 1931, for example, a small Banbury mixer used to mix rubber compound for automobile tires produced 118,000 pounds of rubber compound per day.[3] This one machine produced enough rubber compound for 6700 tires per day if used in standard passenger car tires of the period. If 51 such machines had been in use in 1933, they would have ac-

---

[2] *Ibid.*, pp. 66-67.
[3] B. Stein, "Labor Productivity in the Automobile Tire Industry," United States Bureau of Labor Statistics Bulletin No. 585, Washington, D.C., 1933.

counted for the entire capacity of the industry. In that year there were 44 plants and 33 firms in the tire industry, few enough that competitive performance was not inevitable. But concentration into large firms went beyond this. Four of the 33 firms owned 64% of total industry capacity. The nine largest firms had a capacity of 6000 or more tires daily, accounting for 84% of the capacity of the industry. All of these firms made use of the productive, large-scale Banbury mixer. The remainder of the firms, 24 of them, shared the remaining 15% of capacity, using old-all 24 have disappeared. The Banbury mixer has reinforced the tendency toward control of supply in the tire industry. fashioned, high-cost technology. In the years since 1931, virtually

Economies of large-scale operation may occur for other reasons as well. Sometimes machines used in sequence do not each produce an output that meshes with the others in a 1-to-1 ratio. In that case it is necessary to seek the lowest common denominator for the most efficient size of output. Suppose three different machines, used in succession on the production line, had capacities of 100, 500, and 600 units per day, respectively. To utilize all machines to capacity a firm would need 30 of the first type, 6 of the second, and 5 of the third. Minimum efficient capacity would not be 600 units (the capacity of the largest machine) but, instead, 3000 units per day.

Plants may have to be very large if they are to use the most efficient means of production, but that is not the end of the story. Where great gains may be had through specialization and division of labor within management, firms may grow to be larger than the size established by one efficient plant. One firm may control many plants.[4]

Large-scale operation may also occur when firms react to uncertainty. A firm may wish to produce a variety of products which are sold in different markets in order to spread the risks. If the demand curve for one product shifts adversely (to the left) because of a change of tastes, cyclical variation, or other

[4] For an extensive discussion of efficiency and size of plants and firms, see E. A. G. Robinson, *The Structure of Competitive Industry*, University of Chicago Press, Chicago, 1958, revised edition. Also, P. S. Florence, *The Logic of British and American Industry*, University of North Carolina Press, Chapel Hill, 1953.

they are. The profit motive may lead to larger size because of the gains from market power, which are indistinguishable in the firm's balance sheet from the gains due to technical efficiency. Some of our industrial giants might be broken down into smaller firms without sacrificing a significant amount of managerial or production efficiency. This step would make it easier to prevent outright collusion, but in most cases the larger number of firms would still find themselves in situations of oligopoly with both the desire and the necessity to act like oligopolists.

We are, it appears, on the horns of a dilemma because of these considerations. If we insist on efficiency in the allocation of resources by requiring purely competitive markets, we must accept some inefficiency in the techniques of production. Costs will remain above the minimum. If we want efficient production, however, we must live with less than sufficient competition to allocate resources efficiently. Dilemmas are frustrating. Judges in antitrust cases often depart from the position of economists by treating "rivalry" as a synonym for competition, but this does not dispel the frustration.[6] Justice Department lawyers may have their spirits buoyed by an occasional provable case of collusive price fixing, but tacitly followed price leadership continues practically untouched in industry after industry. With the motive of self-interest primary, intelligent behavior leads each manager to consider the impact of his actions on his rivals so as to preserve the order which exists on his side of the market. To do otherwise might destroy the institution entrusted to his control. While some managers may not be keen enough to anticipate interdependence with other firms, they come to understand by trial and error that ignoring interdependence will bring swift retribution.

If, in many industries, it is not possible to have both technical efficiency in the form of minimum long-run costs and sufficient competition to regulate self-interest for the social good, is there no alternative to detailed government regulation? Are there any other "automatic" regulating devices? Two famous economists, Joseph Schumpeter and John Kenneth Galbraith, have given qualified affirmative answers.

---

[6] Since all oligopolists are rivals by definition, this interpretation makes almost any market structure acceptable. Such a position has proved irritating to many economists for many years.

reasons, the demand for other products may not be so affe
and the firm as a whole may continue to prosper. Some o
impetus for conglomerate mergers in recent years stems
this incentive to spread the risks.[5]

Collusion, price fixing and general noncompetitive behavi
not restricted to situations created by large-scale technology.
all, Adam Smith wrote about the problem prior to industria
tion of England. In small towns today where there are per
two lumber yards, three drug stores, or five lawyers, it is not
possible but probable that there will be parallel pricing.
might still read on the front page of a small-town paper abo
meeting of oil station operators in the area at which it is deci
to end the only gas war in the town's history and restore
initial price structure.

While technological change has created large-scale enterp
it should be noted that it has also reduced the isolation of s
towns and has enlarged effective market areas. When transpo
tion innovations brought New England shoe manufacturers
competition with those in St. Louis for the Great Lakes mark
the possibility of competition being an effective regulator was
larged.

In only a few industries in the American economy do we f
markets large enough and efficient producers numerous enou
to have a market-determined, competitive price. A high prop
tion of production is carried on by firms that operate in situati
of oligopoly because of economies of large scale. This should
be taken to mean, however, that existing firms must be as big

[5] Impetus for mergers also comes from some of our legislation. A sing
merged company can do what two competing companies cannot. With agr
ments, collusion, and trusts outlawed, mergers became the common meth
to reduce competition. Antitrust law has had to be extended to prohibit the
anticompetitive mergers. Moreover, because of our tax laws, it is often a
vantageous for a highly profitable small firm to sell out to a larger firm
convert income into capital gains. Tax law also enables the acquiring fir
to charge off over a number of years the losses of the unprofitable firm whi
it has purchased. Since legislation tends to prevent merger of competi
firms, conglomerate mergers of noncompeting firms have become the answ
for mergers motivated by such financial-legal considerations. Policy maker
it now appears, are striving to develop a legal basis for proceeding again
some of these conglomerate mergers.

B. *Innovation and Competition*

Schumpeter, in his *Theory of Economic Development*,[7] saw a kind of competition at work in the capitalist economy which is different from the price competition of our model. In this important work, Schumpeter placed the entrepreneur or innovator at the center of his theoretical structure. By introducing new things, or new ways of doing things, the innovator puts pressure on already existing products and methods. The new competes with the old in a *process of creative destruction*. It is not inevitable that the new displace the old; sometimes the new is not a close substitute for anything existing at the time of its introduction. The only effect may be the generalized one of competing with all other things for a share of limited income. But oftener than not, the new destroys some or all of the utility of the old. The old must adapt if at all possible, or die.

The internal combustion engine applied to the automobile and bus destroyed the electric street railway. It seriously cut the passenger traffic of railroads for short hauls. The truck reduced the high-grade freight traffic of railroads. While the internal combustion engine of the car, bus, and truck introduced a new, flexible dimension to our transportation system, its innovative character also provided a direct and effective challenge to rail transit. Indeed, the railroad may well be facing a fatal blow to its long-distance passenger traffic from the competition developed since World War II by the commercial airline.

The innovator has a temporary monopoly when he introduces something new, and if he is successful he will receive a flow of monopoly profits. But if the competition of our model now comes into play, he will attract a host of imitators who will compete away his profits. Secrecy, patents, the requirements of large-scale financing, or the advantage of an early start may hold his imitators at bay, but the innovator cannot rest, since another firm, perhaps in another industry, may introduce something new which will displace his process or product.

What are the results of this kind of competition? There is no

[7] Joseph Schumpeter, *The Theory of Economic Development,* Harvard University Press, Cambridge, 1934.

question that the development of aluminum processing created a substitute for many products that had been made of steel. This reduced control of supply by steel firms. Plastics compete with both steel and aluminum as a material for many products. Whereever new products are introduced which can be substituted for existing products, control of supply is weakened and the public benefits. But substitutability does not always develop, and where it does not, a few firms may continue to control supply. There are many uses of steel for which other materials are not close substitutes. In these markets, steel companies control supply. That such control is substantial may be inferred from the fact that steel companies show profit even when the industry operates below 50% of capacity for prolonged periods. All in the steel industry recognize that because of an oligopolistic market, standard competitive behavior—price reductions to produce and sell more—would be detrimental to their interests. Thus, prices are held up (sometimes even increased!) while factors of production remain idle.

Competition provided by innovation does substitute for intra-industry price competition in many cases where concentration of production has decreed oligopoly market structure. Concentration transforms price competition to rivalry by way of product differentiation and innovations to reduce costs. Advertising and product innovation are generated in the first instance, and process innovation in the second. Product differentiation may add to social welfare when product quality is improved or new products are developed. It may subtract from social welfare when a large volume of resources is devoted to creation of superficial differences and their promotion. Process innovation is in the public interest because it reduces production costs. The occurrence of interindustry competition is also in the public interest even though each industry is an oligopoly. Because of such competition, it is more difficult for firms to establish mechanisms for market control. These firms may be under constant threat from firms in industries other than their own.

C. *Countervailing Power*

Thus far we have considered two kinds of "built-in" economic forces that protect the public interest in a market economy; one is our model of competition which illustrates protection by intra-industry competition, and the second is innovation which enlarges this form of competition and creates interindustry competition. A third force which may protect the public interest is countervailing power, identified by Professor Galbraith. In *American Capitalism: The Concept of Countervailing Power,*[8] Galbraith develops the thesis that the existence of power on one side of a market creates a tendency for a countervailing power to develop on the other side. Thus, he claims that if a group of sellers exercises control over supply, we might expect that a group of buyers will try to develop control over demand to offset and neutralize the sellers' power.

There is a strong incentive to develop countervailing power for self-protection. Moreover, the monopoly profits on one side of a market give incentive to develop offsetting power on the other side of the market in order to share in the profits. According to Galbraith, this is why our powerful labor unions are most often found in highly profitable, concentrated industries. Likewise, chain stores have developed to counter the power of concentrated manufacturers. Sears, Roebuck, and Company, for example, was able to obtain substantial price concessions from the Goodyear Tire and Rubber Company in the 1920s, when Sears negotiated with Goodyear to produce a private brand tire.

Countervailing power tends to develop only where there is an initial power that produces high prices and high profits. This appears to be a necessary condition because creation of power on one side of the market without power on the other side would constitute the creation of an initial, as opposed to countervailing, power. Moreover, if prices and profits of the initial power were just sufficient to draw the flow of products, nothing could be gained from the exercise of countervailing power. Such power may be most effectively exercised against oligopolies rather than monopolies because, with several firms, one firm may be played off against another.

In an economy which is characterized by excessive demand, it is difficult for *buyers* to organize effective countervailing power. An individual firm, even though a giant, will not be able to exer-

[8] Houghton-Mifflin, Boston, Second Edition, Revised, 1956.

cise power as a buyer if there are other buyers that are willing to absorb all of the output that sellers can produce. However, if a group of *sellers* (for instance, labor) seeks to counter the established power of buyers (for example, a group of business firms), they are likely to be most successful during inflation. But, in this case consumers continue to pay because higher labor prices are passed on in higher product prices. Higher wages are carved out of high profits, and consumers do not benefit.

What are the conditions under which countervailing power will produce public benefits? When countervailing power is effective, it changes prices and the distribution of income. Whether these changes are a social benefit depends entirely on the individual circumstance. If farmer cooperatives can bring down the prices charged by concentrated farm suppliers, farmers will use more supplies and resources will tend to be allocated more efficiently. This will happen because the farmer sells in a competitive market and the lower costs will be passed on to the buyers of farm products. If a manufacturing firm (or retailer) brings down prices charged by its suppliers, and absorbs the gain rather than passing it on, one economic power group has gained at the expense of another, and there is little improvement in the public welfare. Nothing has been passed on to the consumer.

There must be a broad distribution of the gains from countervailing power for there to be public benefit. Generally, the gains must be passed on to the ultimate consumers. Whether this will happen depends on the degree of market control by sellers through each transaction all the way into the consumer markets.

It should be noted that some legislation forestalls this potential public benefit because it does not distinguish between countervailing and initial power. The Robinson-Patman Act, for instance, prevents price concessions to business firms other than those concessions that can be substantiated by lower costs for that transaction. The act prevents the exercise of countervailing power in situations where there may be no other practical restriction of original power short of close governmental regulation. If countervailing power cannot be exercised, there is *no* chance for its benefits to seep down to the consumer.

Retail price maintenance ("fair trade") laws, passed in the name of competition, have the same effect. By destroying price competition at the retail level, they remove any pressure on this source of countervailing power to pass its gains on to the consumer.

Pure competition cannot be enforced in broad areas of a modern industrialized economy without great social cost in reduced technical efficiency. The void in the protection of the public interest which this situation creates is partially filled by innovation and by countervailing power which create different forms of "competition." Where none of these private regulators are effective, government may be required to regulate in the public interest. Business performance must be studied industry by industry if one is to understand the issues of public policy in the regulation of market power.[9]

II. FRICTION, INDIVISIBILITY, AND IRRATIONALITY

A. *Friction: Lack of Knowledge and Immobility*

For a realistic view of how the market system functions we must understand many problems in addition to that of market power. One such group of problems may be identified as frictions. In Chapter 1, it was noted that the price system works best if all buyers and sellers are well informed of the choices they face. For this reason, we said, the government often provides information to participants in markets. Government has provided agricultural crop forecasts for 100 years. It has provided forecasts of total production in the economy for about 25 years. Collection of data for forecasting is most important if markets are to have stable prices, if there is not to be short-run misallocation of resources, and if public policy is to stabilize the general level of economic activity.

With an understanding of supply and demand, the reader can see why prices for agricultural crops would experience wide swings without data collection for the markets. In the absence of data for forecasting, supply curves in these markets would be based on quantities in storage. The supply curves would shift more and more to the left as the last harvest became more remote. They would jump sharply to the right at harvest time. With a

---

[9] *Case Studies in American Industry*, by Leonard Weiss, in this series provides such a study.

relatively stable demand curve over time, price would be very high just before harvest and very low just after harvest. Regular forecasts of the growing crops, however, help to reduce these price swings as buyers and sellers can anticipate changes in the future supply. Price stability is further enhanced by selling and buying contracts for future delivery, for instance, several months hence. Crop forecasts are essential for these transactions.

Manufacturing firms often require a lead time of as long as six months in planning production schedule changes to meet short-run shifts in demand. Mistakes in forecasting lead to unintended increases or decreases in inventories. As inventories are worked off, or efforts are made to enlarge them, there will be shifts in demand for raw materials and for labor. Where factor prices do not move quickly to clear the markets, there will be unemployment.

A lead time of many years may be required to meet long-term shifts in demand. Often it will require two or three years to build new plants, order new capital equipment which must be manufactured, and install that equipment. If errors in forecasting are made, the firm may face excess capacity with high average fixed costs for many years before either demand shifts to the right or some capital goods are fully depreciated and no longer contribute to cost. Losses from such errors may take many years to absorb.[10]

Provision of market information tends to increase knowledge and, hence, reduce price instability, periodic unemployment, and a misallocation of resources because of errors in forecasting. To accomplish these results, both government and private enterprise strive constantly to gather more complete data for more accurate market forecasts. But despite these efforts, some uncertainty will persist as long as production plans must anticipate future sales

[10] The Edsel automobile required a long lead time for planning and many millions of dollars for capital equipment even though many component parts were common to other Ford products. The Ford Motor Company planned the Edsel to be the principal competitor to Buick, then in third place in total automobile sales. The Ford Motor Company failed to forecast the decline in this automotive price line and consequently experienced gigantic losses. The Ford Motor Company has offset this fiasco in forecasting more recently by anticipation of great growth in the larger-sized sports car market and the resultant introduction of the Mustang.

rather than respond to already received special orders. Errors can be costly because capital is durable. Consequently, business managers will expect a higher return than without such risks. Some capital goods would produce an adequate return without consideration of these risks, but would not be profitable if the risks are included in the calculations. Such capital goods will not be purchased and installed; hence, lack of knowledge adversely affects the allocation of resources. More accurate information will reduce uncertainty and the magnitude of error, thereby contributing to a more smoothly functioning and efficient market economy.

In addition to a lack of knowledge, immobilities are a second friction that interferes with the smooth working of the price system. Simple models of the economy such as ours usually ignore not only time but also spatial considerations. Some immobility of resources is due to lack of knowledge about alternatives and can be reduced by spread of information. Labor market surveys frequently find that workers in one plant do not even know the wage scale for similar work in a plant across the street. Ignorance of wage rates in other parts of the city and other parts of the economy is considerably more widespread. Unionism and government employment exchanges reduce this ignorance, but it continues to be very extensive. Business managers, especially of small retail establishments, also are frequently ignorant of alternatives open to them.

While ignorance reduces the mobility of factors of production so that price changes fail to bring quick adjustment, immobility is also caused by the cost of overcoming distance. Coal mining has to take place at the coal seam. Production that is dependent on the use of coal requires weighing the cost of assembling other factors of production at the coal site against the cost of moving the extracted coal to some other site. Capital also has cost restrictions to its free movement. Usually the cost is prohibitive to dismantle the capital equipment of a factory and ship it to a new location.

A worker faces an economic cost in moving with his family to a new location. In addition, he faces a psychic cost in leaving relatives, friends, and familiar surroundings. (There is even a psychic cost in leaving fellow employees and a known relationship with supervisors for the unknown in a plant across the street.)

The worker must weigh both psychic and economic costs in considering whether to respond to a higher wage somewhere else.

A further restriction on mobility of factors of production relates to specialization. Skilled workers are loath to shift to a different kind of job because they lose the investment of time and money involved in learning their skill. The money cost might include not only an outlay for instruction but also income foregone while being instructed. A worker may prefer periodic unemployment to abandoning these sunk costs and bearing the cost of retraining. The result is a surplus of labor in some localities and occupations as well as a surplus attached to some industries. Seniority, pension rights, and the like also increase the reluctance to move.

Capital equipment generally is more highly specialized than labor, and it does not shift in its existing form from declining to expanding industry. Since many capital goods are durable and are depreciated over 10 to 20 years, the shift of capital occurs over similar periods of time as firms decide about replacing it, rather than the instantaneous adjustment posited in our model. Of course, when the whole system is expanding, all of the additions to capital stock can flow into expanding industries, easing the adjustment process.

B. *Indivisibility*

Continuous marginal utility curves for consumers,[11] and continuous cost and revenue curves for business firms, imply that fine adjustments may be made to changes in market conditions. But business firms long have faced the fact that fine adjustments often cannot be made. Some kinds of capital must be introduced in rather large lumps. A firm may work a plant beyond its rated capacity, but at some point a new plant must be constructed to increase output. Even if a wing is added to an existing plant, there is a discontinuity in the expansion of output. In the steel industry, a firm will have to build a new blast furnace at some point in order to increase the output of pig iron. A blast furnace is big in its smallest efficient size. So is a steel furnace or a rolling mill. The steel industry of the United States operated in excess of rated

[11] Or, for those who studied the appendix to Chapter 3, continuous indifference curves.

capacity for many years after the Second World War and yet had a very large backlog of orders. When the industry finally expanded, the lumpiness of capital led to building more capacity than the existing level of demand required. Demand did not grow according to expectations, but actually lagged for several years, so that unplanned excess capacity was added to planned excess capacity, and the industry operated below 50 percent of rated capacity.

Indivisibility or lumpiness of capital is a special problem for developing countries. A railroad provides an outstanding example of the problem. It cannot be built and used a mile at a time. A railroad, or a highway for that matter, is not useful unless it joins two or more centers of economic activity.

Durable consumer goods produce the same kind of problem for decision making by households. A consumer is often prohibited from weighing the satisfaction from an additional dollar spent in one direction versus the satisfaction from spending it in another. He either buys an automobile or he does not. He either buys a washing machine or he does not. Variations in the elaborateness of these durable goods is of some help in the process of adjusting expenditures. So, too, is the existence of second-hand markets. But even so, the adjustment of expenditure to maximize satisfaction is not so finely attuned as the continuous curves of our model imply.

C. *Irrationality*

Even if all of these frictions and indivisibilities were eliminated, the price system would fail to function in the manner depicted by our ideal market economy. In our model we assumed that all of the market participants are rational. But in the real economy the price system will work out its results in response to dollar "votes" even if they are based on irrational behavior.

Some critics of the theory of household demand argue that it is based on an outmoded hedonistic theory of psychology. It is true that behavior cannot be explained simply as a weighing of pleasure and pain. Psychological explanation of behavior recognizes more complexity today. In consumer behavior, there are compulsive buyers as well as impulsive buyers, and many kinds of expenditure are habitual. Yet the essence of the economic model is defensible because it is not dependent on a psychological theory; it is dependent only on observable facts of which we can be reasonably sure.

It is an observable fact that people choose among alternatives, that choice is constrained by limited income, and that the choices made usually reflect a fairly stable although roughly articulated preference system. Housewives can be seen in any grocery store, momentarily indecisive about whether to put a product in their baskets. Surely they are weighing advantages and disadvantages. Income is a constraint, even if borrowing against future income is included. When habits are broken with changes in income or changes in associations, new choices are made in the formation of new habit patterns. If the individual does not weigh alternatives in considering the purchase of a new car, the banker from whom he seeks to borrow will see to it that he considers at least some of them, just to be assured of repayment of the loan.

There is sufficient stability in the pattern of consumer expenditures that the Survey Research Center at the University of Michigan has had good results forecasting purchases of consumer durables by questioning a sample of consumers as to their intentions. Income, prices, and expectations prove to play important roles in consumer purchasing decisions, as does the amount of existing assets and indebtedness. These are just what we would expect from our understanding of the theory of consumer demand. In constructing his model the economist attempts to produce conceptual frameworks that give precision to these relationships. The difficulty of acquiring data for an empirical indifference map or demand curve may make further refinement of these two concepts improbable, and the two-dimensional character limits their empirical usefulness in any case. However, this does not destroy the usefulness of the concepts in understanding the rational process which underlies the functioning of the price system. Empirical studies do support the relevance of the variables and the relationships deduced in this brand of economic theory.[12]

---

[12] A survey of modern interdisciplinary research on consumer behavior may be found in *Consumer Behavior,* edited by L. H. Clark, Harper & Bros., New York, 1958. For a discussion of the problems mentioned here, see especially pp. 97 ff.

What is the case for rational behavior in the labor market as it is developed in our model? If members of a household are to maximize satisfaction, they must be concerned with more than rational spending choices. As described in Chapter 3, members of households participate in the economy as sellers of labor as well as buyers of products. There the choice to be made in the labor market was treated as a choice between income and leisure. However, this view has very limited applicability in our modern, industrialized economy. Even if we recognize that the supply curve for labor might bend back toward the vertical axis rather than being a positively sloped function, it still may be of limited application. Such a curve may reasonably describe an aggregate labor supply curve for an entire economy with wives, youngsters, and older people moving in and out of the labor force. However, when applied to an individual choosing how much to work during a 24-hour day, it might be relevant to self-employed persons or top managers of a firm, but to few others. Its relevance is restricted to a minute fraction of the American labor force. For most people, hours of work are set by institutional arrangements —by employer fiat affected by community tradition, by legislation, or by collective bargaining. In the main, choices regarding the extent of leisure time are social choices that are not subject to individual discretion. Prices of labor, then, serve mainly to allocate labor among alternative employments. The typical choice facing the individual is between one job and its price, and another job and its price; it is seldom a choice between income and leisure.

Irrationality in consumer behavior usually means to economists that consumers do not weigh choices to maximize utility. That some do not, or that all sometimes do not, may still leave intact the proposition that in the aggregate the relations inferred by economists among employment, income, prices, net assets, and expectations are operational concepts. They do not produce perfectly predictable results so that economists would be delighted if other motives were discovered to improve our predictions, particularly in aggregate consumer behavior.

Irrational behavior of business management might be associated with actions not based on profit maximization. Nepotism, which is widespread in business, falls into this category whenever there is a negative answer to the question: Was the family relative hired by the firm at least as well qualified for the job as the best nonrelated person who could be employed? Other possible motives of business managers, such as output maximization, power maximization, or political equilibrium (within the firm), are being studied in research on the theory of the firm, but as yet no multimotive theory has taken full form.[13]

III. PUBLIC GOODS AND EXTERNAL EFFECTS[14]

In a market-directed economy most goods are produced by private firms and are bought and sold in markets in the private sector. When both implicit and explicit costs are included, the costs to the producer generally encompass all of society's opportunity costs in producing and distributing the good. Likewise, the competitive price charged for the good approximates its relative worth to society. Such goods are marketable in the sense that the producer is able to cover his costs by requiring the purchaser to pay for the privilege of enjoying the benefits of his product. The market price tends to equate the sacrifices (costs) required of society to bring forth the last unit of the good with the satisfactions from its purchase and consumption. As we have seen, because of this equality, the optimum combination of goods is produced and in the most efficient fashion.

A. Public Goods

In Chapter 1, however, we noted that there are some socially desirable goods and services that private firms do not find it profitable to produce. These are goods or services which provide benefits that are not marketable to individual purchasers. In many cases these benefits are not marketable because the good or service must be provided to all members of society if it is to be offered to any of them. Because of this characteristic, these goods are referred to as *public goods*. If the producer is unable

---

[13] For an example of such studies, see R. M. Cyert and J. G. March, *Behavioral Theory of the Firm*, Prentice-Hall, Englewood Cliffs, 1963.

[14] For a further discussion of market failure due to external effects and public goods, see Robert H. Haveman, *The Economics of the Public Sector*, in this series.

to exclude people from the benefit of the good once it is produced, he obviously cannot find anyone who would voluntarily pay a price for the good. When the private producer cannot sell the benefit to anyone, he is not able to recover his costs of producing it, and he, therefore, will not produce it. It is for this reason that governments maintain armies, law courts, and police forces. While there are additional reasons related to justice and equity that argue for the collective provision of these goods, national defense and law and order are clearly public goods.

For a somewhat different reason, fire protection, public health services, and sewage disposal are also publicly produced. Collective action in these cases is required because both fire and disease are "contagious" phenomena. Beneficiaries of protection from spreading fires or disease cannot be separated from these benefits if they do not contribute to payment, which is, as we have seen, a characteristic of a public good. Moreover, society has been unwilling to agree that only those people who are willing and able to pay for it shall receive fire protection or efficient sewage disposal. While these services have been marketed privately in the past, large concentrations of population in cities have encouraged public production of fire protection and sewage disposal.

B. *External (Spillover) Costs and Benefits*

In addition to the failure of markets due to public goods, a second reason that private markets may not function efficiently is the existence of *spillover* or *external* effects. When certain things are produced and sold privately, some people incur costs for which they are not reimbursed or they receive benefits for which they do not have to pay. In short, private costs and gains may not coincide with total social costs and benefits. When this divergence of private and social effects occurs, either too much or too little of the good will be produced and resource misallocation results.

For example, a meat packing firm may cover a residential neighborhood with an obnoxious odor. Citizens are not compensated for this spillover cost which they are forced to bear. Nor does the meat packing firm record this cost so that it can be reflected in the price of meat or in other firm decisions.[15] A manufacturing

[15] This way of stating the problem suggests that one way of bringing private

plant may find its least cost position by using a grade of coal that produces dense smoke and soot which then settles on the surrounding community. A city or a private firm may dump waste into a lake or stream. Farmers, in using pesticides to increase output, may kill a large number of fish as the chemical is washed from the land into the nearest stream. These are all examples of undesirable external effects levied by private production on the rest of society. Because these *external or spillover costs* are not recorded in the accounts of the businesses which generate them, it is likely that they are producing too much of the commodity whose production process imposes these externalities.

The converse of spillover costs is *spillover benefits*. The production of an educated person, for example, confers benefits on the entire society in addition to those private benefits which accrue to the educated person himself. Because of an educated citizenry, the democratic political process works more effectively. Delinquency and family instability are reduced. In addition, an educated labor force enables economic growth be more rapid, production to be more efficient, and costs to be lower.[16] All of these are spillover or external benefits of education. Because of them, private provision of education would probably yield less education output than is socially optimal. The market fails and public action is necessary to correct for market failure.[17]

For some goods and services, however, the case for collective action to correct market failure is not so clear. Some people argue that private provision of certain outputs produces such undesirable

---

costs into equality with social costs would be to tax the meat packers an amount appropriate to compensate the citizens. A second alternative would be to require the firms to install equipment to control the emission of odor. In either case the private firm is required to bear the social cost of production and this higher cost will be reflected in the price of meat products. This in turn will bring a chain of adjustments throughout the market system which will more nearly allocate resources according to household preferences.

[16] For a discussion of the impact of education on productivity, see *Economic Development and Growth,* by Robert E. Baldwin, in this series.

[17] It should be noted that in addition to market failure there are other reasons which account for public rather than private provision of education. One of these is the social judgment that all children should have access to a certain minimum of education even if their parents cannot afford to pay for it. This is an equity as opposed to an efficiency rationale.

side effects (external costs) that government provision of these goods is called for. Others argue that the social cost of discouraging private enterprise is greater than the alleged social benefit from government provision. Water resource development is one such disputed area.

When the government constructs a dam on a river to, say, protect people living downstream from floods, it is acting to correct market failure. The provision of the dam may be socially worthwhile in that the social benefits in the form of flood damage reduction may exceed the costs of building and maintaining the dam. However, private business would fail to undertake the provision of flood control because of the difficulty of recovering costs from the people living downstream who are benefited. The provision of flood protection has some of the nonmarketable characteristics of public goods and, consequently, the private sector market fails to generate an optimum level of production. In a similar way, some of the other "outputs" of federal water resource development may have public good or externality characteristics. How does one economically collect from picnickers and boaters for the improved boating and picnic facilities created by the reservoir behind a dam? Or, how does one economically charge the barges which move goods on the river for the beneficial side effect of a more reliable river channel which is created in constructing the flood control dam? Moreover, should the government not produce and sell hydroelectric power at the flood control damsite once the dam is already there? To fail to do so might mean failure to take advantage of a low-cost production opportunity. Similarly, once the reservoir is there, should the government not use its facilities for low-cost crop irrigation or municipal water supply?

When goods involving these external or public effects are present, the efficient resolution often involves production by the public sector. Even in those cases where production is left in the private sector, public action is necessary to insure the socially optimum amount of production or to correct for undesirable inefficiencies.

Consider, for example, the decision to permit a private power company to build a power production dam on a river in lieu of the public dam. Will the company undertake to provide recreation, irrigation, and navigation facilities when these are socially efficient undertakings? Will it consider that it is producing flood control benefits in addition to power when it designs the dam? In each of these cases the answer is *no*, if the output is external or public, or unassignable to individual beneficiaries, and hence unsalable in a market.

Thus, if the social benefit of these nonmarketable services exceeds the cost of providing them, which it often does, and if the development of the river by a private firm precludes the development of these other purposes, which it often does, then private development of the stream denies society the benefit of these worthwhile yet external or public benefits. Indeed, private development, by failing to provide these services, imposes a cost on society. If society is to enjoy the benefits of these products, the government, in many cases, must undertake the multipurpose development of the water resource.[18]

If it is accepted that the government should be the developer of such multipurpose water projects, how can it decide whether or not any particular project is a worthwhile or economic undertaking? This is not an easy question, but methods for evaluating public projects have been, and are being, devised. The most widely used technique is known as *benefit-cost analysis*. In it, the dollar value today of all of a project's future benefits to society is evaluated and compared with the value today of all costs or sacrifices that society must incur to construct and maintain the project. If the benefits exceed the costs, the benefit-cost ratio is greater than 1—the mark of an efficient project.[19] If the benefits are less than the costs, the ratio is less than 1 and the construction of the project would entail a misallocation of resources.

Although it is difficult and extremely tricky to measure many of the social costs and benefits resulting from such projects, a

---

[18] See John V. Krutilla and Otto Eckstein, *Multiple-Purpose River Development,* Johns Hopkins Press for Resources for the Future, Inc., Baltimore, 1958, for an excellent discussion of the external costs and benefits resulting from alternative plans for river development.

[19] Even where the benefit-cost ratio is greater than 1, there may be insufficient funds to construct all of the projects. Here we must introduce the further allocative proposition—allocate each dollar of expenditure so as to attain the greatest benefit from it, until all of the funds are exhausted.

number of appropriate techniques have been developed. The present value of the stream of power generation benefits, for example, can be estimated reasonably from the generating capacity planned plus estimates of the future growth of demand for power. Irrigation benefits can be calculated in the same way. Benefits from flood control are estimated from historical data of flood expectancy and estimates of future property value in the flood plain. Likewise, by projecting barge traffic on improved streams and comparing transportation costs by barge with the least expensive alternative method of transportation, estimates of navigation benefits can be obtained. In recent years rather successful techniques have been devised for empirically estimating the recreational benefits of water projects.[20]

Notwithstanding the progress that has been made in improving the accuracy of benefit-cost computations, the government continues to construct many inefficient projects. A major reason for this result is clear: an individual state or region need not be concerned with the efficiency of a project constructed within its bounds because it reaps the lion's share of the benefits while the nation as a whole bears the cost. Owing to the political power of its Congressmen or Senators, a region with such a relatively inefficient project may be able to secure federal appropriation for the project even though alternatives which are more highly valued by society exist elsewhere in the nation.

But we would be telling an incomplete story if we implied that government production has been the common collective reaction to goods with spillover impacts. Often the government has sought means of social correction of market failure other than public ownership or production. Consider air and water pollution and the use of pesticides which were mentioned earlier. All of these

---

[20] For a further discussion of the techniques of benefit-cost analysis, see Otto Eckstein, *Water Resources Development,* Harvard University Press, Cambridge, 1958; Robert Haveman, *Water Resource Investment and the Public Interest,* Vanderbilt University, Nashville, 1965; Robert Dorfman, ed., *Measuring Benefits of Government Investments,* The Brookings Institution, Washington, D.C. 1965; Marion Clawson and Jack L. Knetsch, *The Economics of Outdoor Recreation,* Johns Hopkins Press for Resources for the Future, Baltimore, 1968; and U. S. Congress, Joint Economic Committee, *The Analysis and Evaluation of Public Expenditures; The PPB System,* Washington, D. C. 1969.

involve the creation of external or spillover costs by a private firm or government as it goes about its business. In each of these cases the private market fails to take into account all of the costs which a particular action entails. Consequently, in each case it is necessary to go outside the "automatic" price system to assure that *all* costs to society are assigned to the relevant production process. Seldom has the government turned to public ownership and production to remedy this sort of market failure. The most common method has been simply to legislate against the nuisance. Smoke abatement ordinances set standards for smoke density and soot content which require the firm to shift to a different grade of coal or to install mechanisms that will trap offensive materials. Public health and pollution laws control the character of waste that is dumped into public waters .A superior method of imposing social cost on the relevant production process is to charge the production unit an amount estimated to be the cost inflicted on the rest of society from its actions—the external or spillover cost. This concept is embodied in recent proposals for effluent charges on firms and cities that use public waterways for waste disposal.[21] The point is that external as well as private costs should be reflected in the prices and paid by the consumers of the product whose production imposes the costs if resources are to be allocated efficiently to maximize consumer satisfaction.

External or spillover costs and benefits have a time dimension, too. When our generation uses certain resources[22] in the production of something giving present satisfaction, it denies their use to generations yet unborn. Our use of the resources is a cost to these future generations. In order to assess this cost we turn to the rate of interest which is the price that is supposed to allocate production between the present and the future. Since capital is created to produce goods in the future, it must be productive

---

[21] See Allen V. Kneese and Blair T. Bower, *Managing Water Quality: Economics, Technology, Institutions,* Johns Hopkins Press for Resources for the Future, Inc., Baltimore, 1968.

[22] Resources such as oil, coal, and redwood trees are "wasting" resources. Our use reduces the total supply permanently because it has taken many, many centuries to produce each of them. Similarly, use of present, reproducible resources to produce consumer goods rather than capital goods represents a decision in favor of present over future consumption.

enough to cover an interest cost as well as return the amount paid for the resources which created it. When the interest rate is high, only those capital goods which produce a high rate of return over cost will be created. Fewer resources will be devoted to production of capital, hence to future consumption, than when the interest rate is lower.

This function of allocating between present and future is submerged when the interest rate is manipulated for other purposes. When it is regulated by monetary authorities, the rate is set to cope with some contemporary problem such as inflation or a gold outflow. Even when it is set by the relatively free play of supply and demand in the market for loanable funds, the long-term rate probably reflects a time horizon of less than two generations (say, 50 years). To the extent that this is true, the consequences of our actions on people living far in the future are not appropriately taken into account. This phenomenon may require public sector action in the conservation or preservation of basic natural resources, as well as influence the rate of growth in the stock of capital.

When resources are free (or very cheap) and their supply appears to be inexhaustible, the costs of conservation practices often appear unrecoverable. For this reason productive land was maltreated through most of the nineteenth century in the United States. Today, we may be doing much the same thing with the resources of the ocean or with land resources which could be maintained as open space in rapidly growing metropolitan areas.

In much the same way, the free play of the price system is destroying the redwood forests of the West Coast. Redwood is superb lumber for many purposes, and lumbermen can make high profits by cutting it. But continued cutting may be creating contemporary social costs by destroying a unique and beautiful part of the nation's natural environment. Even if all of the contemporary social costs had to be covered by the lumbermen, the timber-felling would likely continue. The interests of future generations in these stands, whether for lumber uses or for the esthetic value of viewing trees that were standing before the voyages of Columbus, may consequently be ignored unless there is social intervention.[23]

[23] This entire discussion, it should be noted, is based on the assumption that

Many other examples will come to mind in which the cost and revenue considerations of the price system may fail to secure the optimal distribution of use of the resources between present and future. The cost of our error falls on future generations if we undervalue the future relative to the present.

The price system then fails to operate in the society's interest both because it fails to produce some goods that are socially desirable and because it produces too many or too little of still others. The latter occurs because the private sector's decisions fail to consider external costs and benefits. The government must provide the worthwhile goods that the private sector fails to produce if the society's welfare is to be maximized. Those external benefits and costs which private decisions systematically ignore must be worked into social decisions if society is to maximize the satisfaction of its members. In both cases the society must make use of other systems of choice in addition to the price system.

As the desire for consumption of social goods grows with the increase of affluence and leisure in American society, it becomes more and more important to devise ways for effective expression of social choice. Voting based on well-informed judgment probably can be effective only in clusters of people small enough that the voters can enter into public discussion. Referenda, as an effective device, seems to be limited to the town or small city. Perhaps ways can be devised to make voting better informed and more effective as an expression of the "will of the people" in large communities. Our experience with referenda to finance local schools indicates that we have a long way to go. As an alternative, representative samples of the population might be polled providing an effective device for expression of social choice that would lead to maximum consumer satisfaction.[24]

---

future generations will have the same general set of values as the present generation. If it is just as likely that future generations will dislike open space in urban areas or standing redwoods as it is that they will appreciate them, our discussion would have little relevance.

[24] For a discussion of means for effective expression of social choice, see A. Downs, *An Economic Theory of Democracy*, Harper & Bros., New York, 1956; and H. R. Bowen, *Toward Social Economy*, Rinehart & Company, New York, 1948. The latter volume is also concerned with many of the other problems in the market system.

IV. THE PROBLEM OF THE DISTRIBUTION OF INCOME

Support for the price system rests on the claim that substantial welfare gains will accrue to a society that relies on the operation of the price mechanism. This claim is based on the following propositions.

1. Each individual knows best what will maximize his satisfaction.
2. The aggregate of these individual maxima will produce maximum satisfaction for the society.
3. The price system provides the best mechanism for making individual satisfactions known and for allocating resources in responses to individual demands.

In this chapter we have recognized problems with all of the propositions.

First, we have seen that the control of supply or demand and the existence of market power are not simply imagined but are widespread and, perhaps, predominant. In Chapter 6, we discussed at length the implications of this control for the ability of the system to allocate resources. Although innovation or countervailing power may weaken this control in some instances, a substantial amount remains.

Second, we have seen that there exists widespread lack of knowledge, frictions, immobilities, and uncertainties in the operation of the market system. Again, the ability of the system to allocate resources efficiently is undermined. Does the typical individual, for example, have any real basis for judging the qualities of two different television sets?[25] Can the worker know the qualities of jobs that are open to him, even if he should know their wage rates? If these very basic things are not known to households, can we expect that their decisions will maximize their satisfaction or that the sum of their decisions will maximize the welfare of the society?

We have seen that irrationality creates difficulty with the functioning of the price system because it may prevent allocation of

---

[25] This particular question is more serious for durable consumer goods than for goods which are purchased frequently and which, consequently, permit reasonably rapid correction of mistaken judgment.

the nation's resources to the production of what consumers want. It raises a fundamental question about proposition one and proposition two. Does the individual always know, or care, what is best for him? Knowing that cigarettes are harmful to health, individuals continue to buy cigarettes; the market continues to allocate a rather large volume of resources to their production, promotion of their use, and their distribution. There is no assurance that households will demand what will ultimately lead to their greatest satisfaction. Again, there is no assurance of a social optimum.

Immobilities and indivisibilities prevent the price system from bringing about nice adjustment in the allocation of resources, and prevent individuals from making nice adjustments in their expenditures and sales in order to maximize satisfaction. The allocation of resources and achievement of satisfaction are imperfect in proportion to the importance of these frictions.

Finally, we saw that some goods are public goods and that some costs and benefits are external to producers and purchasers. Consequently, the price system fails to produce some goods that are socially desirable and fails to allocate some costs and benefits to the production process from which they derive. Because of these qualities, there is "market failure." The price system, by itself, does not efficiently allocate resources or provide for maximum social welfare. It must be supplemented with other modes of choice. Many of these involve some form of government action.

If we prevent or offset control of supply and control of demand, if we reduce irrationality and immobility by education and communication, if indivisibilities are offset by rental opportunities and used product sales, if we find ways to assign external costs and benefits accurately and to measure social choice in the government provision of public goods, then would the price system produce market values that coincide with social values?

Alas, there is another major qualification. The price system grinds out its results on the basis of the particular distribution of income which exists. Change the income distribution, and almost all market values will change.

There is a sense in which income distribution is built into the price system. When the purely competitive system works smoothly and perfectly, and all social benefits and costs are priced, *factors of production receive incomes according to their contribution to the aggregate of satisfaction in the society.* If income according to contribution is the accepted ethic of income distribution, then conscious income redistribution by government is required when for some reason the market system fails to live up to its "ideal best."

However, the market system principle, "to each factor of production according to its contribution," ignores a most basic problem. It treats as of no consequence the fact that the ownership and control of the bulk of the factors of production is in relatively few hands. It makes no social judgment on the equity or justice of any particular distribution which might result from the pattern of resource ownership. Even if the above ethical principle is supplemented by the principle that the laborer (in the broad sense) should own and control the sale of his own labor, the basic "reward in proportion to contribution" principle does not supply an unquestionable value judgment. Neither the principles of "reward according to contribution" nor "human control of human contribution" sheds any light on who should own, control, and receive the income of property—land and capital.

Indeed, some people might go so far as to extend the market system "reward according to contribution" ethic to land and capital, calling them "produced property." This extension is related to the traditional doctrine of private property. "As long as Mr. X has legal title to land parcel A or $B million worth of capital equipment, he is entitled to the income which it generates by contributing to production." However, even this modification cannot reasonably hold in the case of land, for in the natural resource sense, land is not produced.[26] Nor can it hold for inherited property whether it be natural resource or capital, since the heir, himself, has not produced the value. Private ownership of land, inheritance, and the right to the return from these must be justified by argument from principles other than "reward according to contribution." These principles, in turn, must be

[26] A shift from private property to some other form of property control would be complicated because present owners may have paid for it with wages which did reflect their contribution to production.

weighed against the "reward according to contribution" ethic and all other social value judgments.[27]

Moreover, the difference between inherited or "natural" property income and labor income may not be as great as appears on the surface. This is so because even the worker may not be personally responsible for all of the value his labor creates. If he was publicly educated, the society in general paid (and hence is responsible) for most of his training and accumulated skill. Moreover, his physical and mental capacities are to some degree inherited and his parents have contributed substantially to his development. Where discrimination on the basis of race, religion, or sex exists, people of equal innate capacities may receive unequal education, training and, hence, incomes. "Connections" with important people controlling key jobs are not the same for one person as for another. All of these matters cloud the picture of who deserves to get what.

Aside from these serious problems with the "reward according to contribution" principle which is implicit in the price system, what should we do about those who cannot contribute to production, or who cannot contribute enough to live at subsistence or some identifiable level of human dignity? Equity calls for receipt of income above what such people produce. Clearly, the problems of poverty and what to do about it are related to the ethic of income distribution.[28]

Because the economic system does not work smoothly, what about those whose incomes are reduced or eliminated by malfunction of the system rather than their own inability? The problems of economic instability and unemployment also are related to the ethic of income distribution.[29]

Income distribution, then, must be determined by an explicit social decision based on specific social value judgments. These judgments are quite distinct from the workings of the market system. There is nothing particularly sacred about the principle of "reward according to contribution." Indeed, it provides only one

---

[27] For discussions of private property, see G. Dietze, *In Defense of Property,* Henry Regnery Co., Chicago, 1963; and R. H. Tawney, *The Acquisitive Society,* Harcourt Brace & Co., New York, 1948.

[28] See *The Economics of Poverty,* by Alan B. Batchelder, in this series.

[29] See *Toward Economic Stability,* by Maurice W. Lee, in this series.

of the many possible social value judgments on which income distribution can be founded. Where the goals of economic justice and equity come into conflict with the goal of efficiency, some efficiency must be sacrificed. We are optimistic in believing that the sacrifice in efficiency in such cases will not be so great as to offset the enhancement of human well-being which results from greater justice and equity. And, after all, we test economic systems by their net effect on the level of human well-being.

V. CONCLUSION AND SUMMARY

This volume has attempted to explain how prices and markets may be used to organize economic activity in society. When the price system functions well, it generally leads to an efficient allocation of resources, which is an important economic goal of society.

The discussion in this chapter indicates that economic affairs in reality do not conform nicely to our theory, and even if they did, there would be areas in which efficient allocation of resources would not necessarily occur. The reader might well ask why he has been led through the theoretical structure if this is true. Our apologia runs through the volume—in the preface, toward the end of Chapter 1, toward the end of Chapter 2, and so on. Even so, it may bear repeating after this liberal dose of critical comment.

Some of our criticisms merely reflect the fact that that the political and economic institutions of society have not reached perfection. The criticisms point out directions for further striving. Other criticisms stem from the fact that our theory falls short of reflecting reality and fails, in many circumstances, to predict economic behavior accurately. While our theory has many inadequacies, it is, nevertheless, the best we have at present and it does, we would argue, substantially add to understanding. It has helped us to define an important social goal, economic efficiency. It has provided us with sets of concepts and relationships that help us to formulate important economic problems in precise terms. It has been of significant help in evaluating public policy proposals. Although at times there has been insufficient recognition of the limitations of the theory for policy, at other times an understanding of the theory would have led to proper policy applications and closer attainment of the economic goals of society.

Hence, while insufficient in itself, our theory is an essential building block in the construction of more adequate tools for understanding social and economic behavior. Moreover, it provides substantial assistance in understanding the nature of individual choice in economic affairs.

Index